QUESTIONS OF CULTURE IN AUTOETHNOGRAPHY

Autoethnography allows researchers to make sense of the 'ethno' – the cultural – by studying their own experiences – the 'auto'. It links the self to the cultural, allowing for an inductive grounding of theoretical insight into researchers' lived experiences. But what happens when the culture that we research is not conventionally or entirely our 'own'? What happens when our culture does not neatly conceptualise the 'auto' as an individual, Western self? And does autoethnographic writing risk reducing cultural 'Others' if we cannot help but see them through 'imperial eyes'?

Questions of Culture in Autoethnography showcases how cross-cultural autoethnographies might be done effectively, ethically, and reflectively. Chapters include: identity work among Tibetans in India and among the descendants of Spanish conquistadores in Appalachia; insider/outsider identities in myriad contexts from Mexico to Japan; embodied (gendered, raced, sized) intercultural experiences from Samoa to Aotearoa/New Zealand and from Canada to Malawi; and language stories from Korea to Singapore and from Somalia to Australia. It also explores cultural Otherness within 'a' culture, including researchers' accounts of working with Indigenous Australians, of contesting mainstream cultural narratives from a body positive perspective, and as a US American man in New Zealand's 'bloke culture', only seemingly sharing the same English-language-speaking, 'Western' culture.

For all scholars of qualitative methods and autoethnography, the book has a dual purpose – to show *and* to tell. It presents evocative autoethnographies of and about 'culture', as it is variously understood, and discusses the issues inherent in autoethnographic writing.

Phiona Stanley and **Greg Vass** (UNSW Sydney, School of Education) are critical, qualitative researchers working on various aspects of interculturality. They have each worked in various countries and have published and supervised doctoral students in international education, Indigenous education, and language education.

QUESTIONS OF CULTURE IN AUTOETHNOGRAPHY

Edited by Phiona Stanley and Greg Vass

LONDON AND NEW YORK

First published 2018
by Routledge
2 Park Square, Milton Park, Abingdon, Oxon OX14 4RN

and by Routledge
711 Third Avenue, New York, NY 10017

Routledge is an imprint of the Taylor & Francis Group, an informa business

© 2018 selection and editorial matter, Phiona Stanley and Greg Vass; individual chapters, the contributors

The right of the editors to be identified as the authors of the editorial material, and of the authors for their individual chapters, has been asserted in accordance with sections 77 and 78 of the Copyright, Designs and Patents Act 1988.

All rights reserved. No part of this book may be reprinted or reproduced or utilised in any form or by any electronic, mechanical, or other means, now known or hereafter invented, including photocopying and recording, or in any information storage or retrieval system, without permission in writing from the publishers.

Trademark notice: Product or corporate names may be trademarks or registered trademarks, and are used only for identification and explanation without intent to infringe.

British Library Cataloguing-in-Publication Data
A catalogue record for this book is available from the British Library

Library of Congress Cataloging-in-Publication Data
Names: Stanley, Phiona, editor. | Vass, Greg, editor.
Title: Questions of culture in autoethnography / edited by Phiona Stanley and Greg Vass.
Description: Abingdon, Oxon ; New York, NY : Routledge, 2018. | Includes bibliographical references and index.
Identifiers: LCCN 2017057461 | ISBN 9781138908642 (hbk) | ISBN 9781138919587 (pbk) | ISBN 9781315178738 (ebk)
Subjects: LCSH: Ethnology—Biographical methods—Case studies. | Ethnology—Authorship—Case studies. | Cross-cultural studies—Methodology—Case studies.
Classification: LCC GN346.6 .Q47 2018 | DDC 305.8001—dc 3
LC record available at https://lccn.loc.gov/2017057461

ISBN: 978-1-138-90864-2 (hbk)
ISBN: 978-1-138-91958-7 (pbk)
ISBN: 978-1-315-17873-8 (ebk)

Typeset in Bembo
by Apex CoVantage, LLC

Printed and bound in Great Britain by
TJ International Ltd, Padstow, Cornwall

CONTENTS

List of illustrations — *vii*

1 On the difficulties of writing about culture in autoethnography — 1
Phiona Stanley and Greg Vass

2 'Help me': The English language and a voice from a Korean
Australian living in Singapore — 13
Hyejeong Ahn

3 Personal instructions on how to remain a stranger to enforce
a sociological perspective — 23
Silvia Bénard Calva

4 Writing flows: The self as fragmentary whole — 33
David Bright

5 Searching for 'my' Mexico: An autoethnographic account
of unlearning and relearning about the limits of knowing
the Other — 43
Alice Cranney

6 Negotiating the *vā*: The 'self' in relation to others and
navigating the multiple spaces as a New Zealand-raised
Tongan male — 57
David Fa'avae

vi Contents

7 Scene, seen, unseen 69
Fetaui Iosefo

8 How do 'we' know what 'they' need? Learning together
through duoethnography and English language teaching to
immigrant and refugee women 80
Ulrike Najar and Julie Choi

9 Performing problematic privilege in Japan 93
Gabrielle Piggin

10 Nuanced 'culture shock': Local and global 'mate' culture 106
Robert E. Rinehart

11 In which I am sung to, cry, and other suchlike: Reflections
on research in and with Tibetan refugees in India 118
Harmony Siganporia

12 Walking to heal or walking to heel? Contesting cultural
narratives about fat women who hike and camp alone 129
Phiona Stanley

13 Reading Shiva Naipaul: A reflection on Brownness and
leading an experiential learning project in Malawi 142
C. Darius Stonebanks

14 Untangling me: Complexifying cultural identity 156
Gresilda A. Tilley-Lubbs

15 Whose story is it anyway? Reflecting on a collaborative
research project with/in an educational community 167
*Greg Vass, Michelle Bishop, Katherine Thompson, Pauline Beller,
Calita Murray, Jane Tovey and Maxine Ryan*

16 Six tales of a visit to Chile: An autoethnographic reflection
on 'questions of culture' 182
Esther Fitzpatrick

Acknowledgements 191
About the authors 194
Index 197

ILLUSTRATIONS

1	Embodiment of cultural/gendered identities	66
2	Elana (Hediyeh's daughter) imitating us as teachers at the board (© Chris Mertins)	90
3	Members of the Tibetan refugee community engaged in a spontaneous group dance at the end of the Shoton Festival at TIPA, Dharamsala, April 2015 (© Harmony Siganporia)	121
4	Fat girl hiking: Blue Mountains, NSW, Australia (Photo: © Matthew Crompton)	130
5	Me at six (Photo: Fayetteville Elementary School, 1952)	157

1

ON THE DIFFICULTIES OF WRITING ABOUT CULTURE IN AUTOETHNOGRAPHY

Phiona Stanley

SCHOOL OF EDUCATION, UNSW SYDNEY, AUSTRALIA

Greg Vass

SCHOOL OF EDUCATION, UNSW SYDNEY, AUSTRALIA

And so here we go, introducing this book, the topic, the framing. The two central ideas, *culture* and *autoethnography,* have not been taken up smoothly or in trouble-free ways. Moreover, and here we will get confessional, this topic has created a surprising amount of consternation and false starts in our own conversations along the way, not least as we have been writing this introduction. Indeed, we had doubts, disagreements, and differences arriving at this point. And yet, here we are.

We are co-editors of this collection, and we are colleagues with offices a short walk apart. We share much in common in terms of our concerns to do with power, representation, relationships, and ethics in research. In truth, if this cornerstone were not in place, it is likely that we wouldn't have collaborated on this project at all. Over the last few years we have learnt a lot from each other and have grown professionally (and, in many respects, personally) from sharing many laughs alongside of any number of robust conversations. Having said this, in trying to bring our ideas and thinking together for the purposes of writing this introduction, we have also come to realise that there are many unexpected and uncomfortable differences in terms of how we think about, connect with, and talk about the work of autoethnography and the questions of culture raised in this volume.

In other words, we have come to appreciate that methodologically, autoethnography is a 'broad church' and we don't necessarily share the same pew. As such, we feel it is important to note that there is no way of framing a discussion about autoethnography that speaks to or for all that are involved or interested in this approach, and nor is there really much prospect of trying to speak to the middle ground as this runs the risk of narrowing the field and excluding others in problematic ways.

2 Phiona Stanley and Greg Vass

And so, rather than try to establish a somewhat fixed or agreed upon rationale for *Questions of Culture in Autoethnography*, we begin with our origin stories as autoethnographers. These, together, give a sense and flavour of how this book's idea and framing came to be. Concurrently, our stories gesture to some of the similarities and differences in our approaches, understandings, and engagements with autoethnography. This is also a recognisably 'autoethnographic' way to begin. So here we go.

Phiona

I came to academia quite late, in my mid-30s. Now, looking back, I can 'read' my 20s as a time of my own problematic privilege (Piggin, this volume) and neo-colonial adventuring, as an itinerant English teacher overseas, because I was lucky enough to be White, to have a UK passport, and to have English as my native language. This is a legitimate, critical reading of that time, but it is not an emic reading. Then, I thought that becoming 'windswept and interesting', as Scottish comedian Billy Connolly puts it, was a way out of the suburban mediocrity in which I grew up. Those who intimidated me then were worldly in ways to which I could only aspire (Stanley, 2017, pp. 8–11). And although I wanted for nothing material, mine was no intellectual, upper-crust upbringing. What I did want, though, was to *be* someone, because I was a fat, nerdy, bullied teenager, always overlooked and sometimes actively tortured by my prettier, more confident, more streetwise peers. I left school after Year 11 – when I was 16 – because I hated it so much. I just didn't care about who made the hockey team or which queen bee was going out with which rugby player. (Or: I cared. But I had to learn not to care because I was not allowed to exist in that world.)

I scraped into Edinburgh University with just my Year 11 results, because the system in Scotland then meant you could do that. Starting uni was scary but, in many ways, a relief. And although I made some good friends there, among our classmates were plenty of what we then called 'yahs': wealthy and worldly students from southern England who talked about their 'gap years' in far-flung places and described growing up in large, beautiful houses full of books. This was quite different from our shelf of detective-story paperbacks in the wee suburban bungalow that I still lived in with my parents. I went to university so young, and in my home city, and it wasn't until later that I moved out of home. So my peers were all older than me (of course, because I had just turned 17), and they were living out of home, and they talked about places that I could only imagine. This meant that although I had a much better time at university than I had at high school, I often felt that I was on the back foot there, too.

And so, the year I turned 21, I graduated and I went away. I had no interest at all, initially, in English language teaching (ELT), but working overseas was affordable in a way that 'backpacking' wasn't. I did a four-week Cambridge ELT Certificate and it was 'enough'. Honestly, though, during my own post-university 'gap year', which I spent in Peru, I was desperately homesick and I stuck it out only because to give up would make me into someone I didn't want to be. 'Other people' loomed so large in my imagination then. So, I went and then I came home. I ticked that box. Yes, some aspects of my identity meant that it was possible. But other aspects of identity meant that it felt necessary. Identity is such a multi-dimensional thing.

What I now know is this: my going there traced a colonial-type relationship in which, instead of extracting minerals or slaves, I extracted a legitimising narrative that would testify to my own nascent worldliness. And also: until 21-year-old, four-week-trained Peruvians are free to turn up as Spanish teachers in the UK, the relationship is wholly inequitable. I know this, now. But then, within a different framing, I lived it as a different story that is not how I would (choose to) tell it today. Is it a kind of ideo-epistemological imperialism, or historical revisionism, to superimpose a new and more acceptable reading onto an old story? Certainly, framing it critically is not the truth of the story as it was lived.

But isn't this simply a question of temporality? Back then, I lived and performed my 'working in Peru' narrative as part of a discourse of young, British entitlement in which a 'gap year' is a kind of finishing school akin to – and as acceptable, and seemingly desirable, as – the European enlightenment idea of the Grand Tour (Centore, 2004). Whereas now, immersed in activism, academia, postcolonial resistance, and rather more 'woke' discourse communities, I realise that what I did then was highly problematic. If I tell 'my' 21-year-old-me story through a framing of who I am now, I come to see it as a difference in my then-versus-now 'small cultures' (Holliday, 1999, p. 237):

> What has become the default notion of 'culture' refers to prescribed ethnic, national and international entities. This *large culture* paradigm is by its nature vulnerable to a culturist reduction of 'foreign' students, teachers and their educational contexts. In contrast, a *small culture* paradigm attaches 'culture' to small social groupings or activities wherever there is cohesive behaviour, and thus avoids culturist ethnic, national or international stereotyping.

Engaging with such discourses is one way in which we engage with 'cultures' in autoethnography: the framings of the stories we tell may be different from how they were lived.

But back to the story. The summer I came back from Peru I worked at an ELT summer school back in Edinburgh, and there I met people who had just come back from teaching in Poland. And their stories sparked something in me. So, thinking it would be just one more 'year out', I went to Poland for what ended up being the next four, very formative years. Central and Eastern Europe, then, was just emerging from behind what was called the 'Iron Curtain', and people desperately wanted English. So even though life (and the winter!) was grim and grey and cold and difficult, it was also fascinating, quite simply, to live through such profound social and political change.

4 Phiona Stanley and Greg Vass

Unusually, also (for someone living in Warsaw and actively studying Polish), I also wanted to keep up the Spanish I had started learning in Peru, so I enrolled in intermediate-level Spanish classes at the *Instituto Cervantes*. This was where I met Polish people who were also learning Spanish and who ended up becoming my circle of friends. Learning a third language that belongs to no-one is a great leveller, and I was accepted in their context as just another language-school student. So, while I had some access to a world of expatriate privilege – friends who were diplomats and high-flyers – I also made local friends who didn't speak English. Starting out with Spanish as a *lingua franca*, I gradually learned enough Polish to maintain friendships that thrived entirely without English. (Indeed, to this day I have friends in Warsaw and Bydgoszcz with whom I only speak Polish; some of them don't speak much English at all.) To what extent, though, can I legitimately write about my own experiences in Poland at that time? I lived in an immediately-post-Communist world that was so different from anywhere else at that time. But if I write about my own storied experiences there, with my English-proficiency privilege and a passport that let me travel largely visa-free (which Polish passports, at the time, did not), do I write an 'auto' that does not match the 'ethno' to which it purports to relate? This is another way in which autoethnography has to engage with culture/s.

But for now let's return to the 1990s. During this time, I earned a University of Cambridge ELT Diploma (with an elusive distinction grade) and I came to care enormously about English teaching. I also trained up and worked as a local examiner for University of Cambridge ELT exams, became the academic manager of a big, challenging language school in Bydgoszcz, northern Poland, and presented at many ELT conferences. In the years that followed, I worked as an editor in ELT publishing at Oxford University Press and as a teacher in Mexico and Qatar. In short, over the years that followed my 'year out' in Peru, I became credible as an 'ELT professional'.

But then I went to China. Being a Westerner in China was not like being a Westerner anywhere else. Indeed, I don't think I even called myself a 'Westerner' anywhere else. 'Westerners' teaching English in China are pressured to be/perform a certain limited, stereotyped (fun, crazy, confident, free-and-easy, 'relaxed') role. This is what works within a powerful Chinese discourse of homogenised selfhood versus foreign otherness, that in turn legitimises the unelected government (Stanley, 2013). So, Westerners *are* all these stereotypes, necessarily, which lets Chinese people – always conceptualised and portrayed as a homogenous entity – be serious, sensible, demure, loyal, filial, hard-working, and so on. In literary terms, Westernness, as locally constructed, is a foil to Chinese nationalism. In Shanghai, I remember talking to a colleague about a particularly difficult meeting with school owners who were ignoring their contractual obligations to their Western teachers – because by this time I worked in ELT management for a franchised chain of language schools. And he said, simply, 'they hate us'. And although the individual Chinese people we knew probably didn't 'hate us' as such, the nationalism discourse certainly constructed us as lesser, problematic, apart, other. So, while being a Westerner in China was, in some ways, a very privileged experience, we were irreducibly different and constantly othered. It is only in China that that my foreignness, my status as a *waiguoren*, an outside-country-person, has been the subject of taunts, shouts, giggles, and refusals of service.

And so, this was my lived experience, the storied baggage that I brought to 'academic' ELT, when I finally started my Master's in Australia (where, desperate to stay in the country and out of visa options, I enrolled as an international student when I was 32). On the Master's programme, I was greatly outnumbered by Chinese students, most of whom had just finished their undergraduate degrees (mostly, like me, in disciplines other than ELT) and most of whom had never taught English. In contrast, I was a 'native speaker'. I was 12 years into my teaching career by then, and qualified with an honours degree and an ELT Certificate and Diploma.

But suddenly I was *just* a 'native speaker'. On the Master's programme, I engaged with both my Chinese classmates and also the academic ELT/applied linguistics literature. And what I learned was that 'native English speaker teachers' (NESTs, like me) are stereotyped as monolingual, likely unqualified, and certainly lesser than local teachers. NESTs are critiqued as crafty opportunists, illegitimate teachers, and nasty colonisers (see Stanley, 2013, pp. 25–46 for a review of this literature). This narrative relies on a paint-by-numbers postcolonial reading of the ELT industry. Ignored are locally much more powerful discourses, such as the discourse of zero-sum Chinese nationalism. The implied binary of 'nasty imperialist Western teacher' versus 'good, power-resistant, local student' simply doesn't work like that in China (ibid.). Instead, it is much more nuanced, layered with the complexity of contested framing narratives and China's *own* imperialism. But how is it possible, methodologically, to speak back to the power of a disciplinary axiom? And how is it possible to question what looks, on the surface, like a laudable pushback against what looks like postcolonial oppressors? One way is through an autoethnography that sufficiently contextualises lived experience against nuanced and sometimes contradictory framing narratives.

But a problem, ethically and methodologically, arises when autoethnographic insights are applied to a *different* (small) culture than one's own. This is where autoethnography risks adopting the colonial gaze of travel writing (Pratt, 1992), in which the 'other' is refracted through the lens of the self. This is why I cannot tell the stories of, for example, Chinese teachers of English or Chinese students, as to do so risks reducing and stereotyping them. What I can talk about is my experience, as a 'foreign teacher', which was very different in China compared to anywhere else. In Poland, for example, our students demanded that their English teachers have an explicit, detailed knowledge of grammar, and thus weak teachers, both local and non-local, were forced to either learn quickly or leave the classroom. In contrast, a legitimate, grammar-knowledgeable, competent foreign English teacher does not survive long in China if s/he is insufficiently entertaining. Instead of being pushed to get good at language teaching, as foreign teachers in China we learned that 'funny foreign monkey' (Stanley, 2013, p. 138) is the role we are hired to play. This, of course, then reifies the notion that NESTs *can only do the fun stuff* and are not 'proper' teachers (Stanley, 2013). This conclusion is a complexity born of autoethnographic insight into the discourses of native speaker teachers in China and also the scripts, both global and national, that frame this transnational encounter. This, I think, is a complexity too far for most other research methods. This is why I see autoethnography as so valuable: writing about lived experience within a 'small' culture, in this case Westerners teaching English in China, allows for fine-grained, nuanced insights that cannot otherwise be obtained.

So, while I can and *have to* seek to understand the larger, framing discourses that affect my experience (such as Chinese nationalism and the discursive construction of *waiguoren*), I don't think I can legitimately write autoethnographically about those I meet along the way who are outside my 'small culture'. They may be important characters in my own autoethnography, though, so how should I represent them? There's a politics in autoethnography, more generally, of writing others and otherness (e.g. Spry, 2016). This becomes all the more complex when it also involves (large or small) *cultural* otherness.

It appears, from all of the above, that there is much to be gained from questioning autoethnography's engagement with culture. As outlined here, this may include interrogating etic reframings of our 'own' stories from the past, examining privilege across intersectional identities, applying criticality to other 'otherings' beyond the usual suspects (e.g. Chinese nationalism as well as, e.g. Western imperialism), problematising practice whenever the 'auto' doesn't quite match the 'ethno' to which it relates, and engaging in a politics of representation across cultures. For all these reasons, I think we need to talk about culture.

Greg

My story also starts as a 20-something growing up and going to university, in my case in Brisbane, Australia. But, I need to begin just prior to this, when I worked for a few years for what was then called the Department of Social Security, a position that put me in close contact with the sort of institutionalised violence that is directed towards (for example) the young, those from non-English speaking backgrounds, people from low socio-economic communities, single parents, and people who have not been well served by education. It was brutally confronting to hear and work with many of the stories of people coming in to seek help, but what I found perhaps more demoralising and unsettling was the solidarity and collegiality that was created amongst many of the staff. An 'us versus them' disposition encouraged a working culture that framed a situation where self-survival (i.e. keeping your job and health) and systemic protection (i.e. maintaining the state coffers) were bigger priorities than addressing the concerns of those needing assistance. This was an expression of power and problematic relationships that were to resurface many years later, but I can tell you more about that shortly. For now, it is enough to know that I left the Department in search of more skills and knowledge to work with people. So I started a social work degree. I soon realised, however, that it was not really the path for me, as I was more interested in understanding the

Writing about culture and autoethnography **7**

system, and to explore and seek change at the level of influence that impacts on the conditions in which people live. So, instead, I pursued studies with social science majors including history, anthropology and sociology.

It was in these disciplines that I was invited, or more to the point *required*, to investigate and look at the relationship between Indigenous and non-Indigenous peoples in Australia, in ways that my schooling had never attempted to do. As seems the response from many undergraduates that I now witness reacting to the history and legacies presented in teacher education, for me this offered a moment, or sequence of epiphanies (Denzin, 2014), which left a mark on my life. One of the more lasting realisations from this time was that the ongoing injustices and harms faced by many Indigenous peoples and communities were intertwined with the histories and inheritances that afforded many of the privileges and opportunities that I benefited from as a White, able-bodied, educated man living in Australia. It would be easy, but in retrospect overly simplistic and potentially unhelpful, to link this with McIntosh's (1998) notion of a backpack of White privilege, but this was the 1990s and this conceptual tool was still very much in vogue. This was also a time when I first became aware of Freire's (2013) notion of *conscientização*, critical consciousness, and the relationship between the liberation of the oppressed being reliant on the liberation of the oppressors.

Following the completion of my undergraduate studies, I started an honours programme. I wanted to think further about some of the political, relational, and historical issues within the more focused boundaries of ethnomusicology that I had been introduced to and found particularly exciting. So, I decided to consider the international success of the Yolngu band *Yothu Yindi*, from Arnhem Land in the Northern Territory (Australia). This was one of the first and most successful Aboriginal acts to bring musical traditions and language from their communities into the mainstream. Songs such as 'Treaty' also showcased the political edge that the band sought to bring to a wider audience. In addition, and linked to this, I looked at a then popular band from the UK, *Jamiroquai*. They had a band member who played a *yidaki* (didjeridoo) on a number of songs featuring this instrument on their first two albums. In essence, the study looked at concerns to do with cultural appropriation and identity politics within the domain of the global pop music machine around the turn of the 21st century.

It is perhaps also worth noting that my studies were somewhat disjointed in the sense that I took a year off to go to South Korea to teach English. As Phiona and I have discussed, we share many concerns regarding the expectations and pressures to perform an exaggerated characterisation of 'Westernness' in circumstances such as these. My experience echoes concerns that 'teaching' language is much less important than familiarising 'learners' with the sorts of cultural capital that they think can benefit them. However, I also found that in attempting to resist being this sort of 'teacher', I was sought out by many students who were well aware of the pitfalls and dangers of NESTs who start believing in and living the life of a stereotypical Westerner. Okay. This is a somewhat longwinded way of arriving at my point, which is that this was a time of learning about, and experiencing, some of the push–pull

8 Phiona Stanley and Greg Vass

forces that make cultural syncretism and fluidity such complex and challenging phenomena to understand. And what's more, that power is never complete or entirely top-down, as those that have taken up Foucault have shown, there are always possibilities for resistance and claiming forms of power that interrupt or deflect the (full) impact of dominant socio-political frameworks.

In getting back to my story of coming to autoethnography, the most pressing and salient point to make here is my acceptance of the premise that harm and violence are linked to anthropology, and social science research more broadly. This is particularly the case in connection with Indigenous peoples and communities, as has been commented on notably by Nakata (2007), Smith (2012), and Deloria (1997). In the absence of support or motivation to continue further studies at this time, it wasn't until a few years later that I returned to complete my teacher education qualification.

Subsequently, as a teacher, I sat in staff meetings listening to the often-problematic commentary from other educators about Indigenous students, their families, or the teaching of histories and knowledges with which they are connected. As with earlier experiences, this was an environment in which the work culture encouraged colleagues closing ranks in support of each other, at times seemingly more concerned with self-preservation than with the experiences of students. Staffroom encounters were often an expression of the violence and injustices that shape relationships between Indigenous and non-Indigenous Australia. These experiences underpinned my motivation to pursue a PhD.

I knew that there was something about this dynamic that I wanted to understand and address. This is why autoethnography came into my line of vision, as I was exploring methodological possibilities that could help with trying to account for my social location and all the shared insider-ness with other mostly White teachers in connection with the race-making in which they engaged. This became the focus of my study. The primary participants involved were teachers, including my colleagues, as I undertook the project in the same high school where I taught. Hence, there was much we shared in common.

The study, ultimately, was focused on the topic of Whiteness. More to the point, I framed the thesis as a race-critical insider autoethnography that investigated the impacts, operationalising and (re)making of Whiteness in and through schooling practices. However, this was concurrently complicated as the investigation understood race-making relationally in terms of the teachers' involvement and interactions with Indigenous students.

This, then, moved me closer to questioning what autoethnography does with culture/s. Elsewhere, I have described how and why autoethnography constructively contributed to helping me witness Whiteness being discursively reproduced in classrooms (Vass, 2015). And my thesis was infused with reflexive autoethnographic moments that reveal the anxieties, uncertainties, and contradictions with which I was confronted throughout this process (Vass, 2013). But despite these texts, I have enduring worries that persist about the necessity to represent the Indigenous students in the classroom, and the potential for undesirable – yet unintentional – outcomes to later surface.

As such, while the earlier lines of reflexive thinking and writing practices have gone some way in terms of addressing some of my concerns, I still feel there are unresolved or unanswered questions that warrant further attention. I feel I have been aware and open, and yet the tension remains. While the experiences of Indigenous students have motivated my research, my focusing of the (critical) gaze on *teachers'* practices has nevertheless sidelined those same students. So, in common with Phiona, I share methodological and ethical concerns regarding those that are in and part of our autoethnographic stories, but who are not the central players. So, I am not entirely convinced that autoethnography has fulfilled all of its promise in terms of the cultural plurality that is always already present and seems a constant in much of the social research undertaken.

Questioning culture

This is Chapter 1. This is where we start. But as with all books and research, this text is built on the work of others. And, we hope, many of the ideas and practices within it will be taken up and extended in surprising and unexpected ways. So is the notion of making a 'start' misleading?

The emergence of autoethnography has been connected with a time, or a 'turn', that evokes the notion of moving away from something (that is undesirable) and towards something else (that is preferable). Ellis and colleagues (2011) for example, connect autoethnography to the poststructuralist-initiated 'crisis of confidence' of the 1980s, which caused social science to question the increasingly evident 'ontological, epistemological, and axiological' limits to practice. Similarly, Denzin (2010) has linked autoethnography's emergence to the broader 'paradigm wars' of the 1980s, in which qualitative enquiry more generally was pressed to defend and justify its contribution to understanding and addressing an increasingly complex globalising world. So autoethnography was (and still is?) innovative, and was part of the response to the context in which it emerged.

Autoethnography opened up an opportunity to produce knowledge differently, and the possibility of producing different types of knowledge that impact on the world in ways that are potentially empowering (after Lather, 2013). Part of this was the burgeoning realisation that research is fundamentally and inescapably *political*, that the researcher is always far from neutral, that knowledge produced by research practices has 'real-world' effects (that are not always for 'good'), and, as a result, that there is a need for methodology to find ways of navigating these potential pitfalls. This is to say that there has been a growing recognition that, despite good intentions, much of the established research practices have been actively harmful to some groups and issues.

But what *is* autoethnography, and, crucially, what is it *not*? There are no shortage of examples of key foundational texts that have talked about these issues. Here are three recent contributions:

> While all personal writing could be considered examinations of culture, not all personal writing is autoethnographic; there are additional characteristics

that distinguish autoethnography from other kinds of personal work. These include (1) purposefully commenting on/critiquing of culture and cultural practices, (2) making contributions to existing research, (3) embracing vulnerability with purpose, and (4) creating a reciprocal relationship with audiences in order to compel a response.

(Holman Jones et al., *2013, p. 22)*

Autoethnographic and biographical studies should attempt to articulate how each subject deals with the problems of coherence, illusion, consubstantiality, presence, deep inner selves, others, gender, class, starting and ending points, epiphanies, fictions, truths, and final causes. These recurring, obdurate, culturally constructed dimensions of Western lives provide framing devices for the stories that are told about the lives we study. They are, however, no more than artifices, contrivances that writers and tellers are differentially skilled at using. As writers, we must not be trapped into thinking that they are any more than cultural conventions.

(Denzin, 2014, pp. 14–15)

Autoethnography is predicated on the ability to invite readers into the lived experience of a presumed "Other" and to experience it viscerally. Accordingly, we envisioned a project that would "give voice" to previously silenced and marginalized experiences, answer unexamined questions about the multiplicity of social identities, instigate discussions about and across difference, and explain the contradictory intersections of personal and cultural standpoints.

(Boylorn & Orbe, 2014, p. 15)

All of the above say something about the link between autoethnography and culture. These are two of the title words of this edited collection, and they necessarily frame the book. We posit this brief, introductory discussion, and the chapters that follow, in the knowledge that concerns to do with culture have always been central to autoethnography. That is to say that there exists a wealth of material that in some way addresses and explains the complex ways in which culture impacts on researchers, researcher practices, and those with whom we undertake research.

In addition, and as the double meaning of this section, *Questioning Culture*, suggests, the ways in which we have been discussing these ideas are necessarily plural. 'Questioning Culture' can be read either as a gerund-noun combination (the practice of questioning culture) and/or as an adjective-verb combination (a culture in which things are questioned). In our discussions with the book's contributors, and together in writing the present chapter, both readings have been present.

It is our hope, then, that in some way this book can extend current thinking and practices and thus make a contribution to the field. It would be fair to say that we have found the very title surprisingly provocative (and not just evocative!), and that it has given us both cause for alarm and also some encouragement regarding the potential reception of the text. For example, various contributors to the book have come together at two different international conferences over the past 12 months, and have subsequently been challenged and critiqued for various reasons. To be questioned and invited to debate, and further explain, is healthy and productive. So this book is intended as an invitation, a provocation, a series of evocations, and as part of the conversation.

The contributions that follow explore questions of culture in the autoethnographic work that the writers do. Many of the names are new, and most are writing from contexts and perspectives with which readers may be unfamiliar. This is deliberate. The brief, to which the contributors have written, invited them to examine how power and positionality are to be managed in autoethnography and the ways in which writers' appropriated and attributed identities affect their experiences as lived and written. We asked: what happens when autoethnographers write about their experiences in/with cultural groups to which they cannot claim insiderness? It is our hope that the book as a whole encourages readers to reflect on their own thinking and writing. In particular, we are keen to contribute to a conversation about ways in which autoethnography might negotiate instances where the 'auto' does not offer a neat fit with the 'ethno' about which researchers purport to provide insight. And so, here we are.

References

Boylorn, R.M. & Orbe, M.P. (2014). *Critical autoethnography: Intersecting cultural identities in everyday life*. Walnut Creek, CA: Left Coast Press.

Centore, F.F. (2004). *Theism or atheism: The eternal debate*. London: Ashgate Publishing.

Deloria, V. (1997). *Red Earth, White Lies: Native Americans and the myth of scientific fact*. Golden, CO: Fulcrum Publishing.

Denzin, N. (2010). *The qualitative manifesto: A call to arms*. Walnut Creek, CA: Left Coast Press.

Denzin, N. (2014). *Interpretive autoethnography* (2nd Ed.). Thousand Oaks, CA: Sage.

Ellis, C., Adams, T. & Bochner, A. (2011). Autoethnography: An overview. *Forum: Qualitative Social Research, 12*(1).

Freire, P. (2013). *Education for critical consciousness*. London: Bloomsbury.

Holliday, A.R. (1999). Small cultures. *Applied Linguistics, 20*(2): 237–264.

Holman Jones, S., Adams, T. & Ellis, C. (2013). Introduction: Coming to know autoethnography as more than method. In Holman Jones, S., Adams, T. & Ellis, C. (Eds.), *Handbook of autoethnography* (pp. 17–47). Walnut Creek, CA: Left Coast Press.

Lather, P. (2013). Methodology 2.1: What do we do in the afterward? *International Journal of Qualitative Studies in Education, 26*(6), 634–645.

McIntosh, P. (1998). White privilege, color and crime: A personal account. In Mann, C. & Zatz, M. (Eds.), *Images of color, images of crime: Readings*. Los Angeles, CA: Roxbury. Retrieved 11 October 2017 from: http://karenhousecw.org/documents/Undoing RacismWhitePrivilege.pdf.

Nakata, M. (2007). *Disciplining the savages, savaging the disciplines*. Canberra, ACT: Aboriginal Studies Press.

Pratt, M. L. (1992). *Imperial eyes: Travel writing and transculturation.* New York: Routledge.

Smith, L. T. (2012). *Decolonizing methodologies: Research and Indigenous peoples* (2nd Ed.). New York, NY: Zed Books.

Spry, T. (2016). *Autoethnography and the Other: Unsettling power through utopian performances.* Abingdon & New York: Routledge.

Stanley, P. (2013). *A critical ethnography of 'Westerners' teaching English in China: Shanghaied in Shanghai.* Abingdon & New York: Routledge.

Stanley, P. (2017). *A critical auto/ethnography of learning Spanish: Intercultural competence on the gringo trail?* Abingdon & New York: Routledge.

Vass, G. (2013). *White shadows in the classroom: Race-making pedagogies in an Australian classroom.* PhD Thesis, School of Education, The University of Queensland.

Vass, G. (2015). Getting inside the insider researcher: Does race-symmetry help or hinder research? *International Journal of Research & Method in Education, 40*(2), 137–153.

2

'HELP ME'

The English language and a voice from a Korean Australian living in Singapore

Hyejeong Ahn

LANGUAGE AND COMMUNICATION CENTRE, NANYANG
TECHNOLOGICAL UNIVERSITY, SINGAPORE

On my first day in Australia, in Kings Cross, I was confronted with a confused looking, homeless man holding a filthy piece of cardboard, with the words, 'Help me' scrawled across it. The ability to speak English to me, as a Korean, had only ever represented success, power and privilege, all of which I was desperate to have, and thought I would never be able to achieve. Yet, here, incredibly, a homeless man stood before me in the street begging for money in a language that only the wealthy and successful in Korea could call their own. This was the first time that it had ever crossed my mind that English could be owned by 'anyone'. The authority of 'native English speaker' which has positioned me forever as an illegitimate user of the language could be possessed by a homeless man in Australia. I am an English language specialist who has been left with a strong sense of anxiety, inferiority and inadequacy when having to speak in English, who yet still hopes to be freed from this petrifying fear of the language. This chapter explores the process of constructing and continuously reconstructing my multiple identities which are interwoven with my perception of what an ideal English speaker is, and myself as an English language specialist living in Singapore. Three broad categorical themes are presented in this chapter. They examine the change in my perception of English as a language of power, success and privilege to my realisation that the reality of English speakers as presented by English language education is really distorted. The first theme concerns my conflicted relationship with English as a learner of the language. The second and third themes explore my living experience as an immigrant and non-native teacher of English in Australia. These themes focus on how the perceptions of others regarding my status as an immigrant and non-native speaker of English have impacted on my relationship with the English language and as a teacher of the language. The chapter concludes with some insights my experience can offer for English language teaching pedagogy

The language of power and prestige

> 'Help me' scrawled on a piece of filthy cardboard held by a homeless man in Kings Cross, Sydney

On my first day in a conversational English class at a private institution, called a '*Hagwon*' in Korea, Daniel, a handsome, smartly dressed, tall Korean American teacher came into the class saying 'Hello, everyone!' He greeted us in English. I had seen the 'Hello, how are you?' expressions several times in English books in the previous six years of school, and repeatedly practised these expressions in class with my classmates, but I did not recall that I had ever used them in a 'real' interaction. To me, those English phrases had always been something to memorise so that I could produce correct answers in the standardised English tests.

I returned his greeting with: 'Hello'. This was the first time I had spoken English for a genuine communicative purpose. After this first incident of using English as a communication tool, I began to search for English phrases spoken by Hollywood stars in their interviews and paid attention to Daniel's interactions with other students in class. I also searched eagerly for English conversational books and noted that people in the books seemed to look glamorous and attractive.

I started getting the impression that people with good English skills tended to graduate from some of the top universities in Korea and had highly paid and socially well-respected jobs, wearing immaculate suits and dresses. To me, they were glamorous and charismatic. Since that time, it was my ambition to become one of them and English became no longer a boring academic subject full of grammar exercises and memorising vocabulary lists, it was the key to fulfilling my dream.

After two years of burning the candle at both ends trying to become fluent in English and imagining myself as glamorous and successful, speaking fluent and sophisticated English, I was starting to become frustrated. No matter how hard I strived and how many sacrifices I made, I realised that my English skills would never become as good as those of native English speakers. I was starting to become resentful of the privileges that native English speakers seemed to have. It seemed that the proficiency level of a native speaker was something that I fiercely desired but would never be able to achieve. Nevertheless, I was determined to continue my endeavour to master the English language; still dreaming of myself speaking like one of 'those' sophisticated English speakers, although I could not help thinking that life was unfair, mumbling repeatedly, 'Why was I born in Korea and not in one of those English-speaking countries?'

I decided to travel to Australia so I could use the language I had practised so endlessly in Korea. I borrowed AUD $8000 from my uncle to make my first overseas trip. On my first day in Australia, I stayed at a hostel in Kings Cross, an inner-city suburb of Sydney. As I walked out of the hostel, one of the first things that caught my attention was the homeless man begging for money, mentioned above. The ability to speak English to me had only ever represented a special type of success and prestige that I desperately wanted to achieve, but thought was out of my reach, yet here was a homeless man begging for money in a language that only the wealthy and successful in Korea could call their own.

While walking back to the hostel, sulking, complaining, being resentful and frustrated, I questioned myself, 'Aren't English speakers meant to be successful, wealthy and powerful?' How badly have I been misled to think this? How much have I invested to learn the skills that this homeless man uses to beg money for his survival? He was born in the 'right' country to speak this language, I imagined, probably with minimum effort, whereas this ability for me only came with endless dedication, determination and sacrifice. In the past I had got up at 6 a.m. every morning to study English; not to mention that most of my weekends were spent in a library, highlighting and memorising English phrases and vocabulary from the hundreds of expensive English books that I had purchased.

The instance of seeing the homeless man was a moment of realisation for me: 'Why had I been so naïve?' I felt cheated. I saw myself as a foolish Korean girl, believing that what I had seen in textbooks was an accurate portrayal of an English-speaking society. Clearly what I witnessed in Sydney was drastically different from what I had previously envisaged. I was thrown into confusion. I lost my motivation to learn the language of 'power and prestige'.

'The reality' presented in English textbooks has been the subject of critical examination (Bourdieu, 1991; Holliday, 2006, 2009; McKay, 2012) for some time. These studies have argued that the images presented in English textbooks often promote distorted views of the English language and its speakers. The books mainly project a symbolic value of English as the language of power and socio-economic advancement, and, to a large extent, they contain a glamorous and cosmopolitan image of English speakers and their lifestyles. If I had realised earlier that the images constructed in English books only represented a part of English society, just like many other non-English speaking societies, I wonder if I would have been as motivated or as desperate to improve my English profi-ciency skills? If English teaching materials had equipped me with functional skills, instead of projecting a symbolic value of the language as a tool for socio-economic advancement, would my feelings of unfairness and resentfulness have been as strong? Although it may be true to an extent that English proficiency may bring an upgrade in social status and extend the opportunities for success, I felt I was led to believe that the English language was 'a magic wand'. It would have been more appropriate if my education had emphasised the roles of English in a variety of contexts and provided me with a realistic knowledge of a range of different English speakers. I could have been better prepared for what I saw in Sydney and I could have developed a different motivation, that is, to learn the language for international communication.

An immigrant teacher

> Hi, Hyejeong! We have five Korean students visiting our school this month for a short-term study tour. Can you come and work with us for five weeks this term?

In 2005, I had recently graduated from an Australian university having completed a Bachelor's degree in Primary School Education. As I was a first-year teacher, it was difficult to find a permanent employment position at a public school. I decided to apply for several part-/full-time positions advertised by private schools. After sending dozens of resumes, and receiving an equal number of rejection letters, I started to doubt the possibility of me working as a teacher in Australia, a country where I had resided for four years. I was beginning to believe that recruitment committees must only want experienced teachers. I refused to think that I was either racially discriminated against or marginalised because of my foreign cultural and linguistic background.

Although my teaching degree from an Australian university granted me permanent resident status and gave me the opportunity to live and work in Australia, the difference between having the opportunity to work and actually finding work were poles apart. Although the state I lived in was reported to be experiencing a shortage of primary school teachers, local schools were not keen to hire a first-year teacher from a Korean background with a foreign name that they may have found hard to pronounce.

Just as my dream of living and working as a teacher and exploring new places in Australia had started to fade away, I received a phone call from a vice principal at the school where I had recently finished my last teaching practicum. The school is located in one of the most affluent suburbs in South Australia.

'Hi, Hyejeong! We have five Korean students visiting our school this month for a short-term study tour. Can you come and work with us for five weeks this term?'

It was an exciting opportunity and I felt my education, my bilingual ability and my aspiration to integrate into Australian society were finally being recognised. After working closely with the Korean students, assisting their English skills and their early settlement into school life, I felt very proud of myself. After the five weeks had passed, the principal informed me that the school was going to have another batch of students visiting from Korea next term and extended my contract. I felt proud once again, saying to myself: 'I am working at an Australian school as a teacher and the school needs me because I am the only qualified Korean English bilingual teacher in the state.'

However, I soon experienced a creeping realisation that the school only required me to work when there were Korean students visiting. Although I was a qualified teacher who was trained and qualified to be a teacher in Australia with good feedback from my mentor teachers, the school did not hire me to teach mainstream classes. I started to dwell on what the principal thought of me as a teacher. The school had predominantly 'Anglo-Australian' teachers and students from upper middle-class backgrounds, many of whom probably had had little contact with 'non-Australians'.

While I was out of work for a few weeks, I received a welcome phone call from Mark, my mentor teacher from my last teaching practicum at the same school, asking me if I was available to work for him for the duration of the next term as he would be on leave. I was 'over the moon' with the thought that I was going to be responsible for his class for the whole term. 'Mark knew I could be responsible for his class! He had confidence in me that I could teach his students.' But soon after, my excitement was shattered. The principal replaced me with Jessica, another first-year teacher, with the comment that the school would be able to offer me work when the next group of Korean students were visiting. Although his comment must have been made on a subconscious level and with the best of intentions to comfort me that I was not out of a job (Ancheta, 2000), it was a devastating and demoralising moment. I felt vilified, and ignored. I wanted to confront him and ask why I had been replaced despite the fact that Mark selected me to teach his class. I also wanted to clarify with him that I was a qualified primary school teacher in Australia like everyone else that he had hired, who could also speak the Korean language as an additional skill. Not the only skill. I thought to myself, 'Why had my bilingual skills disadvantaged me? Shouldn't this be considered as an advantage?' After I was out of work for a number of weeks, the school called me again to work for five weeks the following term. I accepted the offer, simply to pay the bills. This time, there was no excitement.

The discourse of 'otherness' identifies particular cultures and people from other backgrounds as less proficient and productive than those from within the culture (Kürti, 1997). The principal's comments when offering this type of work with Korean students must have been reasonable to him in his own eyes as being fair, even though his decision was an act of reinforcing the distance between 'him as in us' and 'me as in others', which, I would say, was his conscious production of 'otherness'.

Do I have to supress my Korean-ness? Should I adopt an Anglicised name, like Fiona or Lydia? Or should I try harder to mimic Australian accents? Would these efforts help them perceive me as one of them? What could I do to alter their perception of me from a Korean teacher to being a 'regular' teacher? At the same time, I did not want to reject my deep-rooted ethnic and cultural affiliations. It seemed, however, that how others positioned me was out of my control. Yet, my self-examination of the way I was positioned by the principal and others had significantly influenced my prolonged inner conflict and negotiation in finding my own self within the discourse of 'otherness'.

I had been seeking ways to empower myself in this discriminatory workplace. One way I could have done this at that stage was to pursue further studies, so that in the future I could be in a position where I could train principals of Australian primary schools to increase their awareness of the skills that bilingual and immigrant teachers offered and, hopefully, this would help them to change their deep-rooted attitudes of 'otherness' towards these teachers. Although I had successfully completed my study and empowered myself in some ways, working as a lecturer in Australia and Singapore, I could not help but be bewildered and continued to question myself about whether I had actively sought to decentre 'otherness' in the educational context in Australia or had merely run away from the discourse where I was unable to empower myself. I do wonder how many newly graduated teachers born overseas still experience being 'othered'.

A non-native English teacher

'Where are you from? Your English is really good,' commented John.

While I was completing my PhD studies in 2011, I started working as an ESL teacher at an English language centre in an Australian university. I immensely enjoyed working there. Most of my colleagues seemed to respect my bilingual skills and many of them were bilingual or trilingual with a wide range of lingual and ethnic backgrounds. A majority of them also had experiences living outside of Australia for lengthy periods. I felt comfortable being surrounded by colleagues who understood the educational values of teachers with bilingual skills and international experiences.

One day a new teacher, John, joined me for lunch in the staff room. I was having a discussion about students' assignments with other colleagues. He overheard me talking to the colleagues, then he asked me 'Where are you from? Your English is really good.' I thanked him for his 'compliment'. I carried on the conversation with my colleagues. After the class, I came across John again in the corridor and he repeated his compliment on my English ability again, mentioning, 'I haven't seen many Koreans who can speak English as good as you and your English proficiency is almost as good as an IELTS 8.' I kept walking along the corridor, contemplating 'Why do I have to be the subject of evaluation of my English skills, even by a colleague?' I felt as if he was treating me as one of his students.

After completing my PhD, having resided in Australia for nearly 15 years, I left the country to start working as a lecturer at a university in Singapore. Proudly, I am employed to teach undergraduate and postgraduate students academic English skills. On the first day in class, I introduced myself to students as a Korean Australian and explained my life story in Australia and Korea. Students seemed fascinated by my international experiences.

After a couple of weeks of teaching, I realised I sometimes had difficulties in understanding students' questions. I asked myself, 'Is it to do with the fact that I am not so familiar with their accents?' I started looking at the phonetic patterns and phrases that my Singaporean students frequently used. In the meantime, I also briefly shared my difficulties in understanding students' questions or comments in class with one of my non-Singaporean colleagues, a native English speaker, and thought he might have experienced similar issues when he first arrived in

Singapore. He replied, 'Yes, I sometimes had difficulties in understanding some of their speech but, Hyejeong, it is best not to show your students that you don't understand their questions. They will think you are Korean and that's why you don't understand them.' His intention must have been genuine with his advice to help me out of trouble, but I wondered if his answer reflected his perception of me rather than of the students.

The 'wh' and 'yes–no' questions

'What are you going to do during the Christmas holiday?' asked Peter.
'Are you going to Korea during the Chinese New Year holiday?' asked Jane.

Celebrating Christmas with my friends and family in Australia has become part of my tradition for the past 16 years, whereas the last time that I celebrated the Lunar New Year with family in Korea was in 1998. I started not going home during the Lunar New Year mainly because the air tickets were very expensive for an international student and also because it often fell during the university semester or school term in Australia. Also, my family often spent time together on 1 January rather than on the Lunar New Year, so celebrating the Lunar New Year has not been a 'thing' for me for a long time.

When it was near the Christmas break, many of my colleagues in Singapore during a casual conversation at a lunch break asked me, 'What are you going to do during the Christmas holiday?' Or, 'Any plans for the Christmas break?' I replied to them, 'I am going to Australia.' Then, they also followed up with the question, 'Are you going there for a holiday?', or, 'Do you have a family member in Australia?' I replied, 'I am going there to celebrate Christmas with friends and family in Australia.' I felt that they required a detailed explanation of why I was going to Australia during the Christmas break. Whereas when it was near the Lunar New Year holiday period, I was frequently asked by my colleagues, 'Are you going to Korea during the Chinese New Year?' 'No, I am not going to Korea, I just want to have a rest,' I replied to them.

The open ended 'wh-' questions about my plans for the Christmas break and the close-ended 'yes–no' questions about my whereabouts during the Lunar New Year from my colleagues made me realise that I must be largely perceived as a Korean. They must have assumed that I would participate in one of the Korean cultural celebrations during the Lunar New Year break whereas it would have not occurred to them that I would celebrate the Christmas break. It would not have mattered at all, if I did not feel it was important to me to find out how my colleagues perceived me: either as a Korean or an Australian. Does asking such a question to myself demonstrate my insecurity about my own rooted cultural affiliation, or my desire to be seen as an Australian colleague? Or does this stem from my frustration that my colleagues are not able to see the Australian part of me because of my Korean name and appearance?

At the Australian English language centre and the university in Singapore, it is probably true that I have been largely seen as a Korean colleague; one who celebrates Korean customs and eats Korean food, with my English skills being a subject of 'evaluation'. I was not only complimented on my English skills but I was also advised to pretend to understand when I actually desired further clarification. I was becoming more self-conscious about how I should portray myself to my students and why my colleagues did not see the Australian-ness in me. Why did I feel offended when my English skills were complimented on by a colleague? Why did my colleagues advise me to pretend to understand my students' questions? Why don't my colleagues see me as someone who would celebrate Australian holidays?

These days, I often start a new class by introducing myself as a Korean Australian, giving an explanation of my Australian educational background in a conscious effort to demonstrate my credentials as their lecturer who has been trained in a 'Western culture'. Yet, I have been asking myself, 'Do I continuously let myself be victimised by perceived "native-speakerism discourse" (Holliday, 2006, p. 385) in the English education context?' Holliday (2006, p. 385) problematises native-speakerism as 'a pervasive ideology within English language teaching, characterised by the belief that "native-speaker" teachers represent a "Western culture" and ideal model for English language teaching.' I have been wondering how to find a positive way of validating myself as their lecturer of the English language? I was getting anxious about the thought that my Korean-ness might bring disappointment to my students, most of whom have grown up in the Singaporean education system, where the 'Speak Good English movement' was part of the main discourse (Singapore Government, n.d.). I assumed that Korean English speakers must not be considered as one of the idealised role models for a good English speaker. Would it be better if I reinvented and defined myself as a free-standing person, as opposed to being compared with native speakers of English? Or would it be better if I projected myself as an Australian lecturer? Are these worries from a deeply grounded defence mechanism?

Final comments

The English language has given me a great sense of achievement and simultaneously, also a great sense of uncertainty and resentment. No matter how often and how much I felt frustrated with the status of a recipient of the language of power and success in the discourse of native-speakerism, I have been wondering lately if it is fair to say that the English language has indeed provided me with the tool to achieve the goals that I initially set out to achieve. My initial target goal for English proficiency was that of a native English speaker, which I believed would lead me to accomplish my subsequent goal, which was to finish my studies in a higher education institution and to find a 'high-status' job. I am confident in saying that I have successfully achieved the second goal.

However, my first goal of speaking like a native English speaker requires further examination. It has disheartened me on several occasions as it seemed unattainable and impossible. I have doubted my ability to master the language many times, resulting in feelings of inferiority and bitterness toward native English speakers.

Studies (Ahn, 2017; Kirkpatrick, 2007; Park, 2015) have also proposed that a great majority of English language students in Asian countries often feel inferiority as a result of learning English and these feelings are not only limited to individuals but are also socially rooted. To reduce these adverse effects from having native English speaker proficiency as the target model in English education, it would have been ideal if I had been presented with a different target model for English proficiency.

Canagarajah (2006a, 2006b) has long argued for changes in priorities in English language teaching, stating that the focus should be to teach students to become proficient communicators in English for an international context. According to Canagarajah, even native speakers do not have the skills to negotiate and communicate proficiently in an international context where a number of diversified English speakers from a wide range of linguistic and cultural backgrounds are present. In addition, more people use English today than any other language in the history of the world. English is currently spoken in more than 70 countries as a first language or as an official language and approximately 380 million people speak English as the first language and more than a billion people use it as a second language or additional language (Crystal, 2003). It is common to have contexts where English is spoken and there is no involvement or presence of native speakers. Therefore, English language teaching should aim to prepare students for a realistic landscape of English-speaking contexts, where native English speakers are not always present in English-speaking situations and instead, English is used for international purposes of communicating with other speakers for whom English is their second and additional language. English language teaching should focus on developing students' intercultural communication skills which include a linguistic and cultural awareness of the social linguistic reality of the English-language-speaking context. Effective communicative strategies should be fostered, rather than a focus on mastering native English speaker proficiency (Ahn, 2017). However, an in-depth discussion of the pedagogical problems of native speakerism and a call for a new direction in English language teaching is beyond the scope of this chapter (for more information, refer to Ahn, 2017; Jenkins, 2015; Kirkpatrick, 2007).

I was one of those misled students whose understanding of an English-speaking society was distorted and unrealistic. However, despite my developed and comprehensive awareness of the skills required to communicate effectively in English in an international context, I still cannot help but continue to have an inferiority complex and a conflicted relationship with my rooted linguistic affiliation as a native speaker of Korean and the 'earned' linguistic one of a speaker of English. The opportunity to share my experiences and reflect upon them here makes visible what is generally invisible in personal relations and interactions centred on differences.

In this auto-ethnographic journey, I firstly recounted a number of critical incidents from learning and using the English language and described my ever-changing relationship with the language from seeing it as a 'magic wand' for success to 'merely a tool for communication'. The series of reflections about studying and teaching the language in Korea, Australia and Singapore also portray my own insecurity associated with my rooted ethnicity of being a Korean and an academic, teaching and researching the English language.

The reflections of a small part of my lived experience have explored the perceptions of an immigrant, foreign, non-native speaker of English and an English teacher. They have also examined different methods for accepting or resisting oppressions prevalent in society and questioned if these feelings of resistance have stemmed from paranoia or oversensitivity. It is my hope that sharing and analysing some of my experiences and questions that have accompanied me since starting to learn English has helped to create spaces where critical discussions among students, teachers and researchers in English language fields can occur. Hopefully, this will make a contribution to help empower many people who have the status of 'English learner', 'non-native' and 'immigrant' and to challenge ignorance and prejudice wherever it is found.

References

Ahn, H. (2017). *Attitudes to World Englishes: Implications for teaching English in South Korea*. New York: Routledge.

Ancheta, A. (2000). *Race, rights, and the Asian American experience*. Piscataway, NJ: Rutgers University Press.

Bourdieu, P. (1991). *Language and symbolic power*. Cambridge, MA: Harvard University Press.

Canagarajah, S. (2006a). Changing communicative needs, revised assessment objectives: Testing English as an international language. *Language Assessment Quarterly*, *3*(3), 229–242. doi:10.1207/s15434311laq0303_1

Canagarajah, S. (2006b). The place of World Englishes in composition: Pluralization continued. *College Composition and Communication*, *57*(4), 586–619. doi:10.2307/20456910

Crystal, D. (2003). *English as a global language* (2nd Ed.). Cambridge, UK: Cambridge University Press.

Holliday, A. (2006). Native speakerism. *ELT Journal*, *60*(4), 385–387.

Holliday, A. (2009). English as a lingual franca, 'non-native speakers' and cosmopolitan realities. In Sharifian (Ed.), *English as an international language* (pp. 21–33). Bristol: Multilingual Matters.

Jenkins, J. (2015). *Global Englishes: A resource book for students* (3rd Ed.). Abingdon: Routledge.

Kirkpatrick, A. (2007). *World Englishes: Implications for international communication and English language teaching*. Cambridge, UK: Cambridge University Press.

Kürti, L. (1997). Globalisation and the discourse of otherness in the 'new' Eastern and Central Europe. In T. Modood & P. Werner (Eds.), *The politics of multiculturalism in the New Europe: Racism, identity and community* (pp. 29–53). London: Zed Books.

McKay, S. (Ed.) (2012). *Principles and practices for teaching English as an international language*. New York: Routledge: Taylor & Francis Group.

Park, J. S-Y. (2015). Structures of feeling in unequal Englishes. In R. Tupas (Ed.), *Unequal Englishes: The politics of English today* (pp. 59–73). Basingstoke: Palgrave Macmillan.

Singapore Government (n.d.). *Speak Good English Movement*. Retrieved from http://goodenglish.org.sg/

3

PERSONAL INSTRUCTIONS ON HOW TO REMAIN A STRANGER TO ENFORCE A SOCIOLOGICAL PERSPECTIVE

Silvia Bénard Calva

UNIVERSIDAD AUTÓNIMA DE AGUASCALIENTES, MEXICO

My sociological perspective is very much informed by my personal biography, as a stranger within the broader social context. This problematic weaving of the personal and the social is very much due to ethnic, class, and cultural contradictions that have crossed my family history for generations, because of my father's European ancestry. However, as a family in the Mexican context, we have been unable to name, or explain, how these issues have contributed to or hindered our understanding of who we are. This has not only allowed me to navigate within and across sociocultural settings, but it has given me an unnamed strangeness that has shaped my sociological perspective. The purpose of this chapter is to elaborate on this relationship between biography and profession. This will be done by narrating key 'small epiphanies' that, through introspection, will show how my invisibleness has shaped my inquiry.

> One day I learnt
> A secret art,
> Invisible-Ness, it was called.
> I think it worked
> As even now, you look
> But never see me

This invisibleness, as Meiling Jin so beautifully puts it, has allowed me to navigate within and across sociocultural settings, but has also shaped my sociological perspective (Jin, n.d. cited by DeCaires Narain, 2003, p. 224). The purpose of this chapter is to elaborate on this idea.

Am I Mexican?

Why should I question myself about this? I have often asked myself. Of course I am. I was born in Mexico City and my parents are Mexican. However, I don't

24 Silvia Bénard Calva

feel completely Mexican, because I was born with chestnut hair, fair skin and blue eyes. My father and his sisters spoke in German to each other (not always though, just when they did not want me and my siblings to understand what they were saying), and my grandfather had a strong French accent when he spoke Spanish, despite his second wife being Mexican. His first wife, who had died before I was born, was German.

I am Catholic as well, like most Mexicans. At least, I was raised as such by my mother, who follows a very strong religious tradition. Still, my father often joked about the Catholic Church. He hardly ever attended mass on Sundays, as my mother and we kids did, but my mom and he prayed every night. He even took communion when my brothers and sisters got married. I was the only one who did not marry in the Catholic Church. Nevertheless, my mother proudly recounted: 'When your father asked your grandmother for my hand, she made him promise that you kids would neither speak German at home nor go to a non-Catholic school. Besides, he had to marry in the Catholic Church so he was baptized, took his first communion, and was confirmed before our wedding.' My father did all the things he had agreed to with my grandmother. My parents married in the Catholic Church, all of us kids went to private Catholic schools from kindergarden to high school, and we did not learn German.

Being raised in a Catholic environment, both at home and in a country where, at least during the sixties and seventies, Catholicism dominated and was practiced by most people, meant that my father's non-religious background was apparently irrelevant for us.[1]

Domestic environment

Despite our Catholic upbringing, our way of life wasn't common in Mexico. It was permeated by French and German traditions. We lived next door to the houses of two of my father's sisters. One of these houses was a big French *maison de maître* type, in which my father himself had been raised and where my father's youngest sister still lived by herself, with no company except up to 15 cats. She lived upstairs in the largest bedroom of the house. But there were two other bedrooms, including the one where my sisters and I used to stay, because we had to take turns to keep our aunt company every night. The living room, where we spent most afternoons and evenings with her, was big enough to hold a piano, a big marble-topped table, three different sets of chairs, and another round table in a corner. In that house, with the cats for company, we listened to classical music, practiced our piano lessons, put jigsaw puzzles together, and helped my aunt, *Tía Uli,* to organize her stamp collection. The living room, the bedrooms, and the dining room, where *Tía Uli* and the cats ate *merienda* in the evenings, were connected by a long balcony full of potted plants, bird cages and a big old purple wisteria that had entangled itself around the bars of the balcony railing.

That *maison* was situated on a 7,000-square meter property surrounded by old gardens that had been maintained by three full-time gardeners when my father was a child. But once my grandfather married his Mexican wife and they moved to Acapulco, the garden, along with the rest of that huge house, became terribly neglected. It could not be maintained by my aunt and a solitary gardener who visited only once a week. Nevertheless, there was still a big lawn, of sorts, encircled by two paths, the small track and the big track as we called them, which gave us room enough to ride our bikes. There was also space to play games such as badminton as well as hide and seek, and we managed to roller skate along the paths, too. At the end of the garden there were two hen houses and a duck house next to a pond for them to swim. Beyond the duck pond, I spent hours and hours growing a vegetable garden.

The other two family houses were smaller, located at each side of the big house, and each had garden gates into the big garden. They were originally built by my grandfather for two of his daughters. But while one of my aunts remained single at the big house, my mother and father had gotten married and had started having kids right after. So, as the years passed, there were too many kids crowding our smaller house, while my aunt lived alone at the *maison*. She lived mostly upstairs, though, and so my father settled himself on the ground floor with a studio and a repair shop, next to the old library, which was an extensive room full of all kinds of old stuff; we called it the carcass room. There was also a small photo developing room at the very corner. My other aunt and my uncle lived in the other smaller house, which was the same as ours. They had a child, but my uncle had remarried and moved out of the house by the time I could remember.

Established on the same property as the French *maison*, at the other end of the garden, was the "chocolate factory," a name we used to refer to a cocoa bean processor used to make its derivate products, which kept growing as my father reinvested in it throughout his whole life. That chocolate business was the source of his income and was where my father spent most of his days. It was also where my two brothers sometimes had to work and where, more rarely, the six of us girls helped out. But it was my father who worked and supervised the transformation processes, while my mother did all the secretarial duties that came with administering the factory. She also did most of the housework. My parents were very busy all the time.

That big space was our whole world. We lived there with not much contact with the outside world except for my grandmother on my mother's side and five of my cousins from one of my mother's sisters, who lived a few blocks from our house. There were also our Catholic schools, to which we walked together.

This home environment was unique compared to that of either my cousins on my mother's side or my friends at school. No-one else I knew had such a big house and garden. Nobody else's father stayed at home to work and no-one else's mother did all the administrative and secretarial work for a factory. No-one else had an aunt living with so many cats in an enormous, half-derelict French-style *maison de maître*. And nobody else I knew had hens and ducks in the yard. My acquaintances and friends from school had small to mid-size houses, fathers working in the tertiary sector, a mother who was a housewife, and if they kept any animals then it was a dog or a cat. They also talked about having extended family and friends, and celebrations and parties.

But we only had one celebration a year and it took place in the big *maison*. It was Christmas Eve. That event was carefully planned for months. Macaroons, chocolate stars with sugar lemon icing, pecan and raisins balls, pumpernickel, and other spicy cookies were carefully prepared months in advance by my aunt, with our help. We began by the end of October. I remember sitting on a fallen log with my aunt while shaking pumpernickel through a strainer to clean it from the peels. Then, in the kitchen, we combined the ingredients and either kneaded the dough or beat it by hand, depending on the variety. When the dough was ready, she would let us either press the molds against it, or spoon it onto baking sheets before putting it in the oven. The gorgeous smells that slowly flooded the kitchen as the cookies baked – chocolate, pumpernickel, vanilla, clove – together with the warmth that came from baking all afternoon, slowly changed the coldness of that kitchen and the strong cat odor that was so common inside that house. Once they were done, *tía Uli* carefully kept each different kind of cookie in a big tin jar on a top shelf, out of our reach.

One or two days before Christmas Eve, my sisters and I helped *tía Uli* to clean all the silverware to be used at the party, and our aunt did the cooking while the maid ironed the tablecloths and napkins. On Christmas, all the women worked on setting the table and making the arrangements for the evening. The dinner guests were all of us who lived within the three houses together, and my cousin who had married before I remember, with his wife and three boys. The Christmas tree was carefully set that same day in the anteroom, sometimes with the help of my cousin. But neither of us could see it before the celebration.

Once it was dark and all of us kids were all dressed up and eager to start the celebration, it took more than one visit to my aunt's house before she let us go upstairs. Once we were all ready in the living room, she finally opened the two large paneled doors that led from the anteroom, and let us admire the biggest and most beautiful Christmas tree I had ever seen. It was carefully decorated with ancient adornments and paraffin candles on plates clipped to the tree. The multiple tiny lights, together with the decoration colors and the silver light, drew everybody's attention. We soon refocused our gaze, though, to the bottom of the tree, where there was one carefully wrapped present for each of us kids next to a cellophane bag with cookies and a chocolate Santa Claus.

I was the seventh out of eight kids. There was a nine-year age gap between my oldest sister and I, and five years between me and my youngest sister. Eight kids was too many, even by Mexico City standards at that time: I had three cousins on my father's side, and on my mother's side the families had three, five or maximum six kids. With eight kids, ours was the largest family on both sides.[2]

We lived in our small house next to the French *maison* all the way until I finished high school. We shared books, notebooks, pens, pencils, and coloring pencils in a haphazard way that for me, the seventh, often meant a lack of needed school supplies. The same was the case with school uniforms, shoes and sweaters, which translated into having very limited clothing options and experiencing cold winter mornings at school. We girls sewed our own clothes so that we could keep them more reasonably priced. And to have warm water, each of us heated it in a boiler before showering, making use of dry leaves and sticks we picked up in the big property. Even food was very carefully rationed by my mother.

In short, we were Mexican, but we were white and had many European traditions. We were Catholic, but always listened to my father's critical voice of the Church. And we seemed both rich and poor, because of living in a big property and going to private school while not having enough money for basic needs. Nevertheless, the ways in which all these contradictions intertwined in my family's history were neither understood nor made explicit, either within our family or in the larger Mexican context.

Learning from Max Weber and Georg Simmel

A reading assignment in one of my social theory classes as an undergraduate student was Max Weber's *The protestant ethic and the spirit of capitalism*. Certain characteristics of puritanism Weber describes in the book seamed very familiar to me, although I could not decipher the reasons why until I reached the pages where Weber argues that protestant puritanism remains present even after it is being voided of its religious content. I realized then how much my father resembled that! He was raised with no official religious affiliation, but nevertheless he was strongly influenced by Lutheran ethics, which resulted from his upbringing and his mother's influence. My father, when I knew him, was not a practicing Protestant, but he had many characteristics associated with puritan ethics: he was a hardworking and honest man, with a frugal lifestyle and a strong savings ethic.

My father worked from 5:30 am to 5:30 pm with a one-hour break at 1:00 to have something to eat; the smell of cocoa pervaded the house once he was done with all his self-imposed tasks in the factory. One of his favorite activities, while he was home and relaxing in bed, was to check his stock market account. Many times, I sat down on his bed while he tried to explain to me how the markets worked. He also explained to me that it was necessary to be constantly buying new machinery and expanding the factory to continue being competitive. The factory was a small business so, he often said, "the key for survival is to bet on quality." And quality, I imagined then, required that profit was reinvested in the stock market to make it produce more money for buying machinery. Therefore, I kept thinking, our needs were not germane in comparison.

To make things more complex, my father's frugal lifestyle and his striving for savings was accentuated by his personal biography. He was born in Mexico City in 1909, a year before the beginning of the Mexican Revolution, which brought, among other calamities, economic uncertainty. Then, as a young boy he listened to stories that made him realize how much his extended family was suffering from

28 Silvia Bénard Calva

scarcity in Europe. In 1925, my grandfather decided to enroll my father at McGill University in Montreal, to study engineering. Once he got his degree with honors at such a prestigious Canadian university, he found a job in the United States. But his time there did not last long as he was deported to Mexico in 1931 due to the large unemployment rates during the Great Depression.

As I was growing up, although I wished otherwise, what I inferred from his explanations about financial uncertainty and the need for saving seemed a matter of common sense. But when I read *The protestant ethic*, it very much made me understand how his beliefs, even when voided of their religious content, could derive from his puritan ethic. The lifestyle and ideas about savings, so methodically practiced by my father, were a means to allow for capitalist accumulation.

> This worldly Protestant asceticism, as we may recapitulate up to this point, acted powerfully against the spontaneous enjoyment of possessions; it restricted consumption, especially of luxuries. On the other hand, it had the psychological effect of freeing the acquisition of goods from the inhibitions of traditionalistic ethics. It broke the bonds of the impulse of acquisition in that it not only legalized it, but (in the sense discussed) looked upon it as directly willed by God.
>
> *(Weber, 2005, p. 115)*

Living in a predominantly Catholic country and attending Catholic schools, I had never met a self-confessed protestant in my life. This resulted in an obstacle in realizing that protestantism, which seemed so far away from my background, was a key component of my father's, and thus our nuclear family's, worldview. *This* was what made us strangers within our own wider society! It is also why another classic sociological text, *The stranger* by G. Simmel (1908), sheds so much light on my understanding. Being at a certain distance from the predominant social group contributed to my curiosity about other people's ways of life, while at the same time it facilitated the distancing that allows me to observe social patterns not so easily revealed to the ordinary eye.

The Stranger

Phenomenology and ethnomethodology is the undergraduate sociology course I teach at present. Every time I teach that class, I enjoy discussing the idea of the stranger as it is defined by Simmel, as someone:

> (W)ho comes today and stays tomorrow . . . He is fixed within a certain spatial circle – or within a group whose boundaries are analogous to spatial boundaries – but his position within it is fundamentally affected by the fact that he does not belong in it initially and that he brings qualities within it that are not, and cannot be, indigenous to it.
>
> *(Simmel, 1908, cited by Appelrouth and Desfor Edles, 2008, p. 259)*

As I go on with the class, I verify how those characteristics define my father's family of origin, and my father himself as well, even though he was born in Mexico. A stranger is a person:

- Who "comes incidentally into contact with *every* single element but is not bound up organically, through established ties of kinship, locality, or occupation, with any single one" (p. 404);
- Is characterized by his objectivity. This relates to the above, and because of distance, in the same way as a theoretical observation, his observations come from "a mind working per its own laws, under conditions that exclude accidental distortions and emphasizes whose individual and subjective differences would produce quite different pictures of the same object" (p. 404);
- Has more freedom. "He is the freer man, practically and theoretically; he examines conditions with less prejudice; he assesses them against standards that are more general and more objective; and his actions are not confined by custom, piety, or precedent" (p. 405);
- And he maintains relationships of a more abstract nature with the natives.[3]

As we go through the stranger's characteristics, I am again reminded of my father's extended family, which shared those characteristics depicted by Simmel. This is true even though, as compared to Simmel's Jews in Europe, my father's family was of Christian origin and enjoyed considerably high social status as they were among the few Europeans living in Mexico. Nevertheless, the distance my father enjoyed, I think, allowed him to be more objective and free from certain norms and values that dominated Mexican society. His outsider position was learned by us kids, at least by me, the same way as he had learned puritan ethics from his mother, without noticing it.

Observing and analyzing

The fact that I was the seventh in the family also led me to develop a sociological perspective. As my sisters started having boyfriends and sometimes going to parties, I had to spend long hours as their chaperone, and also helping them sew and iron the home-made garments they would wear when they went out. Since I was seven, when my oldest sister met her boyfriend, and until I was 15, when my next oldest sister decided to rebel against being chaperoned, most of my time outside of home and school was spent with my sisters and their boyfriends.

"I saw you kissing Salvador on the mouth at the wheel of fortune," I say to my sister when we get home.

"I give you ten pesos if you don't tell mother," she says.

"Don't offer her money," my oldest sister interjects. "Just tell her not to tell. She saw me kissing Héctor in the leaving room the other day, and I just told her to be quiet about it."

30 Silvia Bénard Calva

Not another word came from either of them; no more offering money for my silence. Since then it became clear to me that as the chaperone sister, my role was to remain unnoticed and as silent as possible. However, I learned that those qualities didn't prevent me from observing and analyzing what I saw. Isn't that what social scientists are supposed to do?

Christmas vacation

The morning after our Christmas Eve celebration, it is time to visit my grandfather and his wife in Acapulco. The wagon is packed with the ten of us and we are moving out of Mexico City. We are seated quietly, each in our place, just as we were required to by our parents before we could start driving out of the city. My second oldest sister is reading a book, Kosinski's *Being there* (1970).

"This book is great," my sister Elena tells us. "It's about a man, named Chance, who spends his life taking care of the garden in a big property, and he never leaves until the owner, a rich lady, dies. Then, to his surprise, he becomes very popular in the outside world."

"That guy is like us!" one of my brothers says.

Kosinski's book was the closest narrative we had encountered that resonated with our own story. Elena was at the university by then and she was struck by the story of Chance the Gardener, which strongly resonated.

I finished high school a few years later, in 1975, and it took me a couple of years until I finally studied sociology.[4] But by the time I enrolled at university for the first time, as a philosophy major, I could, like my sister, see a bit more of the "real world." This struck me not because I was a successful student, as she was, but for other reasons. My two brothers and one of my sisters were studying at the same private Jesuit University as I was. It was very expensive. I wondered how my father could pay so much for our fees, if he had spent his life saving money. "Take care of cents that pesos will take care of themselves," he used to say. That shows how much education was a priority in my family.

I was only 17 years old at that time and neither of my parents considered philosophy to be a career with a great future for me. Then I invented a crazy plan and I got the courage to ask for permission to do it. We were walking along the street in a small town close to Mexico City, Tonatico, and when the three of us were on the same line and separate from my brothers and sisters, I made the request:

"Do you think it would it be possible for me to spend a semester in Canada with Peter and Lydia? I don't know if I want to continue studying philosophy and I need some time to find out what to do."

"Well, if you think it would help," my mother said.

Then my father said, "Ask them first, and if they agree, you can go."

A couple of months later, I was flying to Canada. I spent five months in Regina, Saskatchewan, with a family that was very close to us even before I went, as we had spent many vacations together in Acapulco, and one of my brothers had gone to spend time with them before.

Canada was another eye-opening experience for me in terms of learning about diversity. I met protestants, found out about Mennonite communities close to Regina, saw many First Nations people on the streets, and took classes with what were considered "typical" Canadian Anglophones. One of the classes I took at the University of Saskatchewan was named *The Decolonization of Quebec*. I chose that subject because I was looking forward to get an understanding of my father's youth, but it did not help much because it was about Francophones, and, like my father, I had never quite understood the reasons for their struggles.

After living in a closed environment for 17 years, I realized being at the university and also in Canada, that people could not only be quite different from me but could also differ markedly among themselves. For this reason, I realized that it would be quite impossible to find a universal criterion to understand everybody's beliefs and actions.

In conclusion

As a sociologist, I have become aware that my personal biography paved the way to my understanding of social phenomena. I was born into a French-German extended family of immigrants who settled in Mexico City at the beginning of the twentieth century. But the latter was not made explicit in a predominantly Catholic and mestizo wider society in Mexico City. Furthermore, I lived a highly isolated childhood within my extended father's family; there, we eight kids lived, played, did homework, housework, and even worked in the "chocolate factory." It was a world unto itself.

When I got in touch with the larger society, it struck me as very unfamiliar and it became the purpose of my reflections. This way, my peculiar background gave me elements to view society from an outsider's perspective, and, as Simmel argues, gave me the opportunity to develop a more objective perspective. Once I started to study sociology, I was able to start making more and more sense out of these issues, helped by the theoretical, methodological and historical material I learned at university.

Viewing my history in light of sociological authors, particularly Weber and Simmel, also allowed me to locate myself within a cultural tradition, framed by protestant ethics, in a predominantly Catholic society. This peculiarity was hardly understood by us as a family, and made us see ourselves as unfit for society at large, and as marginal in very contradictory ways. This was the case even though we were a middle-class family in Mexico City, like our cousins on my mother's side and acquaintances and friends at school.

In the end, writing this text has allowed me to realize how prominent my father's figure has been for the construction of a personal story. Considering my mother's background, and the way in which she dealt with such a multicultural micro world, remains a pending assignment.

32 Silvia Bénard Calva

Notes

1 The total population in Mexico City in 1960 was 4,870,876. Of those, 4,677,685 were Catholic, and 77,152 were protestant (*Censo General de Población*, 1960). In 1970, the population grew to 6,874,165; 6,605,248 were Catholic, and 111,957 were protestant (*Censo General de Población*, 1970).
2 In Mexico City, the average number of children per woman aged 12 years and over, in 1970, was 2.6 (*Censo General de Población*, 1970).
3 This short text, together with two more written by Alfred Schütz, "El forastero" and "La Vuelta al hogar" (1964), are two classic sociological pieces of work on the topic that sociology students should know.
4 In Mexico, students should decide what their major will be in their freshmen year.

References

Appelrouth, S. and Desfor Edles, L. (2008). *Classical and contemporary sociological theory: Text and readings*. Thousand Oaks, CA: Pine Forge Press.
DeCaires Narain, D. (2003). *Contemporary Caribbean women's poetry: Making style*. New York: Routledge.
IX Censo General de Población 1970. Mexico: Instituto Nacional de Estadística y Geografía.
Kosinski, J. (1970). *Being there*. New York: Harcourt Brace.
Shütz. A. (1964). *Estudios sobre teoría social*. Buenos Aires: Amorrortu.
Simmel, G. (1908). The stranger. In K. Wolff (1950), *The sociology of Georg Simmel*. IL: The Free Press.
VIII Censo General de Población 1960. Mexico: Instituto Nacional de Estadística y Geografía.
Weber, M. (2005). *The protestant ethic and the spirit of capitalism*. London: Routledge Classics. First published in 1930.

4

WRITING FLOWS

The self as fragmentary whole

David Bright

FACULTY OF EDUCATION, MONASH UNIVERSITY, AUSTRALIA

In this chapter, I draw on my own experiences of conducting educational research in Vietnam and use Deleuze and Guattari's concept of the assemblage to present a mode of thinking about an autoethnographic Self that is understood as an event: non-essential and constantly becoming in ways that are irreducible to the subjective and personal. I argue that the autoethnographic Self is a product of autoethnographic research; the deed rather than doer. Not pre-existing, the autoethnographic Self is actualised within the complex of cultural, social, and historical encounters between the researcher and the researched, existing in a form of radical alliance from which both researcher and researched are constantly produced and reproduced, constantly becoming in ways that remain resistant to representation, meaning, and understanding.

Introduction

There is a river that cuts through Hanoi, the *Sông Hồng*, or Red River. A Red River that runs a kind of tepid brown colour that is, to my eye, almost but not quite exactly not-red. And, in fact, it's not even named red (*màu đỏ*) but pink (*màu hồng*). A variation of red, I suppose. A tint, red mixed with white. White in red. Is it, I wonder, a matter of perception or a problem of translation?

Sometime during my first year in Vietnam I was told that Vietnamese people couldn't tell the difference between the colours blue and green, with the Vietnamese language having just a single word for both colours: *màu xanh*. I was told and I believed this. It was the result, I think now, of a kind of popularised trickling-down of the Sapir-Whorf hypothesis (Kay & Kempton, 1984); and Brown and Lenneberg's (1954) colour perception experiments; and Berlin and Kay's (1991) colour terms. And I suspect that it was popular and that it did trickle down because it suggested to *us* a reassuring kind of incompetence on the part of *them;* the satisfying superiority of our perceptions and our comprehension of a world that was not, despite what we wanted to believe, ours. Our colours, our words; better than their colours and words. Our words better corresponding with things in the world, with the effect of making us believe that things in the world were ours. Call it what it is, this 'ineradicable distinction between Western superiority and Oriental inferiority' (Said, 1978, p. 42): Orientalism, Colonialism, Imperialism, Racism.

And, of course, it's not even really true. And not only in terms of linguistic relativity but also just simple vocabulary. There is, in *Tiếng Việt*, the Vietnamese language, *màu xanh lá cây* (the blue-green of leaves) and *màu xanh nước biển* (the blue-green of the ocean), and *màu xanh da trời* (the blue-green of the sky) and so on, a way of distinguishing blue and green in language that, it turns out, while different from English colour terminology, is common to many of the world's non-English languages (Kay, 2008; Özgen, 2004). Is this ironic, that it also turns out that rather than being about their inability to name colours properly, this was much more about *our* inability to imagine *them* thinking and naming colours in a different, but no less effective, way to our own?

And so anyway, there is this Red or Pink River that runs thick and brown under the bombed and still-broken arches of the *Long Biên* bridge, feeding the green rice-growing delta that nurtures the city, choked with the silt that is the cradle of Vietnam. The delta is almost entirely devoted to rice cultivation, its intricate layout of ancient dykes and levees arranged prior to history, and testament to the tempestuousness of the river; its violent floods and turbulent fluctuations. The river is Life, this brown, swirling morass that appears to me now more primordial soup than mere water, its infinite atoms of hydrogen and oxygen and carbon forming infinite molecules of water and other stuff that mix in constant motion relative and absolute, producing a water, a river, a city, a country, a people, a language, the name of a colour, and myriad other things in the confluence of particles. Always flowing, the river's eddies and currents are always moving faster and slower as they lay out a body of water. A flow of life, never fixed, never complete, a river that never finally *is*, but that is always becoming: always a water to become river.

Assemblage

Assemblage, the word commonly used to render Gilles Deleuze and Felix Guattari's (1987) *agencement* in English, might also have a problem with translation. Or rather two problems. Or, then again, perhaps none. As Thomas Nail (2017) explains it, the first problem is that 'assemblage' doesn't mean the same thing as *agencement,* and the second is that the French language already has a word *assemblage* that actually does means the same thing as 'assemblage' in English, with all of this suggesting at least the possibility that English readers may be led astray by associating *agencement* with assemblage (Phillips, 2006). Central to the distinction between *assemblage* and *agencement* in French are the notions of arrangement and unity, with the verb *agencer* implying an active arrangement or layout rather than a 'simple coming together', all the while without implying a joined or unified whole (Nail, 2017). Or in other words, as Nail (2017, p. 22) summarises, 'an arrangement or layout is not the same as a unity or a simple coming together'. And yet, Ian Buchanan (1997, p. 81) describes 'assemblage' as 'an apt translation of *agencement*', one that adequately captures what Tomlinson and Habberjam (1977) describe as the active and passive senses of *agencement*: '"a way of assembling or arranging" as well as the resulting "ordering or arrangement"' (p. xiii).

Who knows what it all means?

The river

The red or pink or brown river is neither a unity nor a simple coming together. It is not organismic. It is, rather, a multiplicity. Its parts function without the whole; the whole functions without its component parts or mechanisms. The water and the river are neither part nor whole but rather a 'fragmentary whole' (Deleuze & Guattari, 1994, p. 16), an arrangement of elements that are actively laid out in a certain way at a certain moment, pieced together, but that may and will be and must be removed, recombined, supplemented, and refigured without ever finally producing a unified whole. But this is not a random process. The river is no simple coming together. Its arrangement is active. Untold and unseen forces and relations constitute the river: gravity, flow, pressure, buoyancy, lift, drag, inertia, chaos, continuously laying out a water to become river. And yet the river, nevertheless arranged, has no goal. It is, I reckon, a Nietzschean river, forever incapable of 'being'. In this way, the river is like the world:

> If the world had a goal, it must have been reached. If there were for it some unintended final state, this also must have been reached. If it were capable of pausing and becoming fixed, of "being," if in the whole course of its becoming it possessed even for a moment this capability of "being," then all becoming would long since have come to an end, along with all thinking. . .
>
> *(Nietzsche, 1968, p. 546)*

This river, here and now, is a singularity, an event, not some final state. No pausing. No being. No becoming fixed, only becoming. A river happens.

Assemblage/event

The logic of assemblage, writes Nail (2017, p. 22), 'is the rejection of unity in favor of multiplicity, and the rejection of essence in favor of events.' I sometimes think this makes sense to me, even as I remain unsure what multiplicity *is* or *means*, or if such a question even works anymore (Buchanan, 2008), even though I think I *should* know what it means, because 'what Deleuze and Guattari call

36 David Bright

an assemblage is, in the first instance, a multiplicity' (Patton, 2000, p. 42). And because Deleuze writes important things like:

> there is no being beyond becoming, nothing beyond multiplicity; neither multiplicity nor becoming are appearances or illusions. . . . Multiplicity is the inseparable manifestation, essential transformation and constant symptom of unity. Multiplicity is the affirmation of unity; becoming is the affirmation of being.
>
> *(Deleuze, 1983, pp. 23–24)*

Events seem to offer me firmer ground than multiplicities. Events happen, I guess. They take place. Rivers and cities and people and subjects all occur in moments of time and of space, becoming something even as they lack the capability of finally 'being' and bringing all becoming – and thinking – to an end. Stagoll (2010, p. 89) describes events as 'changes immanent to a confluence of parts or elements, subsisting as pure virtualities (that is, real inherent possibilities) and distinguishing themselves only in the course of their actualisation in some body or state'. Rivers and cities are actualised as bodies or states, distinguished momentarily as events, things that happened or are happening or will happen, here and now, or there and then, or once upon a time, in the confluence of parts and elements. Every river always already the confluence of many rivers. Is this what I am, too? Is 'I' just something that happens?

City/event

This city, too, through which the river flows, is an assemblage of partial objects, arranged and laid out in time and space, only seeming to exist as a unified whole. I can write 'this city *is*' but it isn't really like that at all. Rather, like Nietzsche's world and this uncanny river, the becoming of the city has not and will not and cannot pause or come to an end. It only *is* until you look too closely or for too long. In fact, it shifts and moves. It's nimble, this city, shedding parts and claiming territory, expanding and contracting, never fully determined, becoming such that you can't finally know what it is, or better still what it is capable of, only that it is forever incapable of 'being'.

I arrived and lived in the city, by the river, mapping these spaces that never stood still. I explored and colonised the exotic and unknown, living in the city to conquer the city, distinguishing those real inherent possibilities beyond experience and understanding as I came to know them and name them, representing a city (some city) in words and phrases and sentences that I rehearsed and refined, fixed and controlled within grids of intelligibility and communicability and an appearance of 'being'. I can say and I can write that the city *is* this and that. I can tell people what it's like, or what it was like, rendering the unknown and unimagined recognisable by reducing it to representation, contracting it into a word or a phrase. But something also happens to me in the process. Something that begins from the middle and encroaches outwards as each new pathway is explored and subsumed into the centre. As unknown spaces and entities that previously teased around the outer borders of my imagination are assigned concepts and are fixed and stabilised within the coordinates of common sense and good sense. Distinguished and actualised. Objects begin signifying, and signifiers represent objects. I carve out a territory – my Vietnam – as I traverse the narrow and broken streets and lanes, dusty and exotic and promising, and incorporate them into perception, making them knowable and known. I invade and occupy and colonise. I have become imperious. And in all of this common and good sense is made of the city. And makes the city. And makes me.

Subject/event

I have lately come to suspect that I have, in fact, been assembled. Or perhaps better, continue to be assembled. I feel (fear?) that I am no longer a question of essence, but rather a question of events (Nail, 2017). What will happen once I conclude that I have been arranged and laid out, without forming a unified whole? What forces have actively arranged me as such? What 'external relations of composition, mixture, and aggregation' (Nail, 2017, p. 23) have produced this becoming (what, exactly?) of Little David, existing and subsisting as pure inherent possibility that is distinguished only momentarily? I no longer 'am', as far as I can tell. Instead I happen, time and time again, never identical, never quite the same. 'I' is no longer an essence, rather, it belongs to 'a process of subjectification, that is, the production of a way of existing, [that] can't be equated with a subject, unless we divest the subject of any interiority and even any identity' (Deleuze, 1995, p. 98).

Self/event

And so I am in the city, watching the river, sitting on the bridge, even as I am not sure what 'I' is anymore, having divested it of interiority and identity (*have I really, though?*). I have entered the flow. I observe the river, sitting, listening, watching, and smelling. I perceive water flows, motorcycle flows, people flows, flows of the scents of the *Long Biên* market's food and filth that drift by momentarily, along with the permanent cacophony of human and inhuman sounds, punctuated by the horns of motorcycles and roar of trucks below on *Trần Quang Khải*. The thin or thick brown or pink or red water swirls and swells or sometimes sits still in the river below, speeding and slowing through the smaller nearer channels that form the *bãi giữa*, the farming islands below the bridge. In the main channel, sand and silt-filled barges sit so low in the water they appear all surface and no body.

I am in Vietnam, and Vietnam is in me. White in red and red in white. Only it's not really Vietnam that's in me but Hanoi, and even then it's nobody's Hanoi but my own. And I'm not even sure what this 'I' is that's in it and that it's in. I calculate that I have spent something in the order of four years, or 1460 days, or perhaps as many as 35,000 hours here in the city. Perhaps a tenth of my entire life so far.

38 David Bright

Never long enough to become Vietnamese, for sure, but long enough to be in the middle of becoming something else. Something happening. It is here that I have become recognisable as researcher. Here that I have written. It is in me, part of me. I am in Hanoi, and Hanoi is in me, such that I am no longer that which I was without it in me, that 'I' that had never been, that had never watched the rotting river or eaten its white rice. This I – not that I, even as this I is to become another. This 'I' that still returns, time after time: "'I" after "I" after "I"' (St. Pierre, 2016, p. 8). What happens, ask Lather and St. Pierre (2013), 'if we give up "human" as separate from non-human, how do we exist? Can there be there an instituting "I" left to inquire, to know? Dare we give up that "I," that fiction – the doer before the deed?'

Don't ask me, because I don't know.

Time

Time is a problem. The river is Time. It is duration. Perhaps we have always known this. It is pure flow. It has no precise beginning or end. It neither starts nor finishes, the stuff of river enters the flow at all points, traversing what we perceive as a unified river, producing the flow, exiting the flow, creating or returning to other flows. The river *isn't*, as such. No body of water identical to itself. No unity of river. Only an endlessly repeated flow of river that is each time different, as the flow courses through each valley. Every moment of river constituting an event, a momentary arrangement of particles distinguishing itself in motion and rest, speed and slowness, never repeated, never fully determined, never final, even as the river subsists, once upon a time, a water to become river.

This, as an aside, is or was or will be the secret Hesse's (1971) Siddhartha learned from his river as he lived the life of the ferryman:

> That the river is everywhere at the same time, at the source and at the mouth, at the waterfall, at the ferry, at the current, in the ocean and in the mountains, everywhere, and that the present only exists for it, not the shadow of the past nor the shadow of the future.
>
> *(Hesse, 1971, p. 107)*

All sorts of rivers everywhere, all the time, always returning. But always here and now, always and forever *hic et nunc*: Hesse's river. Twain's river. Conrad's river. All rivers ever. All rivers flowing; still.

End

And so, at any rate, here I am now, looking at my river. Existing only in the present. Only I'm not really, I'm sitting in my office in Melbourne remembering and writing about being there looking at the river, remembering and writing about standing and looking at a red or pink or brown river in a moment that

I can't be sure really happened any more, even though I know that there is a river and I have seen it. I can escape neither the shadow of the past nor the shadow of the future.

But the river is everywhere, or perhaps better, every when. Whatever river I saw is gone, even as the water flows still. The river has changed. The body has changed, its components parts replaced like the planks of Theseus's ship. And the I, too, has changed. This I similar and dissimilar to that which gazed unknowingly at the river, oblivious to what would come. No less or more I than this I – I guess – but not Identical.

Here I am becoming something daily as I ride my small Honda motorcycle across the old bridges to the new schools I study in the back alleys of *Gia Lâm* and *Mỹ Đình*. Across the river, in the city, part of a new flow of money and ideas and teachers and students. Nobody knows who I am or was. I am freed of being this or that, at least to a point. I am an event, a once-upon-a-time becoming-other of Little David. A Little David to become something (*to become what?*). A Little Researcher to become writer. I am arranged and laid out in a certain fashion, by certain forces that remain unknown to me, but also without a goal, never to finally become, such that I would 'no longer be becoming, but would be so' (Plato, 1961, line 155).

And so here's a problem, then: what writing – what representation of Self – might begin from and end with the 'I', without that idea of 'being' that closes down becoming and thinking? Without presuming interiority and identity? How does autoethnography work when we no longer consider ourselves as '*the cogito*, a knowing subject, an epistemological subject, separate from, superior to, and master of everything else in the world' (St. Pierre, Jackson, & Mazzei, 2016, p. 102)? It's not a new problem by any means, but an interesting one, one that has been recognised, but also one that subsists. A problem whose limits remain. Reed-Danahay (1997), for example, suggests that it is autoethnography that:

> synthesizes both a postmodern ethnography, in which the realist conventions and objective observer position of standard ethnography have been called into question, and a postmodern autobiography, in which the notion of the coherent, individual self has been similarly called into question.
>
> *(Reed-Danahay, 1997, p. 2)*

And Gannon (2006), apprehending the paradox of an autoethnographic research that presumes 'subjects can speak (for) themselves' (p. 475), calls for 'an explicit and disruptive poststructural autoethnography, for deconstructive textual practices that represent and trouble the self at the same time' (p. 477), recognising that 'the writing writes the writer as a complex (im)possible subject in a world where (self) knowledge can only ever be tentative, contingent, and situated' (p. 474). I like this idea most: that the writing writes the writer. It seems to me that this arrangement of words, carefully laid out according to forces of grammar and recognisability and meaning and desire and interest and methodology

40 David Bright

and publishing requirements and whatever, this careful and active arrangement of words is writing me, producing this 'I' that writes, rather than the other way around. The 'I' no longer the doer before the deed, but the deed itself. The 'I' distinguished momentarily within a sentence or a clause or a phrase, actualised within a body of writing. Something that happens in the writing, and perhaps returns in the reading.

Does it still work if I say I'm not writing about a Self, nor speaking for myself, but rather writing a self, speaking a Self to become Self? Actualising a Self in writing of the immanent possibilities of self, in the way that all sorts of ethnography have always produced a writer who writes and who has written, to the effect that, as Paul Atkinson (1992, pp. 10–11) observes, 'Whyte is Street Corner Society (1981); Willmott and Young are Bethnal Green; Lacey is Hightown Grammar (1971). They have other personae too, but we know scholars and their fields through the work of the monograph.' It is here, in the writing, that we are arranged, laid out, actualised in some body of writing that has nothing to do with an interiority or identity, but is ordered and arranged according to rules of recognisability and judgement. It is here that we continue to write lines and lines of text, because, 'what's interesting, even in a person, are the lines that make them up, or they make up, or take, or create' (Deleuze, 1995, p. 33). The writing produces the writer. Perhaps we have always known this as well. As Foucault wrote, 'one writes to become someone other than who one is. Finally there is an attempt at modifying one's way of being through the act of writing' (Foucault, 1986, p. 184). And 'the work is more than the work: the subject who is writing is part of the work' (Foucault, 1996, p. 405). And Deleuze:

> Writing is a question of becoming, always incomplete, always in the midst of being formed, and goes beyond the matter of any livable or lived experience. It is a process, that is, a passage of Life that traverses both the livable and the lived. Writing is inseparable from becoming . . .
>
> *(Deleuze, Smith, & Greco, 1997, p. 225)*

Writing, rivers, cities, each always incomplete, each always in the process of being formed, each always distinguished only momentarily in some body or state. This, perhaps, is the secret of the river, and the secret of writing, and the secret of the city. That the writing and the river and the city are neither part nor whole, but rather always a fragmentary whole, comprising elements that are laid out or arranged in a certain way at a certain moment, but that may well and indeed must be removed, recombined, supplemented, and refigured, without finally producing a unified whole, a finished writing, a paused river, a fixed city. And as with the river and the city and the writing, so it is with the self. No unity of self, only this fragmentary whole, arranged, laid out, pieced together, here and now. I am an 'I' arranged of heterogeneous elements, laid out in writing arranged as a whole, the parts functioning without the whole; the whole functioning without its component parts or mechanisms. *This* writing, this city, this river, this self, here and now. This I that is written by the writing, no longer the 'I' that writes, 'I' no longer the doer but the deed. Asked about his life and the relation between biography and bibliography, Deleuze described the process of writing together with Felix Guattari:

> Felix and I, and many others like us, don't feel we're persons exactly. Our individuality is rather that of events . . . a philosophical concept, the only one capable of ousting the verb "to be" and attributes. From this viewpoint, writing with someone else becomes completely natural. It's just a question of something passing through you, a current, which alone has a proper name. Even when you think you're writing on your own, you're always doing it with someone else you can't always name.
>
> *(Deleuze, 1995, p. 141)*

Here lies this I after I after I, laid out beside a river, in a city, on a page, neither unity nor simple coming together, no longer something 'to be', but rather something active and arranged, something that happens, something done in writing, produced in a body of writing, never alone, always returning, always existing in the present, always already here and now.

References

Atkinson, P. (1992). *Understanding ethnographic texts*. Thousand Oaks, CA: SAGE Publications, Inc.

Berlin, B., & Kay, P. (1991). *Basic color terms: Their universality and evolution*. Berkeley: University of California Press.

Brown, R. W., & Lenneberg, E. H. (1954). A study in language and cognition. *The Journal of Abnormal and Social Psychology, 49*(3), 454–462. doi:10.1037/h0057814

Buchanan, I. (1997). The problem of the body in Deleuze and Guattari, Or, What can a body do? *Body & Society, 3*(3), 73–91. doi:10.1177/1357034X97003003004

Buchanan, I. (2008). *Deleuze and Guattari's Anti-Oedipus: A reader's guide*. London: Continuum.

Deleuze, G. (1983). *Nietzsche and philosophy* (H. Tomlinson, Trans.). London: Continuum.

Deleuze, G. (1995). *Negotiations: 1972–1990* (M. Joughin, Trans.). New York: Columbia University Press.

Deleuze, G., & Guattari, F. (1987). *A thousand plateaus: Capitalism and schizophrenia* (B. Massumi, Trans.). Minneapolis, MN: University of Minnesota Press.

Deleuze, G., & Guattari, F. (1994). *What is philosophy?* (H. Tomlinson & G. Burchell, Trans.). London: Verso.

Deleuze, G., Smith, D. W., & Greco, M. A. (1997). Literature and life. *Critical Inquiry, 23*(2), 225–230.

Foucault, M. (1986). *Death and the labyrinth: The world of Raymond Roussel* (C. Raus, Trans.). London: Continuum.

Foucault, M. (1996). *Foucault live: Interviews, 1961–1984*. New York: Semiotext(e).

Gannon, S. (2006). The (Im)Possibilities of writing the self-writing: French poststructural theory and autoethnography. *Cultural Studies ↔ Critical Methodologies, 6*(4), 474–495. doi:10.1177/1532708605285734

Hesse, H. (1971). *Siddhartha* (H. Rosner, Trans.). New York: Bantam Books.

Kay, P. (2008). Synchronic variability and diachronic change in basic color terms. *Language in Society, 4*(3), 257–270. doi:10.1017/S0047404500006667

Kay, P., & Kempton, W. (1984). What is the Sapir-Whorf hypothesis? *American Anthropologist, 86*(1), 65–79.

Lather, P., & St. Pierre, E. A. (2013). Post-qualitative research. *International Journal of Qualitative Studies in Education, 26*(6), 629–633. doi:10.1080/09518398.2013.788752

Nail, T. (2017). What is an assemblage? *SubStance, 46*(1), 21–37.

Nietzsche, F. W. (1968). *The will to power* (W. Kaufmann & R. J. Hollingdale, Trans.). New York: Vintage.

Özgen, E. (2004). Language, learning, and color perception. *Current directions in psychological science, 13*(3), 95–98.

Patton, P. (2000). *Deleuze and the political.* London: Routledge.

Phillips, J. (2006). Agencement/Assemblage. *Theory, Culture & Society, 23*(2–3), 108–109. doi:10.1177/026327640602300219

Plato. (1961). Parmenides (F. M. Cornford, Trans.). In E. Hamilton & H. Cairns (Eds.), *The collected dialogues of Plato, including the letters* (pp. 920–956). Princeton, NJ: Princeton University Press.

Reed-Danahay, D. E. (1997). Introduction. In D. E. Reed-Danahay (Ed.), *Auto/ethnography: Rewriting the self and writing the social* (pp. 1–17). Oxford: Berg.

Said, E. W. (1978). *Orientalism.* London: Penguin Books.

St. Pierre, E. A. (2016). Deleuze and Guattari's language for new empirical inquiry. *Educational philosophy and theory*, 1–10. doi:10.1080/00131857.2016.1151761

St. Pierre, E. A., Jackson, A. Y., & Mazzei, L. A. (2016). New empiricisms and new materialisms. *Cultural Studies ↔ Critical Methodologies, 16*(2), 99–110. doi:10.1177/1532708616638694

Stagoll, C. (2010). Event. In A. Parr (Ed.), *The Deleuze dictionary* (Revised ed., pp. 89–91). Edinburgh, Scotland: Edinburgh University Press.

Tomlinson, H., & Habberjam, B. (1977). Translators' Introduction. In G. Deleuze & C. Parnet (Eds.), *Dialogues* (pp. xi–xiii). New York: Columbia University Press.

5

SEARCHING FOR 'MY' MEXICO

An autoethnographic account of unlearning and relearning about the limits of knowing the Other

Alice Cranney

SCHOOL OF EDUCATION, UNSW SYDNEY, AUSTRALIA

This chapter explores the complications and tensions of researching a field which is not completely 'strange' to the researcher and in which they are not a complete Other. Rather what Bhabha (1994) terms a 'third space' is occupied, the position between the insider and outsider researcher. There has been extensive discussion regarding a researcher's positionality and the possibility of mediating the effects of positioning in research. The focus of this discussion is a PhD journey which began with the expectation of understanding and representing the participants' research to an acknowledgment of the limitations of what a researcher can know. The analysis of two autoethnographic narratives in this chapter aims to demonstrate the ways in which autoethnography can assist a researcher in their exploration and problematisation of their own construction of cultures when conducting research about cultures to which they are neither insiders nor outsiders.

Introduction

I embarked upon a PhD with the intention of exploring how a study abroad experience can alter a student's perception of themselves and the Other, with the rationale that this had been my lived experience. However, the PhD is an 'unmapped journey, and what takes place in between is frequently ambiguous and open to numerous possibilities' (Elliot *et al.*, 2016, p. 1183). This liminal journey transforms the self through a dialogue between society and the self (Deegan & Hill, 1991, p. 324). In doing so, the researcher engages in a dialogue of self-reflection, self-exploration (Deegan & Hill, 1991, p. 322). On completion, the successful dissertation author completes their liminal journey with their absorption into a new community of intellectual experts (Deegan & Hill, 1991, p. 324). Therefore, rather than just the pursuit of professional knowledge, as a result of this process, multiple identities are formed and re-shaped within a web of shifting experiences, positionalities

44 Alice Cranney

and beliefs (Leki, 2003, p. 68). A central element in this is the process of exercising agency as an academic in their negotiation of different professional and personal perspectives as well as their negotiation and presentation of knowledge (Soong *et al.*, 2015, p. 445). The tensions and conflicts which arise on the PhD journey in terms of knowledge and the Other will be the focus of this chapter.

In this chapter, I will discuss two conclusions I drew from my PhD experience, by analysing two pivotal moments in my thesis journey. First, I will explore the impact of my positionality as, as a past exchange student and a researcher, I occupied what Bhabha (1994) terms a 'third space', the position between the insider and outsider researcher. Second, having initially set out to discover the way in which the Other is constructed and then altered when a person is immersed in Other cultural worlds for an extended period of time, I learnt about myself, my construction of the Other and the limitations of what I can know as a researcher.

The aim of this chapter then is to discuss these two ideas as well as the way in which autoethnography can assist a researcher in their exploration and problematisation of their own construction of cultures when conducting research about cultures to which they are outsiders. As a result of this discussion the reader will be challenged to reflect on and consider the implications of their positioning in research. I will discuss two autoethnographic vignettes; the first describes an interview I conducted with an undergraduate exchange student in Mexico as part of my PhD fieldwork. The second narrative reflects on my PhD thesis completion celebration. Through the analysis of two narratives, this chapter will explore, first, my positionality as a researcher in the 'third space' and the tensions and conflicts which arise from such a position. Second, the disconnect between my desire to 'know' the Other and the limitations of what I and the interviewees can 'know' of the Other.

Liquid identities

Rather than reducing the categories of insider and outsider research to a dualistic opposition, I believe that I occupy a 'third space'; a perspective that allows me to acknowledge the nuances of identity and the many factors which contribute to a person's identity (Nakata, 2015, p. 169). Thus, I embrace Bauman's (2000) notion of 'liquid identities', constantly shifting, fragmented, incomplete and contradictory, to appreciate how boundaries in the research process can be 'messily blurred in particular places and times' (Thomson & Gunter, 2010, p. 26). It was this 'moving away from the gaze of the distanced and detached observer to embracing intimate involvement, engagement and embodied participation' with autoethnography that I began to recognise both the strengths and limitations of my own experiences and perspectives in the research process (Ellis & Bochner, 2006, p. 433). A cornerstone of ethnography is the idea of making the unfamiliar more familiar in order to make claims of knowledge or understanding. However, my research context was 'familiar' to me so I was presented with different methodological challenges as I tried to make the familiar unfamiliar. Through autoethnographic reflexivity,

I have sought to delve deeper into my positioning by exploring at 'high deep' conscious level (Saldaña, 2015). I have become more aware, deliberate and purposeful in my research by imploring me to reflect deeply on the knowledge I can gain and represent, and the role of my positionality in this. This is particularly pertinent given the transnational nature of contemporary society and the accompanying changes to conceptualisations of national identity which have affected research activity and require the notions of insider and outsider researchers to be revisited and questioned (McNess *et al.*, 2015, p. 297).

While I had been an exchange student in Mexico, I was confronted with many Others during the course of my PhD candidature. For the purposes of this chapter, Othering will be defined as 'constructing or imagining, a demonised image of "them2, or the Other which supports an idealised image of "us", or the Self' (Holliday, 2011, p. 69). In particular, Edward Said's work on the idea of Orientalism, which is a political vision of reality whose structure has 'promoted the difference between the familiar (Europe, the West) and the strange (the Orient, the East)', has been very influential on the concept of Othering (Said, 1979, p. 43). A surprise for me was that the 'strange' also became the exchange students and their experiences as I realised that their experiences and perspectives on Mexico were not always the same as mine. For me, the 'strange' was Mexico both when I first completed a study abroad and then returned to interview my participants who were on exchange in Mexico.

However, the strange/familiar binary is not so clear cut as the presence of 'Mexicanness' in Australia has increased dramatically in recent years, with the opening of tequila bars, Mexican restaurants and food chains, salsa clubs, Spanish language schools and events like the Agave Love Conference, the Brisbane Mexican Festival and the Day of the Dead Australia Warehouse Project. With Australia's increased exposure to and interaction with Mexico in recent times has come a more concrete and widespread notion of *Mexicanidad*, Mexican stereotypes or what out-groups perceive as inherently Mexican (Australian Bureau of Statistics, 2011). Thus, when I embarked upon exchange I did so with prior imaginings of Mexico.

In young, urban Australia, a positive and vibrant stereotype of Mexico has arisen, drawing upon discourses of exoticised, tropicalised cultural Otherness, such as tequila, *fiestas*, *sombreros*, the Day of the Dead, salsa dancing, *burritos* and Frida Kahlo (Lewis, 2009). In contrast to the U.S.A. where Hispanics comprise over 17 per cent of the U.S. population (United States Census Bureau, 2014), Australia is home to few Mexican nationals, who might contest this misty-eyed Disneyfication of their cultures. As a result, there is an 'imagined community' in Australia that invests in the ideas and practices of *Mexicanidad*, which operates as a vacant conceptual category into which 'cool' yearnings can be inscribed. While at the same time, Mexican nationals, or people who have returned from travelling in Mexico, set up businesses, or engage in dialogue that seem to reproduce the stereotypes of which they may be critical. In doing so, they are actively contributing to the sale and commodification of this idea of *Mexicanidad*.

46 Alice Cranney

To further complicate the construction of Mexico, equipped with 'imagined communities', a person, in this case Australian exchange students, travel experiences and intercultural interactions with the Other can 'reproduce misunderstandings on Otherness, reducing the people and cultures of destination places to the stereotypes circulating in the societies to which the tourists belong' (Brito-Henriques, 2014, p. 321). The us/them binary insists that 'non-modern cultures are not allowed to progress, to grow and change. They are placed in stasis, always ready and available for "Western" consumption of an imagined, nostalgic past' (McRae, 2003, p. 239). The effect of this is the 'exoticisation' of non-Western people and cultures, producing and reinforcing the power imbalance between the creator of discourse, 'the norm' and the subject of discourse, 'a distortion of the norm' (Brito-Henriques, 2014, p. 329). The authenticity sought by travellers comprises a destination image which is a colonial discursive construction of Otherness (Smith & Duffy, 2003). Therefore, imagined communities of the Other create the potential for a contestation between the 'real' and the 'imagined'. However, as will be seen in the narratives, the 'imagined' was preserved and performed through a variety of strategies. In return, colonised people perpetuate their condition as a result of 'colonial mimicry', 'the desire for a reformed, recognisable Other, as a subject of a difference that is almost the same, but not quite' (Bhabha, 1994, p. 126). Thus, the discourse of mimicry is created around an ambivalence as in order to be effective mimicry it must continually reinforce its slippage, its excess, its difference.

Postcolonialism problematizes the duality of coloniser and colonised and the accompanying structures of knowledge and power. This problematising assists me in reflexively reconsidering and interrogating the terms of my research (Hall & Tucker, 2004, p. 1). This involves interrupting the mindset that I, as researcher, and to some extent the participants, am required to render a culture legitimate instead of recognising that I cannot explain the Other. My belief that 'autoethnographic praxes are as profoundly focused upon the sociocultural representations of the Other as those of the self' will be demonstrated through my autoethnographic narratives below in which I explore the Self, framed through my experiences of and with the Other (Spry, 2016, p. 30). The employment of the concept of Othering in this chapter will assist in the examination and identification of what Anderson (2006) terms the 'imagined communities' of Others that permeate discourse and social milieu resulting from the continuing ideology of colonialism.

What counts as the 'real' Mexico?

Slouched in her chair, sunglasses on, the remnants of foam still in her hair from last night's foam party, Izzy chats freely about the adventures she has had, the gorgeous Latinos she has met and the 'authentic' street food she loves.

Opposite, I sit upright, hair pulled back, reading glasses on, tape recorder in hand, listening intently. Despite the connection between us, both having been Australian exchange students in Mexico, my crow's feet, ironed blouse and wedding band mark the passage of time, and my place as an outsider; my occupation of a 'third space' as a past exchange student, now researching current Australian exchange students. A researcher, perhaps a little older, more serious, less spontaneous and definitely not heading to Cancún for a week of heavy partying during the university spring break. But maybe this is also just how I remember life as an exchange student.

Izzy chose the café for our interview today, a salad bar owned by an American expatriate couple. 'What can I get y'all today?', the owner asks with his deep southern drawl. 'An orange juice for me please.' 'Soy latte please,' Izzy responds. 'Sure thing.' When he has gone, Izzy whispers, 'I miss Australian coffee so much. It is just not the same here. Sometimes I just sit here and daydream about Australian coffee.' 'Really?' I ask. As a tea drinker, I struggle to empathise but don't really say anything. She quickly adds that there are lots of things she will miss about Mexico. 'When I'm home I will be dreaming of seafood burritos until I get back to Mexico to have one.'

'Thanks for meeting me here. This is my favourite local hang out.' Silently, I question the 'localness' of this café, listening to the English echoing through the room. 'Stop judging this poor young girl, Alice' I chastise myself, as I remember that I too had a sanctuary in Mexico. The crisp white home of my cousin and his family in Guadalajara, a sanctuary made up of Liverpool Football Club matches on the TV and cheese toasties. My reprieve from the exhaustion, the difficulty and excitement that come from interacting in cultures that are not your own, I understand. Here, unlike on the pavement outside, we are the majority. We feel a sense of belonging. Yet I can't help but feel conflicted, a nagging sense as the researcher that she is not experiencing Mexico. Although my sense of what Mexico is has also blurred as a result of my research. So maybe it is better to say that she is not experiencing MY Mexico.

'No problem. What do you like about it? Good food?' 'To be honest, it is a break from the chaos of this place, and I am just so sick of eating tortillas everyday,' she sighs. The lightness she had before leaves her, furrowed brow and glassy eyes take its place. Izzy opens up to me about the challenges she has been facing day to day: the language barrier, the male attention, her sense that she will never belong due to being a *güera* (a colloquial term in Mexico for a blonde female). She lingers on this last point. I feel myself soften towards her, empathetic of the difficulties that come with being an outsider. I take off my glasses, and lean in, removing my researcher armour. I know that I will chastise myself later, as I listen back to the tapes, for a noticeable change in tone and questioning. A shift to a comforting conversation rather than an interview.

Our drinks arrive. After a few sips of coffee, rejuvenated, her glow returns. She begins to tell me all about the 'real' Mexico she has experienced. Her disappointment that it has been so fleeting and sporadic is evident in comments like, 'This place is so touristy. It is not Mexico. It wasn't until I went travelling that I got to see that.' She asserts, seemingly unaware of the irony in her comment, considering that we are sitting in an American organic salad bar, paying extortionate prices for mediocre Western food. Again, I reprimand myself. I remember feeling these same frustrations in my search for the 'true' Mexico.

48 Alice Cranney

'What do you think counts as "real" Mexico?' I ask. 'Traditional Mexico without the American influence,' she answers definitively, her answer reflecting the imaginative geographies of 'otherness' which are central to her construction of a homogeneous and exotic 'real Mexico' (Said, 1978). It is the Mexico, which exists in the social imaginary of *Mexicanidad* as the unknown, peripheral Other (Holliday, 2013, p. 537). 'I don't want to be surrounded by tourists. I want to live like a local,' she continues. As if to convince herself that she is living like a 'local', she describes the gym she goes to – 'I go to this military hardass gym in this other part of town, not fancy' – and the vegetable market as 'this really cute market at the end of my street with an old lady selling heaps of fruit and veg-etables'. 'What form did my search for authenticity take?' I ponder. I definitely never went to a 'hardass' boxing gym but I can't deny that I did go to some lengths in what MacCannell (1973) terms my search for authenticity, including riding on a tequila-shaped bus. However, from my side of the café table I can't help but feel the critic rising in me.

Her phone pings and her eyes light up, it must be a text from the 'cute' Mexican boy she has been seeing. 'Sorry, I really want to reply to this,' she giggles. As she constructs her response, I further reminisce on my exchange in Mexico. Was my time here filled with the authentically 'Mexican' experiences she describes? Did I seek out the exotic Other as persistently as she appears to? Perhaps my memory betrays me but while on exchange day to day, my mornings were spent at uni-versity while I sipped the afternoons away in Starbucks, or rifling through the sales racks for bargains in Zara, with the other international students. Thrown in were glimpses of 'my' Mexico of the mind, cultural markers of my prior imagin-ings; a piñata at a fiesta, a taco eaten on the curb, the *lucha libre* stadium that was simultaneously oppressive because of the lack of ventilation in a glorified shed and completely enthralling because of the ambience of the crowd. Although these were elements in the reductive and homogeneous version of *Mexicanidad* found in Aus-tralia, I needed these to help me 'make sense of, and negotiate these "other" cul-tures' (Holliday, 2011, p. 70). Later, reflecting on my party, I had an 'ephiphany' as I noticed that in my performance of a worldly exchange student I had drawn on elements of the imagined community of Mexico to conceptualise the Other, just as Izzy had (Denzin, 1989, p. 170). This was a burgeoning realisation as a result of my PhD journey: data collection, interactions in and out of the field and extensive reflections. I realised that now, in my position as a researcher, I was slating her for doing what I had previously done, and undoubtedly still do.

My thoughts are interrupted by her reassurance to me, and perhaps to herself, that she has found home, 'even though it is not very Mexican here, I love it. It is home for me now'. As she talks about all the friends she has made, a stab of long-ing hits me, missing my family and friends. Time and circumstance have excluded me from being invited into the community of which she speaks; the absence of a hangover, and foam in my hair, my betrayers. And it hits me, although not for the first time, that this is no longer home for me. Many of the participants have expressed a sentiment of feeling at home in their exchange communities, no doubt as I had done six years earlier. However, now I wonder whether it ever really was or whether it ever could be home given the deeper understanding of the implications and complications of an outsider claiming insiderness. This research has highlighted to me the oddity of the position of exchange students, the 'third space' they occupy: an intangible, artificial position and the attributed identities which accompany them. As well as the oddity of my position as research.

Although my body aches with sadness at the shattering of my illusion of home, romanticised with each passing year, I sit with the discomfort. The process of interviewing has taught me the importance of asking the uncomfortable questions of both interviewee and interviewer. Indeed, reflections on my positionality are in themselves evidence of a shift in my identity and sense of self as I transition to occupy the ambiguous 'third space'. At that moment, as if sensing my thoughts, she enquires 'what was it like when you were here?', an invitation to enter back into world of exchange, if only briefly.

My third space

As a result of the research process, I came to understand the 'third space' I inhabit. However, as this vignette demonstrates, it was not simple or clean cut but rather messy and blurred as I tried to navigate and understand my positioning. A qualitative researcher's positionality is a paradoxical one: on the one hand, they are required 'to be acutely tuned-in to the experiences and meaning systems of other's while on the other hand 'be aware of how one's own biases and preconceptions may be influencing what one is trying to understand' (Corbin Dwyer & Buckle, 2009, p. 55). My personal experience as an exchange student meant that I was, as Mercer (2007) describes, 'wielding a double-edged sword'. I had a shared understanding with Izzy and the other participants, which I believed would serve as a strength in my research. However, at the same time, the research process highlighted to me the great differences in our experiences and the necessity in distinguishing between them.

Gadamer argues that one's past has a truly pervasive power in the phenomenon of understanding (McNess et al., 2015, p. 305). For me, my past experience as an exchange student was central to my researcher identity and thus my research. Indeed, it was what had initially inspired me to conduct this research. Furthermore, membership gave me, as a researcher, a certain amount of legitimacy as it afforded me more rapid and more complete acceptance by my participants as well as increasing the interviewees' willingness to share their experiences with me because there was an assumption of understanding and shared distinctiveness (Corbin Dwyer & Buckle, 2009, p. 58). When interviewing Izzy, some of her comments and behaviour did resonate, at least at times, with my former self. In particular, her discussion of feeling like an outsider in the local community. Thus, my role as researcher often gave way to my role as an ex-exchange student, such as in this narrative when Izzy discussed the issues she was facing. At this point, I let my guard down and empathised with the difficulties she was facing being on

50 Alice Cranney

exchange. In doing so, my demeanour shifted to engage with the interviewee as a human rather than as a participant. It was particularly this empathy, the capacity to recognise and share thoughts or feelings that are being experienced by others, which made me an effective researcher in this context (McNess *et al.*, 2015, p. 311). It is crucial that researchers reflect on and discuss the blurring tensions in research projects such as these in order to ensure transparency of the researcher and their context.

Despite my past, I discovered that I could no longer be considered by the participants, or myself, as one of them due to the criticality I had gained as a researcher. There are conflicts and complications which can arise from occupying the position of the never-quite-insider researcher. I found that, at times, my perceptions were shaped by my personal experience, which resulted in the data collection being moulded by my experience rather than the participants (Corbin Dwyer & Buckle, 2009, p. 58). This is problematic as holding membership in a group does not denote sameness within that group (Corbin Dwyer & Buckle, 2009, p. 60). Participants made assumptions of similarity to the insider researcher and therefore failed to explain their individual experience fully. Lacking the need to ask more questions for clarification may detract from exchanges of great interest to the research project (Acker, 2001, p. 160). In my case, this was often with Spanish terms for which a non-Spanish speaker, and more specifically a person without knowledge of Mexican colloquialisms, and their accompanying cultural significance, would have needed more explanation, such as Izzy's use of the term *güera*. As discussed above, my past made the research messy and at many points, particularly when beginning my data collection and writing up my findings, I attempted to eradicate this messiness in an attempt to provide clear findings. It was my 'crisis of representation' once I had completed my data collection that led me to seek a method of tackling these issues; autoethnographic writing provided me with a space to do so.

A particular difficulty I faced was that the Other in my narrative was not the locals as it had been while I was on exchange in Mexico the first time but a fellow Australian exchange student, someone with whom I shared many identity markers: nationality, student, foreign, white, female. Izzy's discussion of her partying experiences in Mexico highlighted to me my position as an outsider, as a researcher, in a different stage of life, a Mexican 'expert' in her eyes. As a result, I questioned and recognised my positionality and the fluidity of that positioning. Like Izzy, I had selected Mexico as my exchange destination because of my imagined Mexico as a peripheral, exotic destination. Despite the experience I describe in the narrative, I continued to construct Mexico in alignment with my imagined community as a way of packaging the Other I was experiencing. However, it was not until I had completed my data collection and was in the process of analysis that I began to explore the interpretations I brought to the analysis due to my personal experiences and positioning. In doing so, I challenged myself to interrupt these understanding rather than simply reproducing my imagined version of Mexico; the vignette reflects the beginnings of my questioning of 'my' Mexico. Thus, the tensions in my research did not emerge chronologically but rather 'the reflexive shifts in my understanding emerged diachronically as I learnt to work with this burgeoning sensibility, coupled with attempting the sort of analytical work required of a thesis' (Vass, 2015, p. 2).

The element of self-doubt, so lacking initially in my fieldwork, developed through autoethnographic reflexivity, provided an opportunity for productive reflexivity. A deliberate focus on my representations of the Other caused epistemic discomfort which led me to a 'space of practiced vulnerability' (Spry, 2011). It shifted the aim of my research from a desire to present findings on how study abroad alters one's perceptions of the Other to a commitment to accurately and adequately represent the interviewees' experiences as I can come to recognise my 'own and other's social positionings as both constructed and constructing of knowledge' (Richardson, 1997, p. 108). I found that I could never completely take off my 'research armour' as I continued to critique and assess the interviewees' comments. Thus, there are moments when I related to Izzy as an exchange student, moments when I related to her as a researcher, as well as a continuous blurring between the two due to my awareness of not sharing the identity markers of being a current undergraduate exchange student. In Izzy's discussion of the difficulties of exchange I had to detach my emotions of the difficulty I faced while on exchange as they most likely, at least in part, would have differed to hers. However, it was not until I was out of the field that I realised the extent to which my emotions and perspectives had impacted the ways I read and understood the participants' comments as well as the issues this bought with my subsequent representation of the data. Perhaps the question of whether we are insider or outsider researchers cannot be resolved and rather than attempting such, it is about working creatively within these tensions and conflicts.

Analysing one's own experiences requires that researchers 'acknowledge and accommodate subjectivity, emotionality and the researcher's influence on research rather than hiding from these matters or assuming they don't exist' (Ellis *et al.*, 2011, p. 2). For me, this meant acknowledging the subjectivity I had when the interviewees discussed the difficulties they were facing on exchange, as Izzy did in her interview, and my empathy of them finding a sanctuary, like the American-run café, as I too had had a sanctuary. When Izzy discussed Mexico feeling like home I initially shared that sentiment. However, a result of my research had been my becoming critical of whether it could ever be home to outsiders. As such, autoethnography allows me to 'position myself as an active agent' (Spry, 2001, p. 711). Doing so helps us understand how the kinds of people we claim, or are perceived, to be influence interpretations of what we study, how to study it and what we say about the topic (Ellis *et al.*, 2011, p. 3). Personally, this process was confronting and conflict-ridden as I grappled with my desired self, who I was performing, and my actual self (Dornyei, 2009). For instance, with Izzy, I began the interview with the desire to be considered solely as professional researcher. However, as the interview progressed, my past experiences as an exchange student shaped the path the interview took. The analysis of vignettes, like the one above, helped me

52   Alice Cranney

to separate my experience and accompanying emotions from the interviewees'. Although this dilemma undoubtedly led to internal conflicts and tensions, I believe that it, and particularly my reflecting on these through autoethnography, enhanced my research. Therefore, autoethnography enabled me to first identify such sentiments and second, problematise and reflect upon how to represent their stories, and the power which comes from this position.

The piñata sisters

Nibbling on *totopos*, margarita in hand, I sway along to Santana's *Maria, Maria*, watching those around me greet each other, hugging and laughing. 'Alice, todo bien?', the owner of the bar calls. 'Si, gracias, Pablo,' I reply. The smell of scorched chilies and fresh tortillas hangs in the air.

'Alice!' my friend bounces up to me. She is a radiant *señorita* with flowers in her long, brown hair and a red flowing skirt. As I go in to hug her my *piñata* horn falls from my forehead, poking me in the eye for what must have been the tenth time that night. If only I looked as glamorous as she did. I didn't. The crepe paper on my dress is torn and soggy from spilled tequila shots. How did my sister ever convince me to wear this costume?

The Piñata Sisters, she had said. It sounded so perfect at the time, so exotic, so Mexican. She had spent weeks cutting up and gluing different coloured crepe stripes one by one onto our dresses, for tonight, my thesis completion party. Held at *Calaveras*, a Mexican bar in Sydney's trendy inner-city suburbs, the back wall featured a vivid mural of Day of the Dead, accentuated by the ceilings which were lined with fluorescent *pico de papel*.

The restauranteur had placed sombreros on the tables for his guests to wear. All features which played into a stylised, pastiche version of *Mexicanidad* present in urban Australia.

My friends and family had interpreted the theme 'Mexico' variously. There were stylised *calaveras* (skulls, representing Day of the Dead), cactuses, *lucha libre* wrestlers, and *campesinos* (farmers) in striped *serapes* and improbably large *sombreros*. Their costumes served as exemplars of the constructions of *Mexicanidad* in Australia.

My proud dad, sporting an oversized *sombrero*, circulates the room serving the guests more and more *sangría*. 'Salud' reverberates across the room as people down tequila and *sangría*, their colonial gaze dreaming of a far away Mexico.

Standing in the centre of this fiesta, a few too many *margaritas*, and not enough *tacos*, I wonder how I had got to this night. My PhD journey had begun with my desire to capture the imaginings exchange students hold of Mexico, but during the process it had become very evident that categorisation of the Other was impossible. It had certainly rid me of earlier notions that imagined communities could be packaged homogeneously. Yet somehow here I was, a soggy *piñata* with a horn stabbing me in the eye and a stabbing realisation of how problematic this celebration was.

A researcher's responsibility

On the night of my party I grappled with my decision to have a Mexican-themed party, feeling that it was problematic and that it signalled a failure of kinds as I perpetuated the stereotypes of 'real Mexico' of which I had been so critical during my data collection. However, it was not until I reflected further after the event that I realised that it was through these stereotypes that I conceptualise the Mexican Other. Thus, despite a newfound patina of 'knowing better' in a putative expert voice of critique, these imaginings remain as the exotic, alluring Mexico I had gone in search of eight years earlier. However, now with a researcher's critique, I identify and question such a performance and the intentions behind this. 'Is this identity performance and particularly my replicating of Australian stereotypes of *Mexicanidad* damaging, harmful, insulting, racist? How are these representations trying to understand the Other? Or are they in fact impeding my sense-making of the Other, and future intercultural engagements?'

Although I am bound by institutional constraints of having to produce and present knowledge in my thesis, there is an unavoidable violence with that process due to my accompanying power and privilege (Beňová, 2014, p. 56). My recognition of this is evidence of the development of multiple identities, both personal and professional, and how these intersect in my research. I couldn't come to a clear resolution at the end of my dissertation as I had initially hoped or thought I would. Rather I have learnt that the process of reflecting through autoethnographic narratives of my journey with Mexico, and studying how studying abroad in an exotic destination changes exchange students is that I cannot speak for Others, whoever they may be: Mexicans, my friends, the interviewees. All I can 'know' is about how the interviewees and I construct and present ourselves and the Other, and all that I claim to understand I do so with this caveat.

Conceptualising the Other is unavoidable and necessary. However, pivotal is the extent to which the author is aware of their perceptions, imaginings and positionality and their intention to avoid reducing cultures which are not their own in research. Nonetheless, such an understanding does not eradicate the question of ethics and responsibilities of researchers. The moral step is implicitly recognising, acknowledging and affirming the dignity of our participants, and indeed anyone we discuss (Seidman, 2013, p. 143). Inherent in this is the need to ensure that the way we construct and present people as researchers is, to the best of our knowledge, accurate and fair. In my thesis, a shift resulted from my realisation that I was constructing and performing my imaginings of an authentic Mexico during my PhD. Thus, my Mexican-themed thesis completion party, which encouraged attendees

54 Alice Cranney

to reinforce Mexican stereotypes, bothered me as performing Mexico in such a way was not adhering to my responsibilities as a researcher. Researcher responsibility is an element of my PhD journey which posed a steep learning curve for me and one which I will continue to ponder in later research projects. No matter how ardent we are about ethical principles, acting ethically as a researcher almost always involves a struggle of some kind (Seidman, 2013, p. 139). However, as is the aim of autoethnography, my objective is to 'open up conversations about how people live rather than close down with definitive and analytical statements about the world as it 'truly' exists outside the contingencies of language and culture' (Ellis & Bochner, 2006, p. 435). I incite myself and other researchers to engage further in discussions of how we embrace these tensions and conflicts creatively.

Conclusion

My PhD journey was characterised by a constant battle of trying to establish and recognise my positioning, namely the juxtaposition between my outsider position as researcher and my insider position as past exchange student. The occupying of a 'third space' created complexity and conflict. For me, autoethnography was an effective method through which I could explore, and problematise my own construction of cultures when conducting research about cultures to which I was an outsider. With this awareness came a desire to grapple with those issues rather than eradicating them from my research which, I believe, strengthened my research. This process also led to an understanding of the impossibility of gaining knowledge of the Other as well as the knowledge that whom and what constituted as the Other varied and evolved depending on the context and time. As a result, my research contribution shifted to be how exchange students, including myself, construct and perform their interactions with the Other.

References

Acker, S. (2001). In/out/side: positioning the researcher in feminist qualitative research. *Resources for Feminist Research, 28*(3), 153–172.

Anderson, B. (2006) *Imagined communities: Reflections on the origin and spread of nationalism* (revised edition). London: Verso.

Australian Bureau of Statistics (2011). Migration.

Bauman, Z. (2000). *Liquid modernity*. Oxford, UK: Polity Press.

Beňová, K. (2014). Research(er) at home: auto/ethnography of (my) PhD. *European Journal of Higher Education, 4*(1), 55–66.

Bhabha, H. (1994). Of mimicry and man: the ambivalence of colonial discourse. *Discipleship: A Special Issue on Psychoanalysis, 28*, 125–133.

Brito-Henriques, E. (2014). Visual tourism and post-colonialism: imaginative geographies of Africa in a Portuguese travel magazine. *Journal of Tourism and Cultural Change, 12*(4), 320–334.

Corbin Dwyer, S., & Buckle, J.L. (2009). The space between: on being an insider–outsider in qualitative research. *International Journal of Qualitative Methods, 8*(1), 55–63.

Deegan, M.J., & Hill, M.R. (1991). Doctoral dissertations as liminal journeys of the self: betwixt and between in graduate sociology programs. *Teaching Sociology, 19*(3), 322–332.

Denzin, N. (1989). *Interpretive biography*. Newbury Park, CA: SAGE.

Dornyei, Z. (2009). The L2 motivational self system. In Z. Dörnyei & E. Ushiod (Eds.), *Motivation, language identity and the L2 Self* (pp. 9–42). Clevedon: Multilingual Matters.

Elliot, D.L., Baumfield, V., & Reid, K. (2016). Searching for 'a third space': a creative pathway towards international PhD students' academic acculturation. *Higher Education Research & Development, 35*(6), 1180–1195.

Ellis, C., & Bochner, A. (2006). Analyzing analytic autoethnography. *Journal of Contemporary Ethnography, 35*(4), 429–449.

Ellis, C., Adams, T.E., & Bochner, A.P. (2011). Autoethnography: An overview. *Qualitative Social Research, 12*(1).

Hall, M., & Tucker, H. (2004). *Tourism and postcolonialism. Contested discourses, identities and representations*. London: Routledge.

Holliday, A. (2011). *Intercultural communication and ideology*. London: SAGE.

Holliday, A. (2013). *Understanding intercultural communication: Negotiating a grammar of culture*. London: Routledge.

Leki, I. (2003). A challenge to second language writing professionals: Is writing overrated? In B. Kroll (Ed.), *Exploring the dynamics of second language writing*. Cambridge: Cambridge University Press.

Lewis, V. (2009). Performing translatinidad: Miriam the Mexican transsexual reality show star and the tropicalization of difference in Anglo-Australian media. *Sexualities, 12*(2), 225–250.

MacCannell, D. (1973). Staged authenticity: Arrangements of social space in tourist settings. *American Journal of Sociology, 79*(3), 589–603.

McNess, E., Lore, A., & Crossley, M. (2015). 'Ethnographic dazzle' and the construction of the 'Other': revisiting dimensions of insider and outsider research for international and comparative education. *Compare: A Journal of Comparative and International Education, 45*(2), 295–316.

McRae, L. (2003). Rethinking tourism: Edward Said and a politics of meeting and movement. *Tourist Studies, 3*, 235–251.

Mercer, J. (2007). The challenges of insider research in educational institutions: wielding a double-edged sword and resolving delicate dilemmas. *Oxford Review of Education, 33*(1), 1–17.

Nakata, Y. (2015). Insider–outsider perspective: revisiting the conceptual framework of research methodology in language teacher education. *International Journal of Research & Method in Education, 38*(2), 166–183.

Richardson, L. (1997). *Fields of play: Constructing an academic life*. New Brunswick, NJ: Rutgers University Press.

Said, E. (1978). *Orientalism*. London: Routledge & Kegan Paul.

Said, E. (1979). *Orientalism*. New York: Vintage Books.

Saldaña, J. (2015). *The coding manual for qualitative researchers*. London: SAGE.

Seidman, I. (2013). *Interviewing as qualitative research: A guide for researchers in education*. New York: Teachers College Press.

Smith, M., & Duffy, R. (2003). *The ethics of tourism development*. London: Routledge.

Soong, H., Tran, L.T., & Hiep, P.H. (2015). Being and becoming an intercultural doctoral student: reflective autobiographical narratives. *Reflective Practice, 16*(4), 435–448.

Spry, T. (2001). Performing autoethnography: an embodied methodological praxis. *Qualitative Inquiry, 7*(6), 706–732.

Spry, T. (2011). *Body, paper, stage: Writing and perfoming autoethnography.* Walnut Creek, CA: Left Coast Press.

Spry, T. (2016). *Autoethnography and the other: Unsettling power through utopian performatives.* New York Routledge.

Thomson, P., & Gunter, H. (2010). Inside, outside, upside down: the fluidity of academic researcher 'identity' in working with/in school. *International Journal of Research & Method in Education, 34*(1), 17–30.

United States Census Bureau (2014). U.S. Census 2013.

Vass, G. (2015). Getting inside the insider researcher: does race-symmetry help or hinder research? *International Journal of Research & Method in Education, 40*(2).

6

NEGOTIATING THE *VĀ*

The 'self' in relation to others and navigating the multiple spaces as a New Zealand-raised Tongan male

David Fa'avae

INSTITUTE OF EDUCATION, UNIVERSITY OF THE SOUTH PACIFIC, TONGA

The criticality of *vā* as a relational space whereby the 'self' is constructed and mediated in relation to others is a representation of autoethnographic relativity. This paper highlights the cross-cultural shifting of relationships and the challenges and contradictions as part of navigating the multiple spaces as a New Zealand-raised Tongan male. Though the notion of 'struggle' is often linked to cultural dominance and power, the way that it positions the 'other' as lesser or of little significance is done through a repressive view and is therefore debilitating. As a Tongan male struggling to fit into life in Aotearoa, even when taking a traditional cultural position, this can lead to another form of dominance that invalidates my experiences in New Zealand as in-authentic. To signify fluidity as oppose to permanence, for New Zealand-raised Tongan males, the struggle to walk the two worlds – as a New Zealand-raised and Tongan male – is necessary and required because to emphasise the significance of one over the other is unhelpful and denies the 'self' in and amongst others as lacking possibilities.

Introduction

Negotiating one's positionalities is often a consequence of cultural discernment yet when one understands the very nature of the *vā* or relational ties – where the self and others are constructed and mediated – this can better position one's self to deal with people's judgements. In this chapter, I story the significance of navigating through the multiple spaces that shape one's social and cultural positioning, a process that requires negotiation of the *vā* – between the self and others. 'You're just a *fie palangi* (wannabe white person),' my friend said to me as I answered the teacher's question in our year 10 Social Studies class. Although the young boy's comment was not intended to hurt me as he was my mate and he knew what it was

58 David Fa'avae

like to grow up as a Tongan male, it did, however, remind me of instances where other Tongan elders triggered the same feelings from me. Instances where I felt different from other Tongan males. Despite my attempts in high school to connect with other Tongan boys by joining the Tongan cultural group and playing sport, the two major activities that the majority of the Tongan boys at my school engaged in at the time, I never felt as though I belonged. Instead, I hung out with students of Indian, Vietnamese, Chinese and Pakeha[1] descent because we seemed to have more in common. My goal in this piece is to convey what life was like growing up as a Tongan male in New Zealand. I unfold the shifting relationship between 'self' and the group and the continuous changes as I navigated through the multiple spaces in New Zealand society. For me, learning to be a Tongan male was never in isolation of my *kāinga* (extended family). Navigating through the multiple spaces has helped shape not only my experiences in New Zealand but in doing so have led to better understanding of the *vā* and how it can be negotiated or mediated by the self and others involved.

Me and my Kāinga: Research relationship

Bochner and Ellis argue that the 'self' is never absent or in isolation of others. The 'self' is necessarily always acting and interacting with other people. Attempting to take the role of others and their stories therefore not only brings them into the story, but in doing so, this places our own story/ies and experiences in and amongst theirs (Bochner & Ellis, 1992). In terms of research, the autoethnographic approach has been used by many academics for self-exploration, introspection, and interpretation of the 'self' in relation to others. Armstrong's (2017) utterances signify the link between multiple ways of knowing and, autoethnography as a creative approach to research. A criticality of autoethnographic approach lies in the relationship between personal storytelling and critical theoretical frameworks (Holman Jones, 2016). Chang (2008) used autoethnography to emphasise cultural analysis and interpretation of the researcher's behaviours, thoughts and experiences in relation to others in society. There are very few Pacific Island researchers who have utilised autoethnography for the conceptualisation, interpretation and analysis of their personal experiences within their cultural worlds. In a small way, this piece is my way of filling the space – using and framing my cultural experiences as a Tongan male within cultural and theoretical frameworks of interpretation and analysis.

As in most Indigenous communities, an individual's role and responsibilities lie within the collective. For Tongan people, the *kāinga* (extended family) as a multi-layered socio-cultural unit often frames an individual's *lakanga* (role) and *fatongia* (responsibilities). It is within the *kāinga* that members of the collective learn what to do and what not to do. For Tongan males, knowing one's role within the extended family and the responsibilities that are shaped by your position governs how you interact and behave in front of others in New Zealand and Tonga. An individual's needs and wants were of little value. For instance, when

Negotiating the *vā* **59**

my own needs and wants were not aligned or of benefit to my *kāinga*, then it was deemed as unuseful. Service to others was of greater value. These were cultural values embedded in my upbringing as a Tongan male raised in New Zealand. My *fatongia* within the *kāinga* continues to shift based on the *kāinga*'s needs and our own life situations. Although in the Tongan culture, as the future *ulumotu'a* (highest ranked male), my father's eldest brother's son Sione would one day fulfil his father's leadership role. I too was encouraged to follow suit, not to fill the role as *ulumotu'a* but to be in a leadership position and use my level of education to serve them. Their expectations for me shifted as I navigated life throughout high school and university education, working as a secondary school teacher, and eventually having a family of my own.

Pasifika edgewalkers: Cultural shifting/ walking the boundaries

Today, despite being dispersed throughout the diaspora of New Zealand, Australia and the US, Tongan families are still connected to their *fonua* (land) (Morton-Lee, 2003). Although Tongan culture and the practice of its values outside of Tonga is manifested in different ways by *to'utangata Tonga* (generations of Tongan males) in their new diasporic surroundings – the *fatongia* and function of the collective is still very much a strong force in how individuals live their lives. In spite of Tongan people choosing to migrate overseas primarily to fulfil their *fatongia* towards their *kāinga* through remittances (Morton-Lee, 2009), their transnational ties and connections have now aligned to their new locations. For second- to third-generation New Zealand born and raised Tongans, despite their parents' efforts to instil traditional Tongan cultural values in them, their sense of connection to their parents' *fonua* is not the same. For New Zealand born and raised Tongan youth, their identities and sense of belonging reflect both cultural worlds. Though many minority groups have struggled to live within the cross-cultural boundaries between their cultural worlds, some learn to become resilient to the cultural shifts and are able to maintain continuity wherever they go (Krebs, 1999). For these Pasifika edgewalkers (Tupuola, 2004), these youth of multiple identities have become resilient in the worlds and multiple spaces they live. Some Pasifika edgewalkers are able to shift between their 'cultures in the same persona' (Krebs, 1999, p. 9). Although cultural shifting is a healthy process of the postmodern world (Tupuola, 2004), there are very few narrative accounts of the challenges and contradictions from a Tongan male's perspective. This is what I intend to highlight in this paper.

Vā/vā tapuia/veitapui: The boundaries of relational connections

The *vā/va'* is central to learning how to shift through the cultural boundaries and the multiple spaces in which an individual and others co-exist. *Vā* is an Indigenous concept rooted in worldviews that highlight and emphasise shared principles of

60 David Fa'avae

interconnectedness and participation with the spiritual, natural and social communities. *Vā* is a valued concept in Tongan and other Polynesian ethnic groups which are often diverse based on language, heritage, and cultural norms and traditions. Though Western notions of 'space' are sometimes framed in relation to the space between physical objects, however, for Indigenous scholars, the use of *vā* denotes space that is often unseen – that exists in the mind (Iosefo, 2016; Ka'ili, 2005). From a Samoan female's perspective, Iosefo (2016) articulates *va'* as the space in-between. Her use of Bhabha's (1994) notion of 'third space' adapted by English (2004) as the site of fluidity where one's identity is constructed and deconstructed, has led to her conceptualisation of 'third space' as being akin to the *va'* (cited in Iosefo, 2016, p. 190). Therefore, *va'/vā* is symbolic of relational connections or social relational ties that are significant to how Tongans as well as Samoans construct and deconstruct their multiple identities. Central to Iosefo's claim is that by navigating and shifting through the cultural boundaries, one necessarily experiences 'struggle'. Despite her assertion that 'third space' is a site where minority scholars must learn to emancipate and feel empowered by learning to strip away the ideologies, it is often experiences of struggle that one has to go through in order to learn such lessons (Iosefo, 2016).

As a derivative of *vā*, *veitapui* refers to a sacred space where the relational ties involve a connection between brothers and sisters, or in the case of humans and a divine being such as a deity. *Veitapui* is spiritual in nature and implies a sense of socio-political connection whereby the relational connection is a mutual understanding between individuals that have different social status and power. However, central to *veitapui* is the idea of engagement and interaction that is respectful and sacred. The *vā/ veitapui* are spaces where I have had to learn to negotiate, construct and deconstruct my identities as a New Zealand-raised Tongan male. My struggles and challenges to navigate in these spaces have been manifested in intimate personal experiences depicted as narratives throughout this paper.

To'utangata Tonga: Gender relations

The term gender has no literal equivalent in *Lea Tonga* (Tongan language). Churchward (2015) defined gender as '*ko ha me'a tangata pe ko ha me'a fefine pe ko ha me'a noa pē*' (to do with being male or female or something else) (p. 660). The term *to'u* relates to age/time and *tangata* means man/human being. The concept of '*to'utangata*' denotes generations of human beings and is distinguished across social, cultural, spiritual, political as well as biological dimensions. *To'utangata* implies a sense of fluidity based on the notions of time/history/generations and within these notions are where the aforementioned dimensions are conceptualised and understood. *Tou'tangata Tonga* is a cultural framework whereby 'gender relations' is framed within the *vā/va'/veitapui* that govern one's role, *fatongia*, and relational ties in relation to others within the *kāinga*. This involves knowing my own father's position in relation to his siblings. At another level, knowing my grandfather's position within his own siblings provides knowledge of where his children and grandchildren are positioned in relation to the wider extended family. When considering my mother's position as the eldest female, she then takes on the role of *fahu* (highest ranked female), a traditional rank which places women of higher status than their brothers and their children and grandchildren (Helu, 1995). Although my previous description of *to'utangata* and the *vā* were understood in the context of my father's and mother's *kāinga* however, when church leaders and village nobles are in the mix, this can further intensify the *vā*. For example, the relational ties to the church ministers and village nobles are maintained and practised in different ways compared to one's own *kāinga*. Despite the complex layers involved in how Tongan familial units are structured, such layers indicate nuances in negotiating the *vā* and the relational ties with and amongst others.

The *vā/veitapui* between a brother and a sister is sacred in the Tongan culture therefore there are certain things that a brother cannot say or do in front of his *tu'ofefine* (sister or female cousins) (Helu, 1995). During the 1990s, growing up as a Tongan boy in New Zealand, my brothers and I always got into trouble from our mother and grandmother when we were spotted coming out of our older sister's room. Because my older sister had her own room whereas the rest of us had to share rooms, she had the privilege of having a private space away from everyone else, a space she always used when she had had enough of her 'annoying siblings' as she often referred to us. Despite me urging mum that I just need to use Mel's hair gel, my somewhat egotistical request annoyed her more and led to either a slap on the arm or a stare from her that often left me feeling momentarily paralysed. Respecting my sister's room and her possessions was significant as it was symbolic of the sacredness in how my brothers and I were expected to relate to our sisters as well as female cousins.

To'utangata Tonga: Multiple masculinities

In the past, though most discussions of masculinity related to 'role' or an 'identity', these concepts were problematic (Connell, 1991). Connell (1991) defined masculinity as a 'socially constructed form of life or project in time, which appropriates the bodily difference of men from women into a social process of gender' (p. 143). This form of life or project in time is found in social practice at several levels – in personality, in culture and institutions, and in the organisation and use of the body (e.g. in sexuality) (ibid.). Connell further argues that in any given society, there are likely to be multiple masculinities. The framework of *To'utangata Tonga* encompasses forms of masculinities whereby the 'past molds masculine being, but in changing present practices it is re-membered, both re-embodied and recollected by individual subjects' (Jolly, 2008, p. 5). It is within this cultural framework that the multiple forms of masculinities in the Tongan culture are manifested in how individuals act, think, feel, and do and are inclusive of their diverse contexts.

Hokowhitu (2012) argues that 'masculinity/ies' 'cannot be treated ahistorically, aculturally, or apolitically' (p. 29). For him, masculinity exists through historically

62 David Fa'avae

constructed performance. His notion of 'indigenous masculinities' proposes a 'shift away from the conception of subjectivities as traditional and towards an understanding that Indigenous ontologies have no permanence, but are subject to a morphing biopolitical milieu' (p. 27). As maintained by Hokowhitu, to think of 'indigenous masculinity/ies' in a way whereby an Indigenous person must enact certain behavioural performances to be considered authentically Indigenous is extremely repressive (2012, p. 30). My use of the term Indigenous in this chapter does not mean that my ways of being are solely linked to Tongan traditions because to do so can often lead to issues of authenticity and the privileging of traditional Tongan forms of masculinity. My identity as a Tongan male is inclusive of both the genealogical histories as well as the contemporary histories – that which is 'fluid and representative of moving masculinities across the time and place [in] Oceania' (Jolly, 2008, p. 1), shifting through multiple contexts.

Enacting masculinities

Butler (2009) argues that gender is performative, that is to say, one 'enacts' gender relations based on obligatory norms. An individual enacts gender relations based on a 'negotiation with power' (Butler, 2009, p. i). There was an expectation within Tongan culture for my *to'utangata* to act and behave in ways like our previous *to'utangata*. However, how we enacted 'being a Tongan male' had to align with life in New Zealand. The forbidden rule for brothers/male cousins to be at the same nightclub as our sisters/female cousins was adhered to. Consuming alcohol and hanging out with our sisters was *tapu* (taboo). My sister and female cousins were not allowed to experience the nightlife scene until they were in their twenties. However, my brothers and male cousins experienced the 'clubbing' scene and drinking alcohol a lot earlier when they were in high school. Unlike our sisters and female cousins, there was an unspoken norm that if my brothers and male cousins got 'wasted' from drinking alcohol, this was ok. My choice to not go out or drink alcohol in high school was often perceived as me being a *fakaleiti*, a Tongan term used to refer to a male who behaved like a girl. As a way to serve my extended family, doing well academically was of significance. To please my elders and fit into the norm growing up with other Tongan males was a struggle for me.

Physicality, toughness and sport

Under the term 'hegemonic masculinity', there were stereotypical views of men based on hypermasculine attributes (i.e. an emphasis on physical strength, aggression and sexuality). Playing rugby was one way to enact male physicality and toughness for Pacific Island males. Similarly, for Māori in New Zealand, sport was the 'only mainstream activity where they could achieve success and compete with Pakeha on an even playing field and gain their *mana* (respect or esteem)'. My father and uncles often talked about their glory days when they used to play rugby and laughed at the moments when they were involved in brawls with other players in

Tonga and Niue. The majority of my male cousins and brothers played rugby and rugby league and saw professional sport as a means to benefit the *kāinga*. Despite my attempt to play school yard rugby at primary school, this proved unsuccessful and often left me either in pain, feeling winded or both. Because of my heart condition, this perpetuated a feeling of disconnection not only from sport but also from other male members of my *kāinga*. After realising that rugby or sport for that matter was never going to be something that I could engage in as a means to provide for the family, I relied on the Lord through prayer that He would help find a space where I could fulfil my promise to Him as well as my role and responsibilities to my *kāinga*. As I negotiated the *veitapui* with a divine being – the Lord Jesus Christ – ensuring that I was still able to contribute to my *kāinga's* 'cultural survival and continuation' (Shipman, 1971; Thaman, 1995) as well as serve my heavenly father, this was central to my being able to live life. My heart condition provided a legitimate reason out of the forms of masculinity that were expected through playing rugby. As an individual, the tension to feel a part of the collective and realising that I was not going to be a rugby/rugby league player like my male cousins left me struggling to find ways to fit in.

Spirituality and servitude

Being a Christian was a way to deal with life's struggles. Despite Christianity being a process of Western colonisation in the Pacific, the values associated with the practice were crucial in how I dealt with life's struggles. Historically, as the key protagonist in how Christian values were adopted in Tonga, King Siaosi Tupou I's (Taufa'ahau) decision was based on his desire to unify his people. As a nationalist, Taufa'ahau was firm in his belief that Tongan people needed to understand Western knowledge in order to find empowerment and strength to lead the nation. King Siaosi Tupou I's initial acceptance of Christianity was only 'part of his general desire to adopt the ways of the white man, his wealth, superior knowledge and weapons of war . . . to achieve his ambitions'. Spirituality, the belief in humans having a relationship with a 'higher being', as well as servitude (placing one's self lower than others in order wholeheartedly to serve that person/people) were already inherent in Tongan cultural traditions. So, when Christianity arrived, King Siaosi Tupou I saw how the values embedded in both cultural worlds could complement one another.

Despite Tonga's fearless leader's aspirations for his people and the kingdom, the struggles to empowerment and strength were not foreseen as being a necessary part of the 'edgewalking' process. At the age of nine I was diagnosed with rheumatic heart disease and had to have my valves replaced. Whilst growing up, my impressions of Tongan males were acquired from my own observations of how my grandfather, father and uncles behaved in relation to each other, their wives and children. On the day of my surgery, standing around the bed inside my room were my mother and my father's sisters. My mother could not hold back her tears and before I was pushed out of the room by the hospital orderly, she whispered in my ear, *'Falala kihe 'Eiki he koia pe e lava 'o fakamo'ui koe'* (Trust in the Lord because

64 David Fa'avae

only He can save you). Outside of the room, my father and a few of his brothers were standing together with my siblings and cousins and as I was pushed away my father placed his hands upon my head and said, *'Lotu kihe 'Eiki'* (Pray to the Lord). As a man who often found it difficult to share his intimate thoughts with his children, my father's action showed his love for me and a deep understanding and faith in his maker. As the hospital orderly turned the corner, the view of my mother and family was now out of sight and I started to cry as though I was never going to see them again. The journey from my room to the operating theatre felt long. Lying in the theatre room, everything looked white. Although I was unfamiliar with the Lord Jesus Christ before I was put to sleep, I remembered my parents' advice and it was at that point in time that I gave my life to the Lord and promised Him, 'Lord, if I come out of this, I will gladly serve you'.

Fie palangi: **Walking the white spaces**

Schooling allowed me to navigate its spaces, at times willingly or unwillingly. For example, at Greenlane Hospital in 1989, for nine months I learnt to assimilate; to think and act like a 'white person'. I read books and payed attention to my Pakeha teacher's attempts to make sure I pronounced the words correctly. I was taught to use a knife and fork when eating my food. Almost everyone was white, even the walls that surrounded our rooms. Only the patients were coloured although they soon disappeared – some were discharged whereas others passed away. At the time, I felt as though there was no space for colour particularly in me being able to speak and practise my Tongan culture. After being discharged from the hospital, I then attended the local intermediate school. To other *Pasifika*[2] students, despite me sharing the same skin colour as them, I however, was grouped as a *palangi*[3] because I spoke like a white person. Sometimes I was referred to as a *'fie palangi'* (wannabe white person). In the classroom, I seemed to be doing better academically compared to other Pasifika students. Consequently, my parents took pride in my successes in the classroom. My experience in the hospital helped me fulfil my parents' aspirations for us to do well in education.

It was my father's expectation for us to acquire Western thinking and skills in schooling that would lead to academic success. This was something my father learnt and valued during the late 1960s when he was a high school student at Tailulu College, a mission school in Tonga. He later attended 'Atenisi Institute, a school established by the late Professor Futa Helu. An essential skill promoted by the late Futa Helu and the 'Atenisi Institute was the significance of 'critical thinking' or 'critical thought' through Western philosophies. For my father, academic success would lead to security and financial stability for the family. Though some academics may argue that my father's expectations stemmed as a result of what Franz Fanon refers to as 'colonisation of consciousness' where the ideal was to acquire knowledge of the dominant 'Other' (of *palangi*/Western people), my father's overall desire was not for his children to lose their Tongan cultural values and ideals but to help 'integrate themselves into the dominant society' (Hokowhitu, 2003,

p. 209). To think of these struggles as not being authentic Tongan identities when the notion of Tongan culture or 'Tongan-ness' is not homogenous or unitary, is unhelpful. Rather, to think of Tongan identity and 'Tongan-ness' as fluid spaces provides a consciousness of possibilities instead.

Looking back at my high school experience, the intellectual, social and spiritual learning helped to unfold the context of relationships. We encounter this, and try to understand it to obtain meaning and orient ourselves (Cajete, 1994, p. 193). Negotiating and navigating throughout the intellectual and social spaces and relationships in high school was critical in my learning development. My purposeful attempt to do well in the classroom was shaped by my role and responsibilities within my extended family. Furthermore, my *veitapui* with the Lord was the ultimate source in my capacity to willingly navigate the space and experience the intellectual and social struggles at high school. The more I succeeded at formal schooling the more attention I received from members of my *kāinga*, particularly from my father and his brothers. This was what made me different from my brothers and other male cousins. Though they were proud of my cousins who made representative teams for rugby union and rugby league, however, doing well at school and eventually making it into university was something that I was able to share with them.

Changing my name

Leaving Mangere, a predominantly Māori and Pacific Island suburb in South Auckland, 'the hood' as we used to call it, and travelling to the city for university was an 'out of place and out of touch' experience for me. Despite already feeling like an outsider amongst other Pacific Island students at my high school, my very first experience of university life perpetuated feelings of being different. My first experience of university life was belittling. I started to raise questions related to what it meant to be Tongan, and was it possible to feel less or more Tongan? All I felt at the time was that the more time I spent at university, the less I spent with my *kāinga* and the less Tongan I felt. As a result of learning to negotiate and navigate the boundaries – my *kāinga's* expectations for me to succeed at university and the struggle to fit into Western education at university – I officially changed my name from Tevita to David to avoid my lecturers and tutors mispronouncing it. A person's sense of identity as well as names is 'fluid and depends on [the] context, it cannot be divorced from the interactions which take place with others on a daily basis' (Edwards, 2006, p. 93). Despite my name change, I wanted to keep the rest of my names – Taufui Mikato Fa'avae – because it was my way of maintaining my identity as a Tongan.

Contrasting worlds: The dragon tattoo and cultural patterns

According to Cajete (1994), to reclaim Indigenous people's oral history and cultural tradition for the purpose of constructing a transformative vision requires dialogue about what our visions might be. This requires us to appreciate what others have done in formal and informal ways, big and small, past and present. In this way, we energise our visions as we live and grow (Cajete, 1994, p. 192). Getting a tattoo was a liberating experience for me and it was a way to re-present my Tongan-ness. A tattoo was symbolic of masculinity and I was eager to prove myself to other people. Despite my mother's disapproval, I decided to get it anyway. During my third year at university, in 1999, I received very little from my student allowance. And I used some of it to get inked. Instead of attending my lectures, I caught the yellow bus to Ponsonby, an affluent inner-city suburb in Auckland. After looking at some of the images on the wall, I decided to get a dragon because it was a creature often perceived as strong and fierce. Eight years later in 2007, I was inked again, only this time it was a traditional tattoo with Tongan and Samoan patterns. The tattoo was an embodiment of the negotiation of being between or within two cultures – the contrasting images present a juxtaposition of two cultures that I embraced and authenticated – both internally and externally – in my mind and on my body. The image is a metaphor of in-betweening, the fluidity of cultural/gender identities and how such constructs provide useful possibilities to grow and feel empowered.

ILLUSTRATION 1 Embodiment of cultural/gendered identities

Conclusion

It is not uncommon these days to find young Tongan males with traditional patterned tattoos. In my *kāinga* alone, we have four tattooists. Like our *to'utangata* before us, their inked bodies were symbolic instruments of how they felt at the time. In saying that, we too must learn to appreciate 'time' and what it is trying to teach us and make us feel. The *vā* and *to'utangata* have provided a way forward for Pasifika/Pacific males to construct and deconstruct the ideas of culture and masculinities as fluid constructs that have potential for possibilities. Though we can never really live the life of another person or fully understand their experiences, autoethnography has provided a space where one gets close and intimate and in doing so learns to appreciate others' lives as being central to their *vā* or relational ties with other individuals.

Notes

1 Pakeha is a Māori term used to refer to people of European descent living in Aotearoa, New Zealand.
2 *Pasifika* is a term defined by the New Zealand Ministry of Education as related to recent migrants or New Zealand-born Pasifika people of single or mixed heritage. While identifying themselves as Pasifika, this group may also identify with their ethnic-specific Pacific homeland. Pasifika people are not homogenous and Pasifika or Pacific does not refer to a single ethnicity, nationality, gender, language or culture.
3 *Palangi* is a Polynesian term used to refer to a person of European descent. The term is also often used to refer to a white person.

References

Armstrong, D. (2017). Editorial. *Creative Approaches to Research, 10*(1), 4–5.
Bochner, A.P., & Ellis, C. (1992). Personal narrative as a social approach to interpersonal communication. *Communication Theory, 2*(2), 165–172.
Butler, J. (2009). Performativity, precarity and sexual politics. *AIBR. Revista De Antropologa Iberoamericana, 4*(3).
Cajete, G. (1994). *Look to the mountain: An ecology of indigenous education.* Durango, CO: Kivaki Press.
Chang, H. (2008). *Autoethnography as method: Developing qualitative inquiry.* Walnut Creek, CA: Left Coast Press.
Churchward, C.M. (2015). *Tongan dictionary: Tonga-English, English-Tongan. King Tupou VI Coronation* (Special ed.). Nuku'alofa, Tonga: The Government of Tonga.
Connell, R.W. (1991). Live fast and die young: The construction of masculinity among young working-class men on the margin of the labour market. *The Australian and New Zealand Journal of Sociology, 27*(2), 141–171.
Edwards, R. (2006). What's in a Name? Chinese Learners and the Practice of Adopting 'English' Names. *Language, Culture and Curriculum, 19*(1), 90–103.
Helu, F. (1995). Brother/sister and gender relations in ancient and modern Tonga. *Journal de la Société des Océanistes, 100*(1–2), 191–200.
Hokowhitu, B. (2003). Physical beings: Stereotypes, sport and the physical education of New Zealand Maori. *Culture, Sport, Society, 6*(2–3), 192–218.

68 David Fa'avae

Hokowhitu, B. (2012). Producing elite indigenous masculinities. *Settler Colonial Studies, 2*(2), 23–48.

Holman Jones, S. (2016). Living bodies of thought: The 'critical' in critical autoethnography. *Qualitative Inquiry, 22*(4), 228–237.

Iosefo, F. (2016). Third spaces: Sites of resistance in higher education? *Higher Education Research & Development, 35*(1), 189–192. doi:10.1080/07294360.2016.1133273

Jolly, M. (2008). Moving masculinities: Memories and bodies across Oceania. *The Contemporary Pacific, 20*(1), 1–24.

Ka'ili, T. O. (2005). Tauhi vā: Nurturing Tongan sociospatial ties in Maui and beyond. *The Contemporary Pacific, 17*(1), 83–114.

Krebs, N. B. (1999). *Edgewalkers: Defusing cultural boundaries on the new global frontier*. New York: New Horizon Press.

Morton-Lee, H. (2003). *Tongans overseas: Between the shores*. Honolulu, HI: University of Hawai'i Press.

Morton-Lee, H. (2009). Pacific migration and transnationalism: Historical perspectives. In H. Morton-Lee, H., & S. T. Francis (Eds), *Migration and transnationalism: Pacific perspectives* (pp. 7–42). Canberra, Australia: Australian National University Press.

Shipman, M. D. (1971). *Education and modernisation*. London: Faber & Faber.

Thaman, K. H. (1995). Concepts of learning, knowledge and wisdom in Tonga, and their relevance to modern education. *Prospects, 25*(4), 723–733.

Tupuola, A. (2004). Pasifika edgewalkers: Complicating the achieved identity status in youth research. *Journal of Intercultural Studies, 25*(1), 87–100.

7

SCENE, SEEN, UNSEEN

Fetaui Iosefo

FACULTY OF EDUCATION AND SOCIAL WORK, UNIVERSITY
OF AUCKLAND, AOTEAROA/NEW ZEALAND

Moving in multiple spaces in society as a marginalised person, I have often felt, seen and heard what is in the unseen. It is Friday morning and I am setting up to take a class. A student walks in and asks 'Do you know where my lecturer is?' I smile, and continue setting up. My physical presence is a language which often automatically categorizes me as the 'other' and this example is often my 'norm'. Yes, I/Eye am a chocolate brown skin Pasifika-Samoan woman with a voluptuous body in higher education. My colleague Tessa, asked me a question. She said, 'Fetaui if we taught behind a curtain would people know what colour we were?' I burst out laughing replying, 'No, I don't think so, weird huh? But once the curtain is opened they'll be saying, "pull back the curtain pull back the curtain".' We both continued to laugh. I continued, 'You know Tessa, I didn't come into university to become more palagi (white). I chose to come to university to become more Fetaui.' In this piece, I will explore the Samoan Indigenous Reference (SIR) while negotiating and constructing in the 'third space/Va'.

Opening the curtain

As a Samoan woman born in Aotearoa-New Zealand, being labelled one particular identity is complex. However, at this time and space there are three components that are in negotiation with the complexity of identity. The first is the blending of the Samoan Indigenous Reference (Efi, 2009) and in particular the Va', with post-colonial theorists' (Bhabha, 1990) third space. The Va' is a Samoan term to describe the 'space' and the space in-between (Iosefo, 2014, 2016a, 2016b; Wendt, 1999). Western ideologies often see space as a means of physicality (Montgomery, 2008), whereas space, for Samoans is the *Va'*, not only seen in the physical realm but also in the unseen (Amituanai-Toloa, 2007; Tuagalu, 2008; Wendt, 1999).

70 Fetaui Iosefo

With the influence of Bhabha (1990), English (2004) adds that identity is complex and therefore the construction and deconstruction of identity is fluid. With third space being in the between spaces, and the Va' as well they become complementary to each other.

The second component is autoethnography. Holman Jones *et al.* (2015) highlights five purposes of autoethnography: to manoeuvre; disrupt research norms; break silence; validate insider knowledge and finally make/create work that is accessible. Pathak (2013) seeks to ground autoethnography in a post-colonial space that allows her to be who she is both as an intellect and a person of colour. In doing this, she re-centres herself by positioning post-colonial autoethnography as a mode of inquiry. This allows us to engage with lived experience, without reinforcing oppressive politics (Shuggart, 2003). Gonzalez (2003) contends that post-colonial theory should not be labelled as a means of defiance to the dominant culture but one of strength and mass courageousness; courage which moves from being aware of the dominance and moving to being active agents of emancipatory transformation.

It is with this courage that we employ the usage of the tenets of autoethnography such as critical (Boylorn & Orbe, 2014); evocative (Ellis & Bochner, 2016); interpretive (Denzin, 2014) and performative (Spry, 2011) as fluid notions of discovery. Autoethnography enables creativity within the storytelling as well as the analysis of personal and cultural lived experiences. Ellis and Bochner (2000) argue that there is no logical ordering system, special formula or method for autoethnography; however, they encourage the researcher to explore the complex nature of this process. It is within the exploration that our third component is birthed to analyse and understand the complexities of identity. In the abstract I/Eye is seen. The I/Eye is a representation of what is seen/scene/unseen in the varying lived realities. It is used as a means of comfort to alleviate the cultural/ethnic tension. I/Eye have adopted three writing personas. The first is Jerodeen – she is the academic analyser; second is Fetaui (Samoan for connect) – she is the narrator, and then there is JoFI – she is the poet. JoFI is the acronym for my full name Jerodeen, Olivaigafa, Fetaui Iosefo. My surname Iosefo represents the gift of choice as I have chosen to taken on my husband's family name. Olivaigafa, that identity is yet to be discovered.

The analysing of self through culture presupposes that 'auto' is languaged only as self or as an individual and therefore autoethnography examines self in order to gain culture (Chang, 2007). However, from a Pasifika Samoan perspective the word 'self 'is synonymous with 'relational self' (Lui, 2003, Tamasese, Peteru, Waldegrave, & Bush, 2005). The Samoan 'self' is not a separate entity. It is always accompanied; this is part of the Samoan Indigenous Reference (SIR) Efi (2009). Therefore, autoethnography in the SIR is about the 'relational self' inclusive of all genealogical ties with Va' tapuia (sacred spaces). Efi (2007) describes Va' tapuia as the sacred essence of the relationship between humans and all things animate and inanimate – it has always been, and always will be, part and parcel of being Samoan, being human. Therefore, the term 'auto' is languaged in SIR as the examination of 'auto-self' through I/Eye (scene/seen/unseen as a collective) for the benefit of 'we'.

Over time research perspectives have moved from the coloniser to those who are allies in decolonising. Autoethnography is part of this movement of decolonising. From the margins, I/Eye see the word 'colon' and view autoethnography as the 'cleansing of the colon'. Autoethnography examines storied lives and intricately magnifies the excrements as part of the cleansing process. Nothing about this process is pleasant and at times can feel as though you are constipated on 'self'. It is, however, a time where Richardson (1999) suggests that autoethnographers 'invite Beauty and Truth' (p. 660). The invitation for beauty and truth derives from multiple experiences, some pleasant and some rather unpleasant. It is in these times where Denzin (2006) and Pelias (2004) are revisited to remind me that 'in writing from the heart we learn how to love, to forgive, to heal, and to move forward' (Denzin, 2006, p. 423). Feeling cleansed or imagining feeling 'normal'.

Scene one: Samoa late 1800s: All backed up

JoFI

The swell of her breasts
her pointed nipple,
a sensation
She is being watched
A white man
She looks intently
Fascinated
His face changing colour
White
Pink
Red
His eyes drift lower
Her brown skin is glistening
Her stomach (manava) is lean
A flaxed mat covering her vagina
Her thighs, knees, calves
Her build is like no other
Her muscular sculputured body
She is far from petite
Unlike anything he has seen
She is beautiful
But she is
naked
naked
NAKED
He yells out
Cover up
COVER up
COVER UP
Yet his erected penis
Tells otherwise
. . .

Jerodeen

Interpretive autoethnography allows the autoethnographer to move in and out between culture, history and ideology. It allows the researcher to take up the life of a person in a historical setting, interpret and write from that perspective. Just as Denzin (2006) demonstrates this when he enacts a time in history in Yellowstone Park; he situates himself in the voices of Native Americans and white settlers. *JoFI* has attempted to do the same. She has placed herself as her great grandmother at the time of initial contact between the colonisers and the indigenous of Samoa. *JoFI* explores the tensions of two cultures and their differing views on nakedness and sexuality. According to Denzin (2014), the structures of one's life are lived through performing it. In this performative piece *JoFI* is acknowledging SIR as the 'norm'. In ancient Samoa the exposure of breasts was not afforded the same value of tapu (sacredness) as the vagina. The piece of flax covering her vagina signified the tapu of procreation and its embeddedness in SIR (Efi, 2014), therefore the exposure of breasts was the 'norm'. Interpretetive autoethnography enables multiple juxtapositions. Denzin (2006) closes with 'Today I want to write my way into and out of this history, and this is why I write my version of autoethnography' (p. 426). Through his version the historical cleansing begins for I/Eye.

72 Fetaui Iosefo

Intermission: Voluntary cleansers

In 2014, while embarking on my Masters research I had to consult with my *aiga* (family) about the area of research. There were two topics to choose from, the first 'Unconscious oppression within schools for our marginalised communities'; and an 'Autoethonography on the spaces of higher education from a Pasifika woman perspective'. The *aiga* asked one question: What was the motivation? I explained the first topic came from a place of vengeance whereas the second came from a place of inquiring into identity. Collectively it was decided autoethnography. The *aiga* felt I/Eye would grow from autoethnography and proceeded to set up our '*aiga* (family) ethics' committee.

The *aiga* ethics committee acknowledges Chawla and Holman Jones (2016) whereby they name home, space and place as the beginning of storying. The *aiga* ethics committee also acknowledges Smith (2000) from a Kaupapa Maori perspective that 'Individuals do not hold knowledge for themselves they hold it for the benefit of the whole group' (p. 218). With these thoughts, combined with our epistemological and ontological beliefs, the *aiga* ethics committee was formed. This *aiga* ethics committee currently consists of five matai (Samoan family chiefs) and the family pastor. Two are males and four females. One resides in Samoa, the rest live in New Zealand. Their richness of experience ranges from wisdom and knowledge holders of SIR; psychotherapist; traditional sailing master; teacher/lecturer; PhD holder, and their sexuality is also varied and embraced as part of SIR.

In the last three years, the *aiga* (family) ethics committee has generated guidelines for autoethnography such as:

*   The Samoan Indigenous Reference is to be incorporated as the norm.
*   Every piece of writing that mentions family members or culture needed to go through the full '*aiga* ethics committee'.
*   Write in I/Eye: I to acknowledge the internal (unseen) and Eye to acknowledge the seen, both acknowledging the collective.
*   Each piece of writing must first produce transformation and emancipation within the writer.

Relational ethics, according to Ellis (Ellis, Holman-Jones, & Adams, 2015), is a reciprocity of respect and connectedness between researcher and co-researcher. Anae (2016) discusses the differences between Western relational ethics and indigenous relational ethics. The foundation of indigenous relational ethics without exception to SIR is the inclusivity of the sacred/spiritual dimensions. Efi (2009) states that 'tapu (the sacred) and tofa saili (the search for wisdom) are situated in contemporary Samoan experiences and understandings of the ethical . . . and provide the basis for ethical research in a Samoan indigenous context' (p. 115). Therefore, as a Samoan woman born in Aotearoa New Zealand I/Eye agree with Ellis (Ellis *et al.*, 2015) and her stance on reciprocity and connectedness, however, the SIR validates and invokes the '*aiga* ethics' as the 'norm'.

Scene two: Fetaui and Jerodeen: Constipated, crazy or both?

January 2016, my niece and I met, we discussed how we both wanted to get the traditional Samoan woman's malu tatau (tattoo). The malu begins at the top of the thighs and ends below the knee cap. We arranged a time with my parents and asked for permission to go through this sacred tradition. At this meeting my father spoke about the meaning of the tatau and cross-referenced to being a Christian and the beliefs of spilling blood and how that was not encouraged. We each explained our positionality. Mine was from being named after my grandmother Fetaui; she was the taupou (chief's daughter) and she had a malu so traditionally it should be passed on. Both parents agreed that this decision had to be one where we were all at peace. We left and agreed to pray and let peace be our guide.

The morning of March the 28th I awoke panicked. I had dreamt of my grandmother, my name sake, and two other half-naked Samoan women. I rang my mother freaked out and begun the conversation with '*Mama I think I'm going crazy,*' and relayed what I had seen. At the end, I asked her again if I was going crazy. My mother, a devout Christian, asked about the two half-naked women. I described them to her. Her silence was deafening; I was afraid she would say I needed an exorcism. Instead she said, '*Fetaui if you see these women again speak to them, for now go back to sleep, rest and we will talk about it later.*' I didn't bother calling her back.

The next morning these three women appeared again. This time I rung the pastor and recalled what I had seen and asked him the same question, I asked, '*Am I going crazy?*' He advised me to go over to my see my mum and dad. At my parents' house my two older sisters were there. I explained to them all the scenes and what I had seen. Dad asked about the tatau and what it specifically looked like. I said, '*It wasn't like the traditional malu, the tatau on all three women was like a pe'a (Samoan male tattoo).*' Mum asked me to again describe the woman. I described my grandmother on my right and then described the women on my left. One was tall and beautiful with long wavy hair. Her breasts were pointy but full. Each had flax-like mats covering their vaginas. The other was shorter, she had wild curly hair, her breasts hung like empty sacks. Both women had no stretch marks on their stomachs. My ma choked up with tears and her voice cracked. She said, '*The women on your left are my grandmothers Fetaui.*' She said, '*Next time you see them, I want you to talk to them, ask them why they have visited you.*' At this point I wanted to call the emergency mental health line on my mother and I, we were officially cuckoo and in need of some heavy-duty drugs.

Three days later in the early hours of the morning I saw them again. This time I asked them why they were there. My nana said, '*e sā', nā tā lou malu*' (you are forbidden to have the Samoan traditional woman's tattoo). I replied, '*I wanted to be closer to you, this would make me closer to you.*' She motions for me to look at her tatau and says, '*ē faa'uma i' le tā o le mālu*' (this is where the tattooing ends). I turned to the two women on my left and asked them if they agreed. Leata and Sevao, my

74 Fetaui Iosefo

great grandmothers, nodded. I woke up, journalled and drew the patterns I saw, then rang my mother.

Two days later they reappeared. I spoke with them about how I didn't understand why they had forbidden me and the woman in our line to wear the malu, especially as I wanted it to remind me of them. Sevao said, *'vāai i lou tino, i le meā e auleāga, mā vaivai. O lē nā, ē fai lē tātau. Tu'u lēi' ā, fetu mā manu fēlēlei, ē, āliali lē moānā, fenuā mā le lālolāgi ātoa. Tusi fo'i le* (and she pointed to the diamond) *ē vāai o mātā i lē mea lēnei, onā mānātunātu tātou umā, i tonu lou loto, tātou umā ē puipui mā faāmālosi ai oe'* ('Have a look at your body. Choose the weakest and ugliest part of your body, and use the symbols you have seen. Include bird, fish, and stars; these represent land, sea, and the heavens. Also, include a diamond, that diamond represents the three of us. When you look at what you think is the ugliest and weakest part of your body, you will remember us in your heart and we will protect you and give you strength'). This time I awoke weeping.

I rang my siblings and parents and met with them. I explained the dream and passed around my journal of the patterns that I had seen. My Grandma Fetaui died when I was two, I don't remember her at all. But my sisters who bathed her remembered her well. The patterns and style I had drawn were replicas of what they remembered. We have no photos of my great grandmothers and only have the memory of my mother. The pastor rung during this meeting and I updated him. He said what I had experienced was *'moe manatunatu'*. These visions/dreams come in the early hours of the morning. This is a time where we are at our clearest and where our ancestors create a reflective dialogue. This was relayed to my parents and sisters. My mother smiled and said, *'Yes Fetaui, the Pastor is right.'* 'Aww crap,' I thought. 'Everyone in my "aiga ethics committee" has lost the plot. We all need to be admitted into a mental hospital.'

Following this experience, I researched *moe manatunatu* and Efi (2008) confirmed that the 'aiga ethics committee' were right. *Moe manatunatu* is part of the SIR. Efi (2008) explains that through *moe manatunatu* the ancestors guide the decision making for the family and community. To try and make sense of this I looked for a Western alternative to *moe manatunatu*. 'Hauntology', a term originally derived by Derrida, urged that speaking to ghosts is a respectable subject of enquiry (Davis, 2005; Derrida, 1994). Derrida argues that we should 'speak to the ghost' (Derrida, 1994). Although these readings and findings were somewhat comforting, no offence to the amazing French philosopher, Jacques Derrida, I/Eye needed to fetaui (connect) with someone Pasifika, someone like me.

BOOM. I read Mila (2010); she went through a similar experience where she saw her ancestors in her dreams. Mila (2010) was diagnosed with schizo-affective disorder and was admitted into mental hospital. Earlier this year, I had the privilege of meeting Karlo Mila and shared with her how her story had help validate 'who I/Eye am' within the SIR. The woman I met is definitely not schizo; she is a Tonga, holistic, a gifted poet, an academic, and creative beyond measure. She reeks of beauty and illuminates the seen and unseen. Through Mila (2010) and this experience I/Eye have seen how the unseen of colonisation could have crazily constipated me.

Final intermission: Cleansing identity

In journeying through autoethnography with a critical lens in the evocative, interpretive, performative I/Eye have thus far experienced four stages of identity.

Identity
Interpretive
I.D.   entity
Picture of me: entity: To prove my existence

Evocative
I –den   –t   –ity
I- den (home) –t (Taui) – ity (state or condition)

Performative
EYE-dentity
Acknowledgment of a collective intrinsic lens

Critical
I.dent.it.Y?
What/how and why am I/Eye questioning my existence?

JoFI

Scene three: Consult the excrement

In a moment of road rage a blonde in a BMW drove in the lane next to me on the motorway. I looked across, she winded down her passenger window, I winded down my driver's window and she yelled out 'You black dick'. Then sped off. Initially I wanted to chase her down, and call her a racist and drop a few f-bombs. However, I breathed in deeply and settled on staying in my lane, at the same speed and writing about it later.

In big block letters, I wrote in my journal 'black dick, Black Dick, BLACK DICK'. Paused, then said it out loud "BLACK DICK, BLACK DICK, BLACK DICK". Paused longer, smiled widely, licked my lips, and exclaimed, 'hmmmmm YUM!!!!' These two words that were initially meant to be offensive had sifted through my third space and SIR, and had switched from being vile to delicious.

Inside my skin
Inside my skin
Lays blood & the same colour
Within . . .
Inside my skin . . .
JoFI

76 Fetaui Iosefo

A couple of months after this event, I'm in a line at McDonald's. I've ordered a large latte. I have my heavy backpack on and the place is jam packed. As I turn around I feel my bag connect with a body, I instantly move into apology mode. However, before I am able to say sorry, I face the woman. Her face is filled with anger and disdain. Through gritted teeth says 'YOU . . . BIG BLACK DICK!!' I have but a moment to think about these words. A ridiculously huge smile creeps across my chocolate brown face, I look directly at her, and I reply, 'Why . . . thank you, pink . . . vagina.' Beaming from ear to ear, I walk out with my latte, feeling ever so complimented.

On sharing this story there has been a variety of responses: the obvious one of anger, and then laughter. When asked, 'Why did you respond like that?', for me, it was simple . . . I chose to consult the insult, and chose not to be insulted.

Consult the insult

> Write each word as if it were your last
> Whisper it
> Say it firmly
> Vocalise it louder
> Whisper it softly
> Embrace each word individually
> Grin through the words of hate
> Smile at the scene
> Breathe in what is seen
> Exhale the unseen
> (Re)create your reality
> (Re) claim your identity
> (Re) store your wellness
> consult the insult
> the result
> Incult
> or
> Exhult.
> *JoFI*

Closing curtain: New Zealand/South Auckland: 2017

> The scene
> She is now covered
> A
> Padded bra to cover the swells of her breasts and nipples
> A black top to cover her bra
> A black cardigan to cover the black top
> Bloomers to cover her vagina & her manava (stomach)
> She is wrapped in a Samoan patterned lavalava (skirt)

From her waist to her ankles
No sight of flesh . . .
Black socks to cover her brown feet & toes
Black leather Chuck Taylors
To cover her black socks
He has not changed colour
His face is stoic
His face is white
His erection has soften
He believes
He has won
Because she is covered

. . .

He now believes she is . . .
Invisible
She is oppressed
She is powerless
He believes
He has her on remote control
This scene he created
Is his in-between

. . .

But . . .
Be wary . . .
Because in the UNSEEN . . .

She is
    . . . cleansing
    From the inside
    She is mending
    From the inside
    She is connecting
    From the inside
    She, has the batteries
    From the inside
    With each stride
    She is cleansing . . .
    JoFI

References

Amituanai-Toloa, M. (2007). The 'Va Tapuia' (space made sacred in bridging research and relationship) brown culture and commonsensical ethics. *Alternative: An International Journal of Indigenous Scholarship, 3*(1), 201–219.

78 Fetaui Iosefo

Anae, M. (2016). Teu Le Va: Samoan relational ethics. *Knowledge Cultures, 4*(3), 117.

Bhabha, H. (1990). The third space. In Rutherford, J. (Ed.), *Identity, community, difference* (pp. 207–221). London: Lawrence & Wishart.

Boylorn, R.M., & Orbe, M.P. (2014). *Critical auto ethnography: Intersecting cultural identities in everyday life*. Walnut Creek, CA: Left Coast Press.

Chang, H. (2007). Auto ethnography: Raising cultural consciousness of self and others. In Hopson, R. (Ed.), *Methodological developments in ethnography* (pp. 207–221). Emerald Group.

Chawla, D., & Holman-Jones, S. (2016). *Stories of home: Place, identity, exile*. London: Lexington Books.

Davis, C. (2005). Hauntology, spectres and phantoms. *French Studies, 59*, 373–379. 10.1093/fs/kni143[CrossRef], [Web of ScienceR]

Denzin, N. (2006). Analytical auto ethnography, or déjà vu all over again. *Journal of Contemporary Ethnography, 34*(4), 419–428.

Denzin, N. (2014). *Interpretive autoethnography* (2nd ed.). London: Sage.

Derrida, J. (1994). *Spectres of Marx: The state of debt, the work of mourning, and the new international* (P. Kamuf, Trans.). New York: Routledge.

Efi, His Excellency Tui Atua Tapua Tamasese Ta'isi Efi. (2007). Bio-ethics and the Samoan indigenous reference. *International Social Sciences Journal, 60*(195), 115–124.

Efi, His Excellency Tui Atua Tapua Tamasese Ta'isi Efi. (2008). In Suaalii-Sauni, T., Tuagalu I., Kirifi-Alai T. and fuamatu, N. (Eds.) *Su'esu'e manogi-In search of fragrance: The Samoan Indigenous Reference*. National University of Samoa, Lepapaigalagala, Samoa: The Centre of Samoan Studies.

Efi, His Excellency Tui Atua Tapua Tamasese Ta'isi Efi. (2009). *In search of harmony: Peace in the Samoan indigenous religion*. A paper for the colloquium organised by Pontifical Council for Interreligious Dialogue, Vatican City, Rome, Italy.

Efi, His Excellency Tui Atua Tapua Tamasese Ta'isi Efi. (2014). In Suaalii-Sauni, T.M., Wendt, M.A., Mo'a, V., fuamatu, N., Va'ai, U.L., Whaitiri, R. and Filipo, S.L. (Eds.) *Whispers and vanities: Samoan indigenous knowledge and religion*. Wellington, Aotearoa, New Zealand: Huia.

Ellis, C. & Bochner, A.P. (2000). Auto ethnography, personal narrative, reflexivity. In Denzin, N.K. & Lincoln, Y.S. (Eds.), *Handbook of qualitative research* (2nd ed., pp. 733–768). Thousand Oaks, CA: Sage.

Ellis, C. & Bochner, A.P. (2016). *Evocative autoethnography. Writing lives and telling stories*. New York: Routledge.

Ellis, C., Holman Jones, S. & Adams, T.E. (2015). *Handbook of autoethnography*. Walnut Creek, CA: Left Coast Press.

English, L. (2004). Feminist identities: Negotiations in the third space. *Feminist Theology* (13), 97–125. doi:10.1177/096673500401300108

Gonzalez, M.C. (2003). An ethics for postcolonial ethnography. In Claire, R.P. (Ed.), *Expressions of ethnography* (pp. 77–86). Albany, NY: State University of New York Press.

Holman Jones, S., Adams, T.E. & Ellis, C. (2015). *Handbook of autoethnography*. Walnut Creek, CA: Left Coast Press.

Iosefo, F. (2014). *Moon walking with the Pasifika girl in the mirror, an auto ethnography on the spaces of higher education*. Unpublished Masters Dissertation, University of Auckland.

Iosefo, F. (2016a). Third spaces: Sites of resistance in higher education? *Higher Education Research & Development, 35*(1), 189–192. http://dx.doi.org/10.1080/07294360.2016.1 133273

Iosefo, F. (2016b). Who is eye? An auto ethnographic view on higher educational spaces from a Pasifika girl. In e. emerald, R.E. Rinehart, & A. Garcia (Eds.), *Global South ethnographies. Minding the senses* (pp. 199–208). Rotterdam, Netherlands: Sense.

Lui, D. (2003). *Family: a Samoan perspective*. Wellington, NZ: Mental Health Commission.

Mila, K. (2010) Making the beast beautiful: recovering from a mental illness involves destigmatising one's own life story. The lessons learnt along the way provide value and meaning as one continues on life's journey. *Kai Tiaki: Nursing New Zealand, 16*(8), p. 16(3).

Montgomery, T. (2008). Space matters: Experiences of managing static formal learning spaces. *Active Learning in Higher Learning Education, 9,* 122–138. doi: 10.1177/1469787408090839

Pathak, A. (2013). Opening my voice, claiming space, theorizing the possibilities of post-colonial approaches to auto ethnography. In Sikes, P. (Ed.), *Auto ethnography: Volume IV* (pp. 195–206). London: Sage.

Pelias, R.J. (2004). *A methodology of the heart*. Walnut Creek, CA: AltaMira Press.

Richardson, L. (1999). Feathers in our cap. *Journal of Contemporary Ethnography, 28,* 660–668. doi:10.1177/089124199129023767[CrossRef], [Web of Science R]

Shuggart, H. (2003). An appropriating aesthetic: Reproducing power in the discourse of critical scholarship. *Communication Theory, 13*(3), 275–303.

Smith, G. H. (2000). Protecting and respecting indigenous knowledge. In Battiste, M. (Ed.), *Reclaiming Indigenous voice and vision* (pp. 209–224). Canada: UBC Press.

Spry, T. (2011). *Body paper stage: Writing and performing autoethnography*. Walnut Creek, CA: Left Coast Press.

Tamasese, K., Peteru, C., Waldergrave, C., & Bush. A. (2005). Ole Taeao Atua, the new morning: A qualitative investigation into Samoan perspectives on mental health and culturally appropriate services. *Australian and New Zealand Journal of Psychiatry, 39*(4), 300–309.

Tuagalu, I. (2008). Heuristics of the Va. *Alternative: An International Journal of Indigenous Scholarship 4*(1), 107–126.

Wendt, A. (1999). Tatauing the post-colonial body. In Hereniko, V. & Wilson, R. (Eds.), *Inside out: Literature, cultural politics, and identity in the New Pacific* (pp. 399–412). Lanham, MD: Rowman & Littlefield.

8

HOW DO 'WE' KNOW WHAT 'THEY' NEED?

Learning together through duoethnography and English language teaching to immigrant and refugee women

Ulrike Najar

MELBOURNE GRADUATE SCHOOL OF EDUCATION, AUSTRALIA

Julie Choi

MELBOURNE GRADUATE SCHOOL OF EDUCATION, AUSTRALIA

With the growing intensity of the humanitarian crisis around the world, Australia continues to see a steady increase in the arrival of asylum seeker, refugee and migrant (ASRM) families. As fathers seek work and children begin school, mothers have taken a backstage role supporting the day-to-day needs of their families with very limited knowledge of discourses and cultural practices in English. In this chapter, we draw on an English language teaching project we, as teachers and researchers, undertook from February to May 2016 investigating the language and literacy needs of four ASRM women living in Melbourne, Australia. Rather than starting from university language experts' understanding of what they need or by simply asking the women what they think they need, we used a dialogic and narrative method framed within a duoethnographic approach as a way of exploring their needs. In this chapter, we describe the process of how we came to learn about the women's language needs *together* through class-room activities, the researchers' reflective dialogues steeped in stories of our own language learning and teaching experiences, and finally through the process of writing up the study. In describing the process of how we made sense of the needs of ASRM women, that is, of what gets left out and interpreted from our limited positions, we aim to show how a) making decisions about others' language and literacy needs are vested in practices of power, and b) 'coming clean' in our writing can help to manage the power and positioning of both researchers and participants.

Prologue

Ulrike: I was excited when you asked me whether I'd like to join a duo-ethnographic research project on English language learning needs of refugee and immigrant women. I had done ethnographic work in the past but I had never observed my own teaching practice together with another researcher. And it seemed to fit, the two of us being ethnographers and eager to do work together; that made duoethnography quite attractive for us. Though I still remember how unprepared we were for understanding where the women came from. Our initial morning tea session and the questionnaire we designed to get an initial grasp of the women's English language learning needs was so much more complicated than we thought.

Julie: Yes, it got so much more challenging when we met the women, who didn't even want to hold their pens to write their names and shifted the pen back to us. It was a radical wake-up call and encouraged us to find more creative ways to come to know who these women were and what they would need English for.

(Post-research conversation recording, 25 January 2017)

Introduction

In January 2016, Julie found an ad for teaching English to immigrant and refugee women who live in a housing estate in northeast Melbourne, Australia, put up by a local community centre that organised the lessons. As TESOL teacher trainers and researchers who receive many enquiries of students, teachers, and schools about how to support the parents of immigrant and refugee children, we decided to volunteer and to offer an English language course for low language and literacy women. From February to May 2016, we organised a total of 12, two-hour weekly English language classes in a community activity room within the women's housing estate. The classes were designed for immigrant and refugee women who struggled to attend formal English language classes since arriving in Australia and who identified themselves as lacking confidence and a sense of belonging in their host country. These struggles mostly relate to health and wellbeing issues, childcare responsibilities, restricted mobility and social isolation in Australia (Australian Government Department of Social Services, 2013), as well as traumatic experiences in the past lives of the women (Bartolomei, Eckert & Pittaway, 2002). The women were contacted through the community centre and voluntarily decided to take part in the offered English language classes.

As researchers, our overall aim was to investigate the English language needs of immigrant and refugee women to, ultimately, provide pre-service teachers and other education stakeholders with more guidance on how to support mothers of immigrant and refugee children in using and learning English. Two frameworks were crucial for our teaching and research: a) a critical and b) a participatory framework. As educators who strongly identify with critical pedagogy (Freire, 1968;

82 Ulrike Najar and Julie Choi

Norton, 2013; Kubota, 2004), we aimed for a study design that enabled us to build relationships with the women and that invited them to actively participate in identifying and articulating their English language learning needs themselves. We chose a 'social-contextual approach' to English language teaching (Auerbach, 1989), which focused on *meaningful participation* (i.e., choosing topics and language that is directly relevant in the women's lives) to enact more active written and verbal participation in classroom activities. We also chose language tasks that allowed questions of identity, belonging and social issues to emerge. Throughout our teaching, we constantly encouraged the women to draw on the totality of their resources (i.e., cultural knowledges, multiple languages, gestures, sensory cues, use of electronic devices, etc.) for communication and learning purposes. While we have written elsewhere about the specifics of the study and its findings (Choi & Najar, under review), in this chapter we focus on the methodological process that shaped the study and impacted on the challenges we faced while building relationships with the women and making collaborative decisions about their needs.

In our roles as *teacher-researchers* who investigated the women's English language learning needs *through* teaching, we chose duoethnography, which focuses on 'how the researchers experienced and gave meaning to a given phenomenon and how those meanings were transformed over time' (Breault, 2016, p. 778). Through duoethnography, we engaged in an ongoing, transformative dialogue (which we recorded) about our experience of being teacher-researchers in an immigrant and refugee setting. For reasons of space constraints, here we limit our conversational recordings to focus on issues related to making decisions about other's English language learning needs and processes of repositioning ourselves through writing in the final stages of the project. In analysing selected moments that capture how we made sense of the English language learning needs of immigrant and refugee women, that is, of what is interpreted from our limited positions, we aim to show how a) making decisions about others' needs is vested in practices of power, and b) how 'coming clean' in our writing can help to consider more carefully issues of ethics and 'uncomfortable reflexivity' (Pillow, 2003) in the English language classroom.

Through the processes of holding joint discussions, taking notes, and negotiating meaning, we have created what Latz and Murray (2012) call a 'dialogic and multivocal' text that interweaves the narrative dialogues (post-class and post-research dialogues) with conventional academic writing and extracts of recordings from the classroom. Data consist of recorded dialogues that took place after class and during the writing-up phase of the study, individual field notes, and excerpts from the recordings of classroom interactions.[1] Here, we entangle the multiple sources of data along with our ongoing reflections and analysis. By intertwining these texts, we attempt to illustrate the inseparability of the various strands of teaching-researching and how the tensions that arise in the research process are negotiated back and forth at different times during the research process. By incorporating extracts of our dialogues into the text, we also attempt to give insight into the shared-ness of the meaning-making process of the researchers, whose ongoing dialogues formed the crux of the study and reflection processes.

We focus on two women who, out of a group of about ten women, attended classes regularly. Kotra and Jannah are both from Iran and are speakers of Kurdish and Persian. Kotra arrived as a migrant and has been in Australia for ten years; she has two young children. Jannah arrived as a person seeking asylum with her three adult sons three years ago. Due to childcare, visa and health constraints, both women have not been able to attend English language classes regularly for many years and were motivated to return, or take part in English language classes. While we ourselves have no status as refugees, both of us have had several experiences of migration in the past, with, for example, Julie (who is Korean-American and speaker of English, Korean, Japanese and Chinese) moving to Australia ten years ago, and Ulrike (German and speaker of English, German, Arabic and French) moving to Australia six years ago.

In the following sections, we attend to our understanding of duoethnography, then offer one example from our experience in the classroom to illustrate the complex and often difficult decision-making processes that we encountered in class. Finally, we discuss the challenges we faced when writing up the research and when trying to 'come clean' with the decisions we took before offering concluding thoughts on the processes of learning together in a duoethnographic research project.

Duoethnography

Duoethnography is a relatively new research method introduced by Sawyer and Norris to study how 'two or more individuals give similar and different meanings to a common phenomenon as it was experienced [in] their lives' (Norris, 2008, p. 233). At the core of a duoethnographic study is the *narration of the process* through which two individuals make meaning out of a phenomenon and its embedded power relationships (Sawyer & Norris, 2013). In other words, duoethnography *renegotiates meaning and reality* through retelling, revisioning, and re-understanding of memories of an experience with another person (Latz & Murray, 2012). This includes unpacking the *underlying tensions of roles and positions* that are part of the research process to gain 'insight into . . . current perspectives on and experience of issues related to personal and professional identities' (Breault, 2016, p. 777). Being similar to autoethnography and collaborative ethnography, duoethnography acknowledges and accommodates subjectivity, emotionality, and the researchers' influence on research (Spry, 2001). As such, duoethnography aims for *a shared meaning-making process* that positions the researcher as a participant and an active member of the sharing process – not as an interrogator (Ceglowski & Makovsky, 2012).

In this study, we used duoethnography as a participatory research method that enabled us to develop trust, collaboration, a sense of community in the classroom, to ensure flexibility and reflexivity throughout the research process, and problematise issues of power and positionality throughout the research process. As duoethnographers, we valued our own life stories in that they allowed us to draw on the

84 Ulrike Najar and Julie Choi

larger context and our own cultures when engaging in a mutual and reciprocal research practice. Following Sawyer and Norris, we understand duoethnography as a 'deeply emic form of inquiry', which is 'embodied and relational, thus promoting praxis' (2016, p. 3).

We now turn to one example of our classroom practice to show the complexity of how requests were made by the women, how they were silenced, how new voices emerged, and how moments of critical awareness were negotiated in classroom interactions.

Making decisions about others' English language learning needs

The setup of the classes was rather traditional in that we used a whiteboard, copied worksheets, visuals and a fixed seating arrangement (consisting of one large table and several chairs around it). During the course, we gradually introduced computer and mobile apps for translations into our class routines. We also focused on creating spaces for women-led (often lengthy) conversations around everyday issues they faced in their lives and specific language points they enquired about. The topics that emerged and that were meaningful to the women (such as healthy lifestyles, children's and their own education, family issues or making friendships) were picked up and incorporated into the syllabus and connected to the language points to be discussed in the coming lessons. While our approach to teaching and learning was designed to be in line with Community Language Learning approaches (Curran, 1976; Richards & Rodgers, 2001), Dogme approaches (Meddings & Thornbury, 2009), and Culturally Responsive Teaching approaches (Villegas & Lucas, 2002), the implementation of these methods in our class was difficult because the women came with their own ideas about the roles of teachers (i.e., as agenda setters, leaders, knowledge providers) and learners (i.e., as listeners, followers, etc.) in spaces of learning. We tried to be as careful as possible not to create an environment and relationship where we controlled the direction of what could or couldn't be said or done, but the tensions between different ideological understandings meant acts of silencing and voicing were always present in our interactions, as we show below.

The following excerpt of a class discussion took place in week nine and was planned as a lesson on 'cultural stereotypes' – a social issue that was central to many of the women's previous conversations on how to build relationships with Australians or the teachers of their children. The language points we had prepared for this lesson focused on new vocabulary and phrases related to the overall social issue of discrimination. By this class, we had already established rapport with the women who were accustomed with our use of visuals. In this lesson, we used visuals that captured socially unjust scenarios which stimulated their own stories of such experiences. The following classroom conversation took place at the beginning of the lesson and is a combination of the classroom interaction recording and our memories of the event (in italics).

How do 'we' know what 'they' need? **85**

Julie: Today, we are going to talk about 'stereotypes'.

Julie writes the word on the whiteboard and Ulrike explains the term.

Jannah: *(talks to Kotra in Kurdish)*
Julie: What did she say, Kotra? *(laughs)*
Kotra: She say 'why stereotypes? I need learn "hello", "how are you",
            more grammar'.

*Jannah is still saying something in Kurdish, puts down her pen and looks dissatisfied.
Kotra is silent.*

Julie: *(hesitates)* Oh, OK. *(short break)*
Ulrike: Jannah, it's good to learn about other things than 'saying hello'. To
            speak about your life in Australia, and what you find difficult can
            help you every day (. . .)

*The women remain silent and the situation remains unresolved. Ulrike points towards
some of the 'grammar points' we have already learned in class and reassures the women
that we will continue talking about grammar. Julie then moves on with the visuals we
had prepared for the class and that dealt with social injustice. The women continue to
contribute to class and, after some time, we reach the word 'discrimination'.*

Julie: Kotra, do you know the word 'discrimination'? *(Julie spells the word)*
Kotra: Dis-cri . . ., disc-ri . . ., long word! *(Kotra starts searching for the word
            in Kurdish on her phone and translates for Jannah)*
Julie: Yes, it's long but you have to know this word. It's a very important
            word. (. . .) Have you had this experience in Australia? Or any
            other place?

*Kotra starts to tell us about falsely being called a thief by a shop assistant. Jannah joins
in the discussion in Kurdish, which Kotra briefly translates but Kotra doesn't seem to
be interested in her story. Julie moves back to the whiteboard and points to one of the
key phrases that says 'I stand up for myself'. Kotra isn't as interested in learning a
new phrase now. She wants to tell another story that happened to her.*

Kotra: Yes. One time my husband. He say, he go to the nightclub. He
            say, I drink. He is Muslim but he is drink *(laughs)*. He say, he is just
            relaxed sitting in the chair with friend (. . .). But when this security
            come, 'YOU, go outside!'
Ulrike: You have to leave?
Kotra: You have to leave in here. (. . .) My husband say, 'Yes, OK, I go out-
            side.' You see, he leave it, and like, ah, five people, big guys, come,
            go outside. He nearly died. Everybody, his body [was injured].
            REALLY, REALLY BAD! *(stresses these three words strongly)*

Jannah puts her hands over her mouth and shakes her head, asking her something in Kurdish. Kotra explains very quickly in Kurdish to get back to continue telling the story to us in English.

Ulrike: Why did they do that?

Kotra: He say, 'I don't know.' He say, he call the police. Police come, they say 'what happened?' Five, six people, not good. Police say, they are bloody or see everything, but . . ., because he is not Australia. But OTHER guy Australia. Police talk with them, talk with the other people, security. Police say, 'go home, go home.' (. . .)

Julie: And did nothing?

Kotra: Nothing. *(Jannah knows this word, sighs loudly in disbelief and continues to say something in Kurdish which Kotra ignores.)* But few people told my husband, if you want to go to the court, I . . .

Ulrike: To be a witness.

Kotra: Yes, a witness.

Julie: So, if you could say something to the police, what would you say?

Kotra: *(She points to the whiteboard)* This one. THIS IS DISC . . . *(Kotra struggles with the pronunciation of the word.)*

Julie: Dis-cri-mi-na-tion. This is discrimination.

(Class recording, 26 April 2016)

In one single class, we can see a call for 'more grammar' and more conventional English language instruction and, at the same time, the use of situated English for social action by the women. Jannah makes a reasonable point in that she needs to learn more basic language and grammar points but, intuitively, we silence her request, pressing on with our lesson as planned. We watch the women's body language, we 'read' the silence and feel the tensions spoken in English through the Kurdish translations but we remain attached to our agendas. The following dialogue is an extract of our recorded post-class conversations and illustrates how we responded to what happened in this class.

> Julie: Jannah saying, 'I can't even say "hello". Why are we talking about social issues?' really threw me off. I wasn't sure what to say because what she said makes total sense. We say we are taking up a participatory stance, yet, in the classroom, when utterances like these are made, we don't really listen. This incident was the first time I started to see the downside of combining research and teaching together.
>
> Ulrike: But interestingly, we were trying to create a space in which the women feel comfortable enough to give us direct feedback and to participate by voicing their needs. And, as you said, when Jannah did voice what she wanted, we somehow silenced her by moving on with the lesson as planned. I really wonder if we taught more for us, that means the objectives of the research project, than for the women themselves.
>
> *(Post-class conversation recording, 26 April 2016)*

As teacher-researchers, our research agendas were in the back of our mind when navigating through interpersonal, intercultural, and pedagogical issues, that required us to act at the same time. The unpredictability and complexity of the teaching and researching brought us to situations in which we used our power as teachers by silencing the women's request and moving on as planned. However, we also saw Kotra communicating her stories of discrimination in a way that demonstrated that something has shifted for her – there is an urgency in her voice, the tone of her story, the stress placed on certain words and the speed of sentences that fly out of her mouth in both English and Kurdish. While she is interrupted by Jannah, having to be her interpreter, and also by Julie and Ulrike who continue to ask for more details, Kotra is able to tell her story in English in ways everyone understands and that builds on previously learned words (e.g. 'witness'). Jannah picks up on new vocabulary also (e.g. 'nothing') combined with her sensory interpretations of where Kotra puts the stress on words. Jannah knows more than she let on and she also had stories she wanted to tell (and we wanted to hear them), but Kotra is too tied up with her own story. In our post-class dialogue, we, once again, wonder about the implications of these narratives for our role as not only teachers, but also researchers.

> Julie: While the women tell us their stories, I always get this niggling feeling I am stealing their stories. I'm not sure how to really reconcile that idea. But the stories that are told through our 'pushing' still make me think there is something very important about that we can learn from them such as not making assumptions that low language and literacy learners cannot engage in high-level genres of speaking.
>
> Ulrike: Yes, they were enthusiastic during the lesson and eager to tell us about their experiences of injustice in Australia. And, if you think about it, they were able to say a lot with very little English. It was in their power to decide whether they wanted to share those stories or not and it did feel empowering to see them telling the stories they want to tell, and acquiring words that are useful for social situations like these at the very same time.
>
> Julie: Yes, and in many ways, I realise the women need a safe space to share their stories. They need a place for their stories to be heard. Perhaps it also means something else to tell those stories in English to their English language teachers.
>
> *(Post-class conversation recording, 26 April 2016)*

We were flooded with stories from the women on unjust events, realising we knew very little about the kinds of language they could use in these crucial moments. Over time, we saw the women taking more charge of their own learning and, most importantly, identifying and articulating their own English language learning needs. So, what did 'we' need to say? How could 'we' know what 'they' needed? In situations such as the one illustrated above, we seemed to reach for intuitive strategies, focusing on what *felt* right in the moment, based on the development of a close relationship with, and understanding of, the women. Benesch's work on emotions in critical English language teaching is central here, in that it reminds us

88 Ulrike Najar and Julie Choi

to focus on 'what emotions *do,* and how they interconnect with power and bodies in classrooms, postsecondary institutions, and societies' (Benesch, 2012, p. 4). In other words, we 'feel our way' (Ahmed, 2004, p. 12) in making decisions about silencing or voicing as we are teaching, having reflective dialogues and negotiating the use of power in the teaching-researching process. Situations like the one illustrated above are not necessarily about 'resolving', but about engaging with the situation through an 'ethics of care' (Kubanyiova, 2008), a point we will discuss in more detail below.

We now turn towards the process of research writing and the ways in which it enabled us to make sense of the complex dynamics that crisscrossed the spaces of teaching and practices of research.

The challenges of 'coming clean'

In reflecting, analysing, and writing our study for publications, we continuously grappled with the questions: *Did we do what was appropriate for the women and based on their needs? Or did we end up doing research that was more 'about' the women than 'with' or 'for' them?* 'Writing as a method of inquiry' (Richardson & St. Pierre, 2005) helps us to bring matters of transcription, positioning, othering, representation, and care to the fore. However, at the same time, by writing out our story, stitching bits and pieces of our past and present together, here, we continue to wonder if these acts of writing are simultaneously acts of attempting to 'come clean' through writing to 'give an account of ourselves' (Butler, 2005), to make sure we did all the 'right' things. In writing our first draft of this chapter, the following post-research conversation emerged:

> Ulrike: The text, as it stands, looks as if we were doing the 'right' thing. Although much of what we did was of a temporary, almost incomplete nature and based on issues that were meaningful to this particular group of women. And it might not have helped them at all. How do we come clean about these issues without making it look as if everything was 'OK' at the end?
> Julie: 'Coming clean', that's a very strong word. What does it mean anyway? It almost sounds like 'I've washed my hands and it's clean now'. There's a sense of finalisation to that term.
>
> *(Post-research conversation recording, 20 January 2017)*

In critically thinking about the concept of 'coming clean', Pillow's concept of a 'reflexivity of discomfort' (2003) resonated with us and helped us to reposition ourselves as emerging duoethnographers in the overall academic discourse on qualitative research methods. Pillow argues that 'practicing uncomfortable reflexivity interrupts uses of reflexivity as a methodological tool to get better data while fore fronting the complexities of doing engaged qualitative research' (2003, p. 175). Repositioning ourselves through a 'reflexivity of discomfort' meant for us to acknowledge how we as researchers accrue capital from presenting and publishing our work while potentially shifting away from real-world problems (Kubota, 2014). Thorstensson Davila (2014) encourages researchers in this light to continue pursuing 'representations that have meaning, albeit temporary, or partial' and to engage in 'representation as an act of caring' (p. 30). The act of caring, which Rinehart and Earl (2016) identifies as a valued and aspirational construct in qualitative research, was at the core of our project. Our often-contradictory responses in class were characterised by, and based on, an 'ethics of care' (see Kubanyiova, 2008) for the women and our project. As Pittaway, Bartolomei and Hugman (2010, p. 231) put it, 'the ethical challenge is for researchers to add value to the lives of the people they are researching, recognizing them as subjects in the process and not simply as sources of data'.

Conclusion: Learning together through duoethnography

> Ulrike: Often, we taught in a particular way, because we bounced off each other with our positivity about the project and the women. We cared for them and they cared for us as well. There were many feelings involved that you couldn't put into words.
>
> Julie: There's so much that goes on in my mind while we're teaching-planning-researching. I say something to you and you say, 'that's interesting' or 'yes!' – that kind of response helps me sift through the chaos and get on with the job of research. I really like that dialogic angle duoethnography enables.
>
> *(Post-research conversation recording, 10 February 2017)*

Duoethnography is not a formula but a concept that stimulated and guided us to work within specific contextual structures. While we aimed to work towards enabling creative language use, criticality and participation, we are aware we wield and yield power as we negotiate the structures of our research interests. Duoethnography represented for us an alternative within the current neoliberal and accountability-oriented research discourse by *allowing a focus on experience, affect, and the body* (Rinehart and Earl, 2016). In investigating immigrant and refugee women's needs we gave credit not only to what the women said, but also to the cultural knowledges, health/body states, gestures, electronic devices, and affective responses that were present in the classroom. Spry's (2001) argument that autoethnographic work can be considered an embodied methodological praxis also holds for duoethnographic work. An embodied methodological praxis acknowledges that not everything can be put into words and that, often, our bodies and feelings take over when having to make decisions as we work within tight schedules and heavy workloads.

In our duoethnographic movements, we engaged not only in shared planning, revisioning, re-telling and reflecting, but in positively caring for the project, the women and ourselves. It was this shared process of doing the research *together* that we could begin learning about what we *all* need.

Epilogue

ILLUSTRATION 2 Elana (Hediyeh's daughter) imitating us as teachers at the board (© Chris Mertins)

In our last class, Hediyeh, another new-arrival refugee woman in our group, told us that she started going to playgroups offered in a nearby community centre, indicating that through the English language lessons she rebuilt her confidence to make friends and use English in unfamiliar environments. As we chat, we see Elana, Hediyeh's two-year-old daughter who had joined our sessions frequently and hasn't learned to read and write yet, standing on a chair she has organised herself, scribbling on the board, possibly imitating us as teachers (Illustration 2). This moment reinforced to us again the ethics of what was being exchanged in these spaces – that what we say and do bears some responsibility in what they may be able to imagine and become.

Note

1 Ethics approval was granted by the university, housing estate, and community centre.

References

Ahmed, S. (2004). *The cultural politics of emotion*. New York: Routledge.
Auerbach, E. (1989). Toward a social-contextual approach to family literacy. *Harvard Educational Review, 59*(2), 165–181.

Australian Government Department of Social Services (2013). *Getting settled: women refugees in Australia*. Canberra: Commonwealth of Australia.

Bartolomei, L., Eckert, R., & Pittaway, E. (2002). "What happens there . . . follows us here": resettled but still at risk: Refugee women and girls in Australia. *Refuge, 30*, 45–56.

Benesch, S. (2012). *Considering emotions in critical English language teaching: Theories and praxis*. New York: Routledge.

Breault, R.A. (2016). Emerging issues in duoethnography. *International Journal of Qualitative Studies in Education, 29*(6), 777–794. doi.org/10.1080/09518398.2016.1162866

Butler, J. (2005). *Giving an account of oneself*. New York: Fordham University Press.

Ceglowski, D. & Makovsky, T. (2012). Duoethnography with children. *Ethnography and Education, 7*(3), 283–95. doi.org/10.1080/17457823.2012.717197

Choi, J. & Najar, U. (under review). Immigrant and refugee women's resourcefulness in English language classrooms: Emerging possibilities through plurilingualism. *TESOL Quarterly*.

Curran, C.A. (1976). *Counseling-learning in second languages*. Apple River: Apple River Press.

Freire, P. (1970). *Pedagogy of the oppressed*. New York: Continuum.

Kubanyiova, M. (2008). Rethinking research ethics in contemporary applied linguistics: The tension between macroethical and microethical perspectives in situated research. *The Modern Language Journal, 92*(4), 503–518.

Kubota, R. (2004). Critical multiculturalism and second language education. In B. Norton & K. Toohey (Eds.), *Critical pedagogies and language learning* (pp. 30–52). Cambridge: Cambridge University Press.

Kubota, R. (2014). The multi/plural turn, postcolonial theory and neoliberal multiculturalism: Complicities and implications for Applied Linguistics. *Applied Linguistics, 37*(4), 1–22. doi.org/10.1093/applin/amu045

Latz, A.O. & Murray, J.L. (2012). A duoethnography on duoethnography: More than a book review. *The Qualitative Report, 17*(14), 1–8.

Meddings L. & Thornbury, S. (2009). *Teaching unplugged: Dogme in English language teaching*. Brooklyn: Delta Publishing.

Norris, J. (2008). Duoethnography. In L. Given (Ed.), *The Sage encyclopaedia of qualitative research* (pp. 233–236). Thousand Oaks, CA: Sage Publications.

Norton, B. (2013). *Identity and language learning. Extending the conversation* (2nd ed.). Bristol: Multilingual Matters.

Pillow, W. (2003). Confession, catharsis, or cure? Rethinking the uses of reflexivity as methodological power in qualitative research. *International Journal of Qualitative Studies in Education, 16*(2), 175–196.

Pittaway, E., Bartolomei, L., & Hugman, R. (2010). 'Stop stealing our stories': The ethics of research with vulnerable groups. *Journal of Human Rights Practice, 2*(2), 229–251. doi.org/10.1093/jhuman/huq004

Richards, J. & Rodgers, T. (2001). *Approaches and methods in language teaching*. Cambridge: Cambridge University Press.

Richardson, L. & St. Pierre, E. (2005). Writing: a method of inquiry. In N. Denzin & Y. Lincoln (Eds.), *The Sage handbook of qualitative research* (3rd ed., pp. 959–978). Thousand Oaks, CA: Sage Publications.

Rinehart, R.E. & Earl, K. (2016). Auto-, duo- and collaborative-ethnographies: "Caring" in an audit culture climate. *Qualitative Research Journal, 16*(3), 210–224. doi.org/10.1108/QRJ-04-2016-0024

Sawyer, R. & Norris, J. (2013). *Duoethnography: Understanding qualitative research*. Oxford: Oxford University Press.

Sawyer, R. & Norris, J. (2016). *Interdisciplinary reflective practice through duoethnography: Examples for educators*. New York: Palgrave.

Spry, T. (2001). Performing autoethnography: An embodied methodological praxis. *Qualitative Inquiry, 7*(6), 706–732.

Thorstensson Davila, L. (2014). Representing refugee youth in qualitative research: questions of ethics, language and authenticity. *Diaspora, Indigenous, and Minority Education, 8*(1), 21–31. doi.org/10.1080/15595692.2013.803466

Villegas, A.M. & Lucas, T. (2002). *Educating culturally responsive teachers: A coherent approach*. Albany: State University of New York Press.

9

PERFORMING PROBLEMATIC PRIVILEGE IN JAPAN

Gabrielle Piggin

SCHOOL OF EDUCATION, UNSW SYDNEY, AUSTRALIA

Endeavours to snapshot the phenomenon of any Western lived experience in the Japanese context often encapsulate the atypical Occidental experience in the 'mysterious far East'. Casting aside awareness of neo-colonial concerns, these tend to revel in the romanticized Oriental Other in contrast to the Occidental Self. However, non-Japanese-speaking, cultural faux pas-ing Western foreigners are, in fact, Japan's ideal temporary guests, in models of intercultural competence institutionalized in local educational and political discourses. Performances outside of these bounds are outside the norms of Japanese societal expectations of the 'them' to Japan's 'us'.

But what is life like as an 'Other' in Japan beyond touristic events or travel sojourns? My narrative seeks to disrupt the normative mythologizing of 'culture- crossing' to probe the complicated intersection of race-gender-language-age-occupation, embodied by my individual lived experiences as an English-speaking, white woman educator living and working in Japan. The descriptors that define me are those that have given me the privilege of working and living in Japan. And yet these same positionalities are also innately problematic in the performances I am sanctioned to embody.

Introduction

Few countries make such conflicting claims on the imagination as Japan. The mere mention of the word Japan is enough to set off a cascade of contrary images: ancient temples and futuristic cities; mist-shrouded hills and lightning-fast bullet trains; kimono-clad geisha and suit-clad businessmen; quaint thatch-roofed villages and pulsating neon urban jungles [. . .] The fact is, whatever

94 Gabrielle Piggin

> your image of Japan, it probably exists somewhere on the archipelago – and is
> just waiting for you to discover it. So what are you waiting for?
>
> *(Rowthorn* et al., *2003, p.13)*

The above introduction from the Western travel bible of the pre-social media age, *Lonely Planet*, poses Japan as a passive entity 'just waiting for you' – the intrepid discoverer – to arrive and manifest 'your image of Japan' into existence. Such imaginings and re-imaginings of C/culture (Holliday, 1999) in all its shapes and forms are dependent on whose hand is doing the writing. Yet in so many writings, travel, academic and otherwise, the positionality of the author, and how their individual intersection of discursive traits transforms their own lived experiences, is often an unconsidered factor; just as the assumed 'you' of Lonely Planet readership is a monolithic 'Westerner' in contrast to the travel destination's definably exoticised and Otherised attributes. C/cultural imaginaries prevalent in cross-cultural texts are comparable to Pratt's (1992) explication of how imperial travel writings acted as effectual ideological tools in that they remain 'social transmitted representational assemblages that interact with people's personal imaginings and are used as meaning-making and world-shaping devices' (Salazar, 2012, p.2). The American anthropologist Ruth Benedict was hired by the US War Office of Information to delineate Japanese cultural behavior and her tome *The chrysanthemum and the sword* (1946) still exerts a worryingly far-reaching influence 'despite the enormous empirical and theoretical flaws' (Clammer, 2000, p. 204). Benedict's acclaimed analysis's foremost failing for qualitative researchers is that it was written without ever setting foot in the country she so famously decoded for the West. Lummis (2007) illuminates the continuing deification of Benedict's account (tellingly in Western and Japanese business circles), in that it:

> is useful, however, not as an accurate account of Japanese society, but as
> a work of political literature. The same could be said of other works of
> anthropology. Long before anthropology was invented, drawing detailed
> pictures of Another Country was a time-honored method of political theory,
> a method of establishing a "standpoint" from which one's own society could
> be viewed in a different perspective, thus enriching self-praise.
>
> *(Lummis, 2007, p. 4)*

This piece of autoethnographic writing seeks to explore what comes about when a sojourner remains and resides in Japan and from this standpoint interrogates how they as a *gaikokujin* (literally translated as 'outside country person' and abbreviated as *gaijin*) traverse the privileges that are problematically granted to their performances of imaginary Westernness.

Inside–outsider

In the context of Japan, how does one who is ascribed a foreign/outsider identity write robustly about their 'insider' experience? Geertz (1994, p. 220) alleges that 'anthropological writings are themselves interpretations, and second and third order ones to boot. (By definition, only a "native" makes first order ones: it's his [sic] culture.)" Therefore, how exactly does a writer write legitimately about a culture which is not 'their own'? An example of a supposed successful and non-ethnocentric 'interpreter' of Japan is Lafcadio Hearn (1850–1904) who has been hailed as the ultimate outside–insider writer and successful 'culture crosser' into Japan's historical exclusive sphere (Askew, 2009). Hearn managed to capture his outsider's sentiment and appreciation for the Japan he saw as being in danger of disappearing during the Meiji Restoration. His written representations were in stark contrast to other Western visitors who 'would often arrive in Japan as part of the grand global tour, expecting to be met with gratitude and for their innate superiority to be recognized' (Kendall, 2001, p. ix). Hearn has also been framed as one of the preliminary (and perhaps unwitting) scribes of the more ultranational-ist *Nihonjinron* (theories of Japanese-ness) by elevating in his analysis of Japanese culture 'the fanatic nationalism which was then being constructed by politicians and ideologues on Shinto foundations' (Guo, 2001, p. 106). Japan, albeit question-ably, is considered in its *Nihonjinron* representation to be a homogenous, ethnically definitive cultural entity via clearly drawn 'pure' bloodlines and thus imaginary racial borders (Befu, 2001; Ching, 1998; McVeigh, 2002; Sugimoto, 1999).

Akin to many discursive concepts, the veracity of authentic 'Japaneseness' is an imaginary, as are some Western writers' worlds re-created in their words when they are exemplifying the Other to their Self. Endeavours to snapshot the phenomenon of any Western lived experience in the Japanese context in travel writing/autobiography has often inevitably encapsulated the atypical Occidental's experience in the 'mysterious far East'; casting aside any awareness of neo-colonial concerns to revel in the romanticised Oriental Other in contrast to the Occidental Self (Adelstein, 2009; Ferguson, 2010; George & Carlson, 2005; Rauch, 1992; Williamson, 2006). The non-Japanese-speaking, cultural faux pas-ing Western and phenotypically white foreigner *gaijin* is in fact Japan's ideal temporary guest in touted models of intercultural competence; a Westerner imaginary which is institutionalised in educational and political discourse as the 'sociohistorically con-structed idealized other' (Rivers & Ross, 2013, p. 330). Performances outside of these bounds are outside the norms of Japanese societal expectations of the 'them' to Japan's 'us' (Bailey, 2006, 2007; Hashimoto, 2000; Seargeant, 2009).

What is life as an Other in Japan beyond touristic events or travel sojourns? Lowitz writes in her introduction of acclaimed author and critic Donald Richie's collection of *The Japan Journals* (2009) that Richie has been:

> like any foreigner, restricted to the role of spectator. Even though he has lived most of his life in Japan he has never become a citizen, only a per-manent resident. He pays full taxes but he cannot vote. And, given Japan's peculiar attitude towards foreigners, he has been powerless in many other ways as well.
>
> *(Lowitz, 2009, p. xi)*

96 Gabrielle Piggin

The 'peculiar' attitude to foreigners has enabled Richie to have experienced 'power-lessness', that in itself is incongruous; a white American man, who is world renowned as *the* leading Western authority concerning Japanese film (i.e. an interpreter of Japa-nese C/culture for the West) is located as an individual without agency or autonomy by being framed as a 'spectator'. Such exclusion which occurs in the Japanese context is marked because in Western dominated imaginaries 'discourses of whiteness are very much like those of Westernness in that both "white" and "Western" subjects are distinguished in part by being "not Other"' (Frankenberg, 1993, p. 193). In recent years a more critical approach by non-Japanese, Japan-based scholars is offer-ing more critical viewpoints on the complexity of power and privilege of members 'belonging' to a non-majority demographic in Japan (Appleby, 2012; Bailey, 2006, 2007; Houghton & Rivers, 2013; Simon-Maeda, 2004).

Introducing an I into the musings

This is where the stickiness of my own research starts to seep in: how can individu-als in a privileged positionality outside of their 'own culture' align their experiences with narratives such as powerlessness? How can this complex contradiction be parsed and unpacked? Could a dense literature review justifiably speak of expe-riences of otherisation of upwardly mobile individuals compared to the disen-franchisement that marginalised migrants endure? Of course, it cannot. However, scrutiny of different positionalities and complex nexuses of power may bring to bear new important threads of discussion of the variable structures of 'truths' and imaginaries in transnational lived experiences that have not been at the forefront of insider perspectives of Japan thus far.

My narrative seeks to chop and change the normative mythologising of the culture- crossing archetypal Westerner to probe the complex intersection of race-gender-language-age-occupation embodied in my own individual lived experi-ences as an English-speaking white woman educator living and working in Japan. To examine how privileged positionalities such as mine engage with the worlds around them it is useful to consider how the concept of intersectionality works to unpick the morphing and constitutive interplay of discursive tropes as '[i]ntersec-tionality has, since the beginning, been posed more as a nodal point than as a closed system – a gathering place for open-ended investigations of the overlapping and conflicting dynamics of race, gender, class, sexuality, nation, and other inequalities' (Cho, Crenshaw & McCall, 2013, p. 788). These adjectives that intersectionally define me are constitutive of hegemonic gaijinness (cf. Stanley, 2008) and innately 'privilege-conferring' (Carbado & Gulati, 2001, p. 707), allowing me to work and reside in Japan. Yet these traits that afford me undeniably problematic privileges are also inherently problematic in the performances I am sanctioned to embody; a 'Westerner' imaginary in Japan may be pushed up by the privilege they wield by embodying a foreigner script, but also how such privilege can be simultane-ously reductive. The complexity of status and identity is elucidated by Carbado and Gulati (2001) in that '[A]n identity intersectional that is marginalized in one context might be privileged in another' (p. 708).

Apart from the central role researcher subjectivity takes in some methods of qualitative inquiry which is rich, thick and iterative, often the researcher-self's positionality is conspicuously absent due to academic practices of research and research writing. So to disclose my perceived subjectivity I am phenotypically identifiable as a white, Western woman; this is important as '[f]undamental to intersectionality theory is the notion that race and gender are interconnected; they do not exist as disaggregated identities' (Carbado & Gulati, 2001, p. 706). I am in my late thirties and I have resided in Japan for 15 years. I am from an urban area in New Zealand and English is my first language and a variety which is considered to be of the 'inner circle' of World Englishes (Kachru, 1997). My trajectory in Japan began as an 'international exchange' in education which eventually led to a career in Japanese higher education within the realms of TESOL, Applied Linguistics and Cultural Studies. Currently I am a non-tenured lecturer on a five-year capped contract at a private university in a department that benefits its graduates with prestigious paths in life. To rehash on the road I wandered (oft travelled by those who share some of my own positionality traits) I was:

> initially spurred on by the opportunity to be 'the stranger', my sojourn metamorphosed into a transnational life and career. How and why my foreignness affects my perceived and performed positionalities has burgeoned into this exploration of the lived experiences, perceptions and negotiation of selves.
>
> *(Piggin, 2016, p. 68)*

Now, the tricky bit is to ensure that for you, this is 'a tale worth telling' (Carless, 2012, p.2) and that I may confidently shoulder epistemic justification post-tale.

From this point, I seek to decrease the distance between myself and the assumed 'you' even further. I will try to reveal fragments of my lived experience from behind the curtain of research metalanguage as so far 'I' have been largely absent and speaking through academic discursive conventions. Conventions will not be entirely left behind as I attempt to explore my autoethnography across C/cultures: as Chang (2007) outlines there are very definite conventions and 'pitfalls to avoid' doing autoethnography. Why I use the verb 'attempt' is because I am not only laying bare accounts of my life in public view, but am doing so within stretching boundaries of scholarly discourse. Therefore, I am attempting to embody my research rather than maintaining 'a mind/body dualism' (Butler, 2011, p. 16) while also trying to evade buying 'into the false dualism of theory and story' (Ellis, 2004, p. 18).

Romanticised uncomfortableness in boutique internationalisation

> We tell ourselves stories in order to live [. . .] We interpret what we see, select the most workable of the multiple choices. We live entirely, especially if we are writers, by the imposition of a narrative line upon disparate images,

98 Gabrielle Piggin

by the "ideas" with which we have learned to freeze the shifting phantasma-
goria which is our actual experience.

(Didion, 1990, p. 11)

I was drowning in awkwardness behind the driver's seat with no-one in the
doily-clad seat next to me. It was even more unsettling that the car was not a
taxi but driven by an enthusiastic senior teacher (I hoped) from the countryside
high school where I would apparently become an 'agent of internationalisation'
for an exchange programme. The senior teacher had bundled me into a car once
I stepped off the train with no formal greetings but a knowing and loudly voiced
'a-ha' as I was evidently the only white person on the train and at the station.
Little notice had I taken that all my other fellow 'agents' at orientation were also
white. Naively I thought the index of my skin pigment was incidental to my
privileged new occupation, not a privilege which Frankenberg (1997) surmises
as the 'unmarked marker' (p. 5) that had opened the gates for my entry to begin
with. The dichotomous 'cultural value profiles' (cf. Hofestede, 1986) distributed
by the orientation leaders at the time seemed like a useful code to make sense of
this experience; a culture of kindness and politeness as my welcome committee
of one (perhaps he drew the short straw) assured me the back seat was the safest
if he had an accident and how important it was that no harm come to me while
I was a guest in Japan. My Japanese-speaking Australian neighbour would later
tell me that kindness is the barrier between Japanese and non-Japanese; a way to
keep the parameters in place between the outside and the inside. At that time,
I was really puzzled how such an attitude could ever possibly be construed as a
negative thing.

From the car window, I saw a mass of colour I was not used to seeing. On the
southern hemisphere horizon a blazing red ball high in the heat-frazzled blue sky
and . . . the flag semiotic finally clicked. Verdant-green waving rice paddy after rice
paddy yet once in a while a vending machine was just . . . there. I was in the land
of archetypal juxtapositions for my grassroots adventure, following the script of
foreign English teacher arrives in the Japanese countryside. An hour ago I had been
a bullet train ride away in the Japan with sky blocked by snarled entanglements of
power lines and apartment buildings. Then there were only mountains and woods
and blue-roofed hamlets until an arrival at a country train station with huge and
startling plaster red-and-blue smiling ogres on either side of the entrance and a
hot spring bath inside the train station. The blanket of summer's cloying, oppressive heat was intensified by the full-length suit I wore as I was very conscious as
'a woman's modesty being representative of their professionality and upper arms
and décolletage should be hidden from view at all times' according to all the guides
I was armed with. In future weeks, my supermarket basket contents from the night
before would be reported back to me the next day in the office in a way that my
everyday movements outside work became small talk to engage with. Food and
my literal body of foreignness was a hot topic at work desks; the school nurse
warned me and any possible lunch companions that my delicate foreign and female

stomach was unsuited to eat sashimi and it was best avoided for my health. The roles I attempted to perform to the 'professional' standards expected were marked by boundaries of not only othered hegemonic femininity (cf. Schippers, 2007) but also *hegemonic gaijinness*; '[p]ut another way, the social meaning of a person's phenotypic racial identity is a function of the ways in which that person performs her identity' (Carbado & Gulati, 2001, p. 723).

The destination of my initial car ride was a 'welcome to our prefecture' homestay where I discovered my autonomy was negligible and I was to experience a somewhat discordant state of adult infantilisation in my new role as a cultural representative. I was not allowed to leave unaccompanied the well-intentioned but suffocating homestay for four days where I was the 'special' guest: I was reminded each night that all windows and doors to the room where my futon mattress was placed on tatami mats every night had to be shut and locked so 'no bad people could get in as everybody in town knew there was a very special foreign guest staying there'. Every night I dreaded my embarrassment of having to use the searing family bathwater first as the 'honoured guest', which resulted in a steamy bathroom on a stifling summer's night beside the kitchen where my hosts waited for their turn on the other side of the door. I never imagined that I would have to fake a bath for four nights running to avoid sweating in the water the family members would have to subsequently use. Attempts at independence and moving into my own apartment were taken as an affront to my hosts' generous hospitality – laughably in hindsight, I wanted to purchase a 'double futon mattress' which did not exist and was no doubt perceived as extremely inappropriate and suggestive of a sexuality which had no place in the boundaries of a correct feminine performance. Over the next 15 years in Japan, my identity would recurrently be determined as a guest, as a temporary visitor, and by my attributed performances; no matter how long I stayed, how much Japanese I spoke or how much I strived to contribute civically. My identity was contested in a way that was familiar because I was a young woman and my body could be breached so I had to ensure its boundaries. Embodying uncomfortableness in that first week gradually morphed into an identity of the non-negotiable professional boutique Other, which I was expected to perform, which for me came with the frustration of daily 'struggles which occur when certain identity options are imposed or devalued, and others are unavailable or misunderstood' (Pavlenko & Blackledge, 2004, p. 20).

Illegitimate professionality and permanent visitor

How do I position myself? Or the bigger question is to address how *can* I position myself as an outsider attempting an inside view of another C/culture (Merriam *et al.*, 2001)? Conceison (2004) writes of her time as a white Western woman in China defining the guilty resentment as '"a significant Other," a privileged marginalized Other rather than a dominated colonized object – which results of course in a vastly different dynamic' (p. 3). How may I attempt to address the uncomfortable knottiness of the problematic privilege that I embody in my own professional

100 Gabrielle Piggin

positionalities in Japan? Undoubtedly the white privilege I carry in my identity backpack as an educator has been a salient feature (McIntosh, 1989). Although privilege is responsively becoming part of media vernacular, I would like to situate my usage of it overtly through Black and Stone's (2005) definition:

> First, privilege is a special advantage: it is neither common nor universal. Second, it is granted, not earned or brought into being by one's individual effort or talent. Third, privilege is a right or entitlement that is related to a preferred status or rank. Fourth, privilege is exercised for the benefit of the recipient and to the exclusion or detriment of others. Finally, a privileged status is often outside of the awareness of the person possessing it.
>
> *(p. 244)*

Just as my positionality benefits me with a smooth passage as a mobile migrant with a privilege to live and work with ease in education, has my career path been justifiably based upon my own merit or have I solely been able to propel myself forward on a myth of self-made meritocracy, or more accurately, a well-performed hegemonic gaijinness? A former colleague once told me that I was well liked by my university department colleagues as 'a good example of a foreigner for Japanese students'. Seemingly the equation of my embodied positionality plus a perceived affability warranted my employment rather than the actual work performed. This 'revelation' did not entirely rock me to the core as I was well down the road to problematising my mobility, yet the fact that it was said out loud induced a corporeal response of ickiness and pushing pins and needles into any legitimate professional worth I thought I had. Hegemonic gaijinness, or the ability to adhere within the sticky boundaries of a working cultural script, encompassed my paid and unpaid roles in education as a 'cultural broker' (Bruner, 2005, p. 6). Essentially I exchange my performed and embodied foreignness as my own cultural currency. Lan (2011) adroitly coined the concept '"flexible cultural capital conversion" to describe how Western migrants in Taiwan, given their linguistic habitus and privileged locations in the global geography of power, are able to convert their English language capital into economic capital, social capital and status privilege' (p. 4).

My attributed identity of nothing more or less than a Native English speaker educator was further expounded in a conversation with a senior tenured colleague: '*The students like you though.*' '*They like your courses.*' '*You are genki (cheerful) so people like you.*' '*Between you and me you got on the yes pile despite your TESOL specialization . . .*' (the irony of 'despite' lies within the fact that this was a department where over half the students are studying second language acquisition courses in their second language), '*but then your photo was plucked out as someone who our students would like . . .*'. Seemingly my career trajectory was out of my hands and reduced to my performance of inferred likability from a photo; a nexus of my race, gender, appearance and age. Indubitably I had to have the desired qualifications and experience to be considered for my position. But would any of those variables matter if my facial features deemed me unfeminine? Or my haircut was different on the interview day? I could see clearly for the first time how much rode on my 'likability', physicality, attributed femininity and performances of hegemonic gaijinness, And how I was complicit in these performances. The emotional labour (Constanti & Gibbs, 2004; Hochschild, 1983) of my likability and ensuring that it remained intact as an educator plays out day after day in interactions with students, colleagues and administration staff. Performing outside the boundaries of expectations is unlikely to successfully secure an employment position (Carbado & Gulati, 2000), or positive course evaluations as my professional positionality is directly indexed to a successful embodiment of hegemonic gaijinness. This tension of emotional labour and working of identity (Carbado & Gulati, 2000) hinged on my openness, friendliness and ultimately gaijinness is exhausting, frustrating and partly provided the impetus for me to seek out why my professional identity was so precarious and ostensibly never-ending as '[p]erformativity is not a singular act, but a repetition and a ritual, which achieves its effects through its naturalization in the context of a body, understood, in part, as a culturally sustained temporal duration' (Butler, 2011, p. xv). Perhaps I am merely place holding for the next version of another Other to fulfil what is required in the professional performance of the Westerner imaginary; as beyond travel guides imaginaries are so firmly established and all-encompassing that they are difficult to escape and 'are alienating when they take on an institutional(ized) life of their own' (Salazar, 2012, p. 864).

Challenges to legitimacy and habitual trivialisation

A non-native English-speaking international student looked incredulously around my office bookshelves and exclaimed, 'Gosh, they treat English teachers really well here, don't they?' When I asked her to clarify she stated that she considers the 'native teachers' (a term she used to describe white faculty on campus) as not 'real lecturers' but 'just conversation teachers' in Japan. This ascribed identity can come from all sides: whether it was students who by the end of a Media Studies semester-long course said, 'Thank you for the English class'; several strangers who surrounded me in a gym sauna and requested free lessons 'as friends'; Japanese colleagues and administration staff who tell me in Japanese not to go to meetings because it will be in Japanese and there is no point . . . as I am not . . . How do I contest the privileged identity bestowed upon me that concurrently beleaguers me? In public interactions, I am always assumed to be lost in incompetency, or/and perpetually available to impart English practice sessions; when these assumptions are challenged it undoubtedly disturbs, as it rips up the Westerner-in-Japan imaginary script of ascribed expectations in 'cross-cultural encounters'. Such prescribed reductiveness is disquieting as 'residual effects of such encounters over time can be quite negative' (Conceison 2004, p. 4). I have also observed that in my conversations with different white, western women who share my age, and occupation in higher education, that from the romanticised tourist imaginary of Japan emerges a more cynical imaginary affected by the individual's positioning within

102 Gabrielle Piggin

its structures. One colleague often quipped, 'You know what they say . . . you're no one until you've had a stalker'; 'Professional blondes for hire'. My own pertinent incidents of burning irritation, blotchy humiliation or clenching frustration became daily moments making up my life. I have found that any association of a Westerner with education in Japan immediately connotes a signified non-skilled occupation and their worth is seen in their enactment of the imaginary C/culture they represent and that 'the most valuable capital they carry across border is not money but their English-speaking abilities' (Lan, 2011, p. 4). It has left me with the question of how do I eke out an imaginary of Self based upon preconceived roles I am supposed to perform?

Perpetual Otherness

> The knowledge produced and reproduced through reading a personal narrative and an autoethnography is what I refer to as a privileged knowledge. I argue that it is a significant form of knowledge because it provides an insider account and analysis of weaved power structures that an outsider cannot dismantle. This makes autoethnography a genre and a way of knowing for the unknown and the rarely spoken of.
>
> *(Hamdan, 2012, p. 587)*

Does residing for 15 years in a culture that is not my own by birthright or citizenship bestow upon me valid insights to impart? Does this time period itself lend my voice an authority and/or authenticity? Ellis outlines autoethnography as 'research, writing, story, and method that connect the autobiographical and personal to the cultural, social, and political' (2004, p. xix). As demonstrated in this chapter, autoethnography allows researchers and readers to address the murkinesss and messiness of cultural crossing where power and privileges shift and move outside marked boundaries. In addition to the unjustified and discriminatory privileged imaginaries which allow perceived Western/white native English-speaking teachers such as myself a monopoly on many sought-after Japanese university positions, and to also be tokenised as ideal others, it is crucial to face these issues head on as Kubota and Lin (2006) advocate that:

> Rather than being silenced by the discomfort of discussing race, racialization, and racism, the field of TESOL could initiate unique and vibrant inquiries to build on these topics and *investigate how they influence identity formation, instructional practices, program development, policy making, research, and beyond.*
>
> *(p. 473, emphasis in the original)*

No matter what path I tread in Japan, I will always have to negotiate my liminal identity, limited social inclusion and contested legitimacy through a lens of hegemonic gaijinness, yet of course any 'resentment at being treated as Other is accompanied by feelings of guilt due to recognition of this privileged status'

(Conceison, 2004, p. 4). Despite such privilege and the transnational gates I have been able to walk through (or really be escorted as a special guest) so freely, I still find that every day I am compromised to successfully perform the good foreigner by holding my tongue through a racist stereotype; an unrequested intervention on my behalf to perform an everyday task; an inappropriate question about my personal life; a disapproving 'tsk' through sucked teeth in my direction (Carbado & Gulati, 2000, 2001). Such 'discordant experiences of privilege and precarity' (Botterill, 2016, p. 16) are definitely not Japan-specific and are unequivocally a gentle avenue to be differentiated in light of how systemically debilitating and dangerous Othering can be. There remains a deluge of issues which need considerable unpacking beyond this chapter as to: how this particular white, gendered, nationalised problematic privilege is performed by the inside–outsider and, what C/culture crossing really reveals about the practices of life when performing passive or active manifestations of hegemonic gaijinness beyond the platitudinous tourist narratives.

References

Adelstein, J. (2009). *Tokyo vice, an American reporter on the police beat in Japan.* New York: Pantheon.

Appleby, R. (2012). Singleness, marriage, and the construction of heterosexual masculinities: Australian men teaching English in Japan. *PORTAL Journal of Multidisciplinary International Studies*, 10(1), pp. 1–21.

Askew, R. (2009). The critical reception of Lafcadio Hearn outside Japan. *New Zealand Journal of Asian Studies*, 11(2), pp. 44–71.

Bailey, K. (2006). Marketing the *eikaiwa* wonderland: Ideology, *akogare*, and gender alterity in English conversation school advertising in Japan. *Environment and Planning D: Society and Space*, 24(1), pp. 105–130.

Bailey, K. (2007). Akogare, ideology, and 'Charisma Man' mythology: Reflections on ethnographic research in English language schools in Japan. *Gender, Place and Culture*, 14(5), pp. 585–608.

Befu, H. (2001). *Hegemony of homogeneity: An anthropological analysis of "Nihonjinron"* (Vol. 5). Melbourne: Trans Pacific Press.

Benedict, R. (1946). *The chrysanthemum and the sword: Patterns of Japanese culture.* Boston: Houghton Mifflin.

Black, L.L., & Stone, D. (2005). Expanding the definition of privilege: The concept of social privilege. *Journal of Multicultural Counseling and Development*, 33(4), pp. 243–255.

Botterill, K. (2016). Discordant lifestyle mobilities in East Asia: Privilege and precarity of British retirement in Thailand. *Population, Space and Place.* doi:10.1002/psp.2011.

Bruner, E.M. (2005). The role of narrative in tourism. *Urbana*, 51, 61801, accessed 28.01.17 from: http://www.nyu.edu/classes/bkg/tourist/narrative.doc

Butler, J. (2011). *Gender trouble: Feminism and the subversion of identity.* New York and London: Routledge.

Carbado, D., & Gulati, G.M. (2000). Working identity. *Cornell Law Review*, 85(5), pp. 1260–1308.

Carbado, D., & Gulati, G.M. (2001). The fifth Black woman. *Journal of Contemporary Legal Issues*, 11, pp. 701–729.

104 Gabrielle Piggin

Carless, D. (2012). Negotiating sexuality and masculinity in school sport: An autoethnography. *Sport, Education and Society*, 17(5), pp. 605–625.

Chang, H. (2007). Autoethnography: Raising cultural awareness of self and others. In. G. Walford (Ed.), *Methodological developments in ethnography* (Studies in educational ethnography, Volume 12, pp. 201–221). Boston: Elsevier.

Ching, L. (1998). Yellow skin, white masks: Race, class, and identification in Japanese colonial discourse. In K. H Chen, H.O.L. Kuo, H. Hang and H. Ming-Chu (eds.). *Trajectories: Inter-Asia Cultural Studies* (pp. 65–86). London and New York: Routledge.

Cho, S., Crenshaw, K. W., & McCall, L. (2013). Toward a field of intersectionality studies: Theory, applications, and praxis. *Signs – Journal of Women in Culture and Society*, 38(4), pp. 785–810.

Clammer, J. (2000). Received dreams: Consumer capitalism, social process and the management of the emotions in contemporary Japan. In J.S. Eades, T. Gill and H. Befu (eds.), *Globalization and Social Change in Contemporary Japan* (pp. 203–223). Melbourne: Trans Pacific Press.

Conceison, C. (2004). *Significant other: Staging the American in China*. Hawaii: University of Hawaii Press.

Constanti, P., & Gibbs, P. (2004). Higher education teachers and emotional labour. *International Journal of Educational Management*, 18(4), pp. 243–249.

Didion, J. (1990). *The White Album*. New York: Farrar, Straus and Giroux.

Ellis, C. (2004). *The ethnographic I: A methodological novel about autoethnography*. Walnut Creek, CA: Altamira Press.

Ferguson, W. (2010). *Hitching rides with Buddha: Travels in search of Japan*. Canada: Vintage.

Frankenberg, R. (1993). *White women, race matters*. Minnesota: University of Minnesota Press.

Frankenberg, R. (1997). *Displacing Whiteness: Essays in social and cultural criticism*. Durham: Duke University Press.

Geertz, C. (1994). Thick description: Toward an interpretive theory of culture. In M. Martin & L.C. McIntyre (Eds.), *Readings in the philosophy of social science* (pp. 213–231). Cambridge, MA: MIT Press.

George, D.W., & Carlson, A.G. (Eds.) (2005). *Travelers' tales Japan: True stories*. Palo Alto, CA: Travelers' Tales, Inc.

Guo, N. (2001). Interpreting Japan's interpreters: The problem of Lafcadio Hearn. *New Zealand Journal of Asian Studies*, 3, pp. 106–118.

Hamdan, A. (2012). Autoethnography as a genre of qualitative research: A journey inside out. *International Journal of Qualitative Methods*, 11(5), pp. 585–606.

Hashimoto, K. (2000). 'Internationalisation' is 'Japanisation': Japan's foreign language education and national identity. *Journal of Intercultural Studies*, 21(1), pp. 39–51.

Hochschild, A.R. (1983). *The managed heart: Commercialization of human feeling*. Berkeley, CA: University of California Press.

Hofstede, G. (1986) Cultural differences in teaching and learning. *International Journal of Intercultural Relations*, 10, pp. 301–320.

Holliday, A. (1999). Small cultures. *Applied Linguistics*, 20(2), pp. 237–264.

Houghton, S.A., & Rivers, D.J. (Eds.) (2013). *Native-speakerism in Japan: Intergroup dynamics in foreign language education* (Vol. 151). New York: Multilingual Matters.

Kachru, B.B. (1997). World Englishes and English-using communities. *Annual Review of Applied Linguistics*, 17, pp. 66–87.

Kendall, N. (2001). In Lafcadio Hearn's *exotics and retrospectives* (pp. xv–xvi). New York: ICG Muse Inc.

Kubota, R., & Lin, A. (2006). Race and TESOL: Introduction to concepts and theories. *TESOL Quarterly,* 40(3), pp. 471–493.

Lan, P.C. (2011). White privilege, language capital and cultural ghettoisation: Western high-skilled migrants in Taiwan. *Journal of Ethnic and Migration Studies,* 37(10), pp. 1669–1693.

Lowitz, L. (2005). Introduction. In Donald Richie's *The Japan Journals: 1947–2004* (pp. vii–xiv). Berkeley: Stone Bridge Press.

Lummis, C.D. (2007). Ruth Benedict's obituary for Japanese culture. *Asia Pacific Journal: Japan Focus,* 5(7), pp. 1–21.

McIntosh, P. (1989). White privilege: Unpacking the invisible knapsack. *Peace and Freedom,* 49(4), pp. 10–12.

McVeigh, B.J. (2002). *Japanese higher education as myth.* New York: M.E. Sharpe.

Merriam, S.B., Johnson-Bailey, J., Lee, M.Y., Kee, Y., Ntseane, G., & Muhamad, M. (2001). Power and positionality: Negotiating insider/outsider status within and across cultures. *International Journal of Lifelong Education,* 20(5), pp. 405–416.

Pavlenko, A., & Blackledge, A. (Eds.) (2004). *Negotiation of identities in multilingual contexts* (Vol. 45). Bristol, UK: Multilingual Matters.

Piggin, G. (2016). Problematic privilege: Female western native English speaker English educators in Japan. In V. Longden (Ed.), *Situating strangeness: Exploring the intersections between bodies and borders* (pp. 67–79). Oxford, UK: Inter-Disciplinary Press.

Pratt, M.L. (1992). *Imperial eyes: Travel writing and transculturation.* New York: Routledge.

Rauch, J. (1992). *The outnation: A search for the soul of Japan.* Boston: Harvard Business School.

Rivers, D.J., & Ross, A.S. (2013). Idealized English teachers: The implicit influence of race in Japan. *Journal of Language, Identity & Education,* 12(5), pp. 321–339.

Rowthorn, C., Bender, A., Ashburne, J., Benson, S., Atkinson, D. & McLachlan, C. (2003). *Lonely Planet Japan* (8th ed.). Melbourne, Australia: Lonely Planet Publications Ltd.

Salazar, N.B. (2012). Tourism imaginaries: A conceptual approach. *Annals of Tourism Research,* 39(2), pp. 863–882.

Schippers, M. (2007). Recovering the feminine other: Masculinity, femininity, and gender hegemony. *Theory and Society,* 36(1), pp. 85–102.

Seargeant, P. (2009). *The idea of English in Japan: Ideology and the evolution of a global language.* Bristol: Multilingual Matters.

Simon-Maeda, A. (2004). The complex construction of professional identities: Female EFL educators in Japan speak out. *TESOL Quarterly,* 38(*3*), pp. 405–436.

Stanley, P. (2008). 'The foreign teacher is an idiot': Symbolic interactionism and assumptions about language and language teaching in China. *Linguistics & the Human Sciences,* 4(1), pp. 67–89.

Sugimoto, Y. (1999). Making sense of nihonjinron. *Thesis Eleven,* 57(1), pp. 81–96.

Williamson, K.T. (2006). *A year in Japan.* New York: Princeton Architectural Press.

10

NUANCED 'CULTURE SHOCK'

Local and global 'mate' culture

Robert E. Rinehart

FACULTY OF HEALTH, SPORT, AND HUMAN PERFORMANCE,
UNIVERSITY OF WAIKATO, AOTEAROA/NEW ZEALAND

In ethnographic identity work, stark differences between individuals are highlighted. Classically, such identity markers as race, class, gender serve as contrasts with the ethnographer's own 'home' culture. In such cases, there is an implied hierarchical structure contrasting the home culture of the ethnographer with the 'exotic' culture of the comparative culture. When the differences are stark, it seems, comparisons appear more obvious; when differences are more subtle — as in moving between one English-speaking country and another — discovering 'difference' and 'similarity' can sometimes be more 1) time consuming, and 2) confusing.

In this piece, I look at markers and exemplars of aspects of 'bloke' or 'mate' culture in Aotearoa/New Zealand from the perspective of a so-called 'Permanent Resident' raised and biased by a United States' upbringing. Using a fictionalized writing approach, I story some of the experiences of male-to-male relationships, particularly in sport culture, that are both similar and different between the various instantiations of these two cultures.

My 19-year old son and I moved to Aotearoa/New Zealand in 2008. Earlier, he had moved to live with me, after much legal rancour, in the States, and the opportunity for a new set of work challenges had presented itself to me. Transitioning from a relatively secure Associate Professor role at a Research 1 institution in the United States to the English-speaking but decidedly 'foreign' culture of New Zealand was both exciting and frightening – for both of us. Professionally, it might prove to be a bad move on my part, but life consists of risks we take, and, in addition to the professional challenge, I wanted to model curiosity and wonder for my son.

As my son was growing up to be a man, I found that the male cultures of the United States, even in a university town, were problematic and complicated at best.

Local and global 'mate' culture **107**

What Jackson Katz (in Jhally, 1999) has referred to as a 'tough guise' produced a dominant socialization that lead to maladjustment, bullying, and anger issues for many young American boys and men. I meant to raise an aware son, one who was sensitive to others' emotional, spiritual, and physical issues; I meant to raise a child who did not respond to frustration with anger or fear (the two emotions males seemed to be allowed to express), but rather with empathy and understanding; I meant to raise a boy who could dance between the 'hard' sub-cultures of 'tough boys' and the 'softer' sub-cultures of creativity, self-expression, hope, and love for the world. My naiveté as a father of a young lad was stunning. As with many parents, I felt I could shield him from the world, but the only 'shield' would be his own knowledge and confidence born of sometimes-hard-learned experience.

As all kids do – as I did at his age, as everyone I know did – his interactions with the outside world, the myriad subtleties of 'male' cultures, was sometimes a rough period of values clarification, mistakes, and adjustments. His grades in early high school suffered perhaps in part because he was over-committed to making friendships and becoming accepted. He tended, like some of us often do, to blame others for things over which he, ultimately, had control. Only he did not see that. Growing up, becoming socialized, is a process, not an end point, for all of us humans: males, females, transgender, questioning. As Denzin (2014) reminds us, 'there is no empirically stable I giving a true account of an experience' (p. 2). There is no final point; there is no singular story; there is no definitive account: my son's experiences may touch with mine in some ways, yet the changing nature of both of our performative accounts attests to the variability of this kind of recounting of experience – and, at the same time, the acknowledgement of our universally singular experience and values.

I don't know if he yearned for the gun culture that is a prevalent sub-theme of white male acculturation within much of the United States. He was not exposed to it from me. I owned no guns – pistols or rifles – and never wanted to own one. I believe the admonition that accidents happen in homes. If guns are available, accidents can be catastrophic. Anger can also be a mitigating factor in violence during passionate moments. Though I learned to target practice as a Boy Scout – and my son did too – I did not want a weapon in the house.

I had a childhood friend whose father verbally bullied, sometimes in front of me. This friend was a genius, but cowered to his dad. He was slight, not physically powerful as a child. But he grew up. Bought a Toyota 4 x 4, with lifters. Packed a loaded .45 semi-automatic pistol underneath his car seat, 'just in case'. Bragged about it.

I once was sitting around the kitchen table at his house. We were in our early 40s, grown men. His father had died. He had been married twice, and was angry about that. He went into his bedroom, and came out with two high-powered rifles, a shotgun, and a revolver. Placed them on the table.

I flashed back to when my father, drunkenly, had threatened my brother and me with a loaded pistol. Reactive fear made me, ironically, freeze. My friend decided to swing the barrel of a .30–06 Browning BAR towards my chest. I pushed it away. He laughed at me.

108 Robert E. Rinehart

'What's the matter?'
'I don't like you pointing that at me,' I said.
'It's not loaded.'
'Yeah, that's what they all say.'
'It's just for self-defense.'
'Then why isn't it loaded?'

In the United States, the National Rifle Association (NRA) runs rampant over the logics of intimidation of fellow citizens. In fact, an ad for a type of 'round' or bullet used in a Browning BAR .30–06 makes this claim:

> Sure, there's the old adage about the placement of a shot being the most important part of the terminal ballistics equation, but this round makes it a bit easier. Any animal hit within their terminal area is going to be hard pressed to take even a few more moments in life.
>
> *(Ben W., 2012)*

The term 'animal' in this review of the Browning BAR .30–06 hunting rifle is also code, and can be interpreted by many racist readers to roughly mean game – or those they term less-than-human. That is a sub-text, though of course there are many hunters who only want a weapon to hunt deer and big game. One of the keywords for this article is 'Self Defense.' And, of course there is no need for self-defense against a deer.

So we moved to New Zealand. This chapter is meant to be about a contrast of the 'bro' culture in the USA and the 'bloke' culture of Kiwis in New Zealand.[1] Myself, I know the USA male culture more intimately than the NZ one, but, for me, the Kiwi one stands out in starker relief due to my normalizing of United States' male socialization. So here are some particular stories and observations, and perhaps even generalizations. The fictionalization / factionalization and universal / singular divides may preclude the extent to which we can apply our own autoethnographic 'tales' for general use, but for now, perhaps it would help to listen to some of these tales.

The pub

My son's friend Aaron (pseudonym) visited from the United States. Coming from the US, and yet critical of George W. Bush's embarrassing social clumsiness, we all clearly carried *perceived* privilege to the locals in this west-coast New Zealand town. By American standards, none of the three of us was highly advantaged either monetarily or materially; but traveling in the rest of the world – and simply by virtue of being 'United States' Americans – we automatically fit into a cultural stereotype. To be honest, travelling halfway across the world is a privileged position for many tourists.

Our clothes identified us as 'rich' Americans. Our accents gave us away. Most Kiwis, in social situations, were lovely, asking how we were enjoying the country,

Local and global 'mate' culture **109**

what did we like best about New Zealand. They would avoid talk of Bush and his cronies, as if knowing that we were not our government.

I dealt with much of their questioning the way I would if I had won a large amount of money in Harrah's casino at South Lake Tahoe: I downplayed it. I would shift the conversation to another topic, asking them questions about their work, where they grew up. I would try to become less visible, attempt to take up less space. As a male in both cultures, this was a decidedly 'feminine' ploy. This, for me, was a more comfortable position than being the centre of attention. But not for Aaron.

We went to the pub. Now, this pub is laid out with a veranda, where ageing bikers, smokers, and surfers co-mingle drinking beer; a front dining room, meant for families to enjoy a pub supper; a mixed-sex bar area, filled on All Black rugby test nights; and, in an homage back to settler-England values, what has come to be known as a 'sports bar', a generally male-dominated space filled with pool tables, 'pokies', television screens, a TAB (Totalisator Agency Board) wagering station (for Australian and New Zealand horse and dog racing). In summer months, the pub opens up an outside family area with shade and trees, picnic-tables and benches, pizza, and kids running around freely. During different times of the day, the gendered nature of some spaces is more or less salient. Some spaces, with the inclusion of lots of alcohol (and drugs ingested prior to coming to the pub) and crowding, become less safe, mildly confrontational, somehow more 'blokey'. Only occasionally, these elements combine to create a dangerous situation – but, by United States[2] standards, there is very little risk. In the early 2000s, even the violent exchanges were usually between younger males and generally were alcohol-fuelled with knives the preferred weapon of choice.

In Aotearoa/New Zealand, as implied by the double name for this magnificent country, there are two official oral languages, te reo Māori and English (and a third official language, New Zealand Sign Language). This reflects the original owners of the land, the Māori, who, like many Indigenous groups throughout the world, resisted colonization, 'containment, appropriation, [and] assimilation' and exploitation (Coombes, 2006, pp. 1–2) –and the British settler-colonialists (cf., Smith, 1999). The Indigenous Māori and the *pakeha*, or European-derived New Zealanders, enjoy a mostly amicable relationship, in part due to events (and Te Tiriti o Waitangi, the Treaty of Waitangi) during settler-colonist times. As Tapsell (2006) points out, 'the media [have a] propensity to put all Maori into one racially biased basket' (p. 90); Bell (2006) reinforces this tendency:

> the . . . characterisation of [New Zealand *pakeha*] identity now appears simplistic, partial, even clichéd. Particularly wanting has been the implication that this sense of distinct identity was unified and unproblematically subscribed to by the European New Zealand (Pakeha) population – in a *settled* condition.
>
> *(p. 101)*

Both Māori and *Pakeha* push back against attempts to generalize their characteristics, tendencies, or identities. Though Māori are numerically low in relation to the total population – 15 per cent self-identify in the 2013 census (Statistics New Zealand, 2015) – the 14 tribes (or *iwi*) comprise just over 600,000 members. Rata (2011) notes that numbers of Māori 'may include people who identify as Maori but who do not know their tribe' (p. 363); she also mentions that there is the 'social reality of ethnic fluidity in New Zealand' (p. 359). Historically, it was only due to settler colonialism that the complex of tribes saw mutual benefit in uniting against a common enemy (Tapsell, 2006).

Nipples

Aaron knew nothing of any alcohol-fuelled tensions rumbling through the sports bar of the pub. Barely there for a year, even my son and I still kept to ourselves. But Aaron was his outgoing self, responding openly and honestly in that sometimes-charming and naïve 'American' way. He identifies as cisgender male, I believe, but his openness and sensitivity, especially in greeting and meeting newcomers, belied a certain fear of rejection: as most of us do, he wanted to be liked. Interestingly, his generation (and my son's) has enjoyed playing with, testing out, their sexuality in a wider array of performances than my generation ever did.

An aside: in 'America', there are *many* 'Americas'. The one my son and his friend lived in was upper-middle class, in the mostly-white enclave demarcated from urban America that house some land-grant, state-owned universities. There are many vestiges of unexamined privilege in the life of an academic. There were murders – there was danger – of course. This was in the United States. But the safety factor of children growing up in this town was quite high. People simply were not 'mean' to white male children of professors. There was an inculcated – or perhaps learned – assumption that strangers would like them (and me, for that matter). Being an American was a non-issue: we were all Americans. We were the dominant group, privileged, felt we had a right to belong, and shocked if the storyline went counter to that narrative.[3]

Bringing that white-privileged confidence of his likability into the sports bar that night, Aaron started up a conversation with a middle-aged Māori man. 'As you do,' they say here. They were playing pool with two others. But Aaron's accent, or his false bravura, or the man's drunkenness – something – triggered a response in this man to where he started teasing Aaron. Only Aaron didn't know he was being teased. The man was 'taking the piss'.

We were all drinking beer. The place was filling up. When this man and Aaron came to the table to fill up their glasses from our jug (a small pitcher of beer), I looked in the eyes of this man. They looked straight through me. The only other time I had seen these eyes was in a courtroom in San Bernardino, California, when two shackled murder defendants shuffled by me in their orange suits. Their eyes were vacant, like they'd already been executed. They contained no humour or light: they were black holes.

I hadn't seen this guy around the pub – ever. He was thin and wiry, muscled, and had a teardrop tattoo: all clues to how he viewed masculinity. But also, all stereotypes. In the reality of the moment, my fear button – again, based on theoretically unfair stereotypes – went into alarm mode. Aaron's didn't. My son's might have, but I think he was caught up in an Aaron-induced nostalgia of Americana and some trusting kind of belief. You want your kids to have and hold that hope forever, but when they are exposed to pure hatred, xenophobia, or irrational rage, you want them to identify it, and either run from it or prepare for battle. Aaron didn't see it coming. I saw it, and was seemingly helpless to intervene.

The guy asked each of us a question. Looking back, he was measuring where we all were from by the colour in our shirts, the types of shoes we wore, our accents. My son and I appeared semi-Kiwi, because we'd lived here for a year. However, we all failed the accent test: we were either Canadians or Americans.

Then, pouring himself another beer from our jug, he proceeded to stumble, catching himself full on with Aaron. He lingered a bit, as if making up his mind about something.

They all three went back to the pool table. I whispered to my son, 'Be careful with that one.' My son, at the age when taking advice is a mark of lack of courage, looked at me as if I were crazy.

When they came back to the table for more beer, this guy was slurring even worse. At one point, he pinched and twisted Aaron's nipple through his shirt. At first Aaron giggled, certain this was a show of acceptance by his new-found friend. But it wasn't: it was more a show of power, a show of sexuality, an attempt at dominance.

It was about Americans coming to live in his country. It was about slights he'd suffered at the hands of white colonialist settlers – and their ancestors. It was about an outsider to town. This guy did not care about the tourism trade or economics or treating a young adolescent with some basic humanity.

It was an attempt at humiliation.

His twisting of Aaron's nipple made me think of one of the meanings of a teardrop tattoo in the United States: it meant the owner was in a gang, and had killed someone as a part of an initiation ritual. I wondered if this was the case in New Zealand.

I said, 'Let's get out of here.'

'Why?' asked Aaron. He was obviously trying to 'man up', to ignore or meet the threat. We were all reading this differently. Perhaps because of age, I wanted no part of a guy I thought might be a felon. My son's reaction was a bit in the middle: he wanted to stay but I think he also sensed some peril. I believe Aaron, new to the country like an innocent abroad, thought his American-ness would protect him from all dangers.

Shooting

Growing up male is fraught with symbolism. In the United States, the National Rifle Association (NRA) and its massive lobbying efforts to skew legislation sympathetic to pro-gun culture has effected 'what it means to be a man'. But the encouragement to use weapons – and to kill things – seems to start early in a young man's life.

112 Robert E. Rinehart

I was talking with a Kiwi retired farmer, 15 years my senior. He told a tale of receiving an air rifle as a young lad. He and his brother wanted to try it out, test its power. Knowing a pellet would hurt them, they decided to take the nub off of a pine needle sheath—below the needles, near the branch, the bit the length of a pellet—and load it into the rifle. His brother pointed it at his leg, pulled the trigger, and it broke the skin. Rather than cry out, he staunched his yelp, took the gun, saying, 'No, didn't hurt a bit!' (though it hurt like hell). 'See?' He then proceeded to shoot his brother in his leg.

Of course, I had a similar story: BB gun, no BBs in the chamber, pump action – meaning you could pump it up to make the pressure stronger. I pointed it at my friend's leg – he just stood there, willing it to happen. And I pulled the trigger. A blue dot appeared in his leg, and he howled with pain. To this day, he will point to the dot (almost 50 years later) as if to say, 'You owe me, sucker.'

Is this a tale about boys, and how they are socialized to become stoic? Is it about stupidity, and the freedoms that kids had 50 years ago as opposed to now? Is it about one-upmanship, power, showing who is tougher in ridiculous test situations? Is it about trial and error, and the grace that allowed us to survive our own mistakes?

The Kiwi told me he still hunts, mostly game birds. In fact, he said that he thinks it is tragic to see beautiful mammals shot for 'sport'. At about age six, I shot that pump BB gun (this time loaded with BBs) at a robin singing in a tree above. The suddenness of its drop to the earth was breathtaking. Its stillness made me cry. I nudged it with my shoe, but it never came back to life. About eight years later, I went deer (sport, not food) hunting, saw a shockingly large buck panting out his last rattled breaths after being shot in the heart. There he lay, with six of us around him just watching, mesmerized. Such a magnificent animal. The older men in the hunting 'party' were beside themselves with joy, exclaiming, 'Great kill!' and 'Nice shot!' Juxtaposed with the death throes of the deer, its eye panicked and hurt and sad, their celebrations seemed obscene to me.

And today, with all the wars and killing of humans, conflicts entered into almost haphazardly, these animal deaths seem almost insignificant. But they still haunt me. Clearly, I'm not a full member of the bro society that so famously is represented in American caricatures of 2nd Amendment defenders – or for that matter, simply gun owners (cf., Springwood, 2007).

The Kiwi farmer is not representative of *all* Kiwi farmers. The young boy I was is not representative of *all* young male Americans raised in the 1950s. This is one of the main keys to unpacking this notion of 'bloke' and 'bro' 'cultures': representational efforts only reveal a part of the picture.

In New Zealand, children climb trees outside of restaurants and in school; when I first moved here, three- to four-year-olds would climb sign-poles, shimmying up them to touch the sign, then gliding back down. This independence, born of a combination of a staunch 'do-it-yourself' attitude and a sense of Kiwis 'punching above their weight', results in university students who speak confidently in front of

Local and global 'mate' culture   **113**

their classmates and young men who are polite and somewhat shy when they try to 'chat up' prospective partners.

Picking up

'Care for a drink?' he asked.

'Aw it's my shout, mate,' she replied, somewhat keeping him at arm's length. It may have also meant that she was interested, but *just not yet*. It was a contemporary form of social ambivalence, social capital. It also meant that she was, for now, independent. Not aloof: independent.

They sat in a group of ten. Six women, four men. They were all in their early twenties. Glenn was single; so were Charlotte and Brittney. For that matter, so was Kenda, but she seemed quite uninterested in the male–female dynamic of the party.

Glenn was homing in on Brittney. His tone respectful, his wit trained to interest but not show off, his interest deflected to include the others while simultaneously creating a special intimacy: this was his particular style of approaching women. That and self-effacing humility.

'So, Charlotte. How'd you and Brittney meet?'

Charlotte warmed to the subject. 'We were at camp. We've known each other since – what? We were nine? And we met at camp, abseiling, rock-climbing, kayaking, orientation: you know the drill. We were in the same group. She was fierce!'

'We were the Kowhai Group,' Brittney said. Her eyes wandered back 12 years. 'We were all trees.'

'All native trees?' Glenn asked, hoping Brittney would answer.

'Yes, they were!' Charlotte said, too loud. 'There were kauri, the rimu.'

'– and totora?' asked Brittney. 'I think Marg was in the Totora Group?'

'Attractive trees, all,' put in Glenn, smiling. He avoided looking at Brittney.

Kenda rolled her eyes. 'So lame.' There was an uncomfortable silence.

'Ah, Kenda,' said Mark, 'you think everything's lame! You didn't even like Bruno Mars!'

'Totally lame,' she grinned.

They all laughed; Brittney looked at Glenn and, a split second later, he looked at her. They smiled.

In both the United States and Aotearoa New Zealand, boys and men are generally limited to expressing ranges of two emotions: anger and fear. In the US, all males – and particularly males of colour – have had their emotional and affective lives stunted, limited, and constricted (cf., Katz, 2006). The tenderness, uninhibited joy, frivolity: these and more have been tamped down, shaped and modulated, to demonstrate a coolness, or what Majors and Billson term 'cool pose' (1993). Male children, in effect, learn to be hard. But in Aotearoa New Zealand, the level of acceptable antisocial behaviour as boys grow into men is much lower than the norms in the United States.

114 Robert E. Rinehart

'Bloke' behaviour in Aotearoa New Zealand generally has as its intended object a harmless bantering with others, a 'we're in it together' kind of male subculture: an innocence. 'Bro' behaviour in the United States – especially with the public stretching of 'acceptable' antisocialism in the Trump era – seems to have as one of its primary intents the demonstration of power over others. This is a fundamental difference; though, with a creeping globalization, even Aotearoa New Zealand is beginning to be affected by so-called American values.

The recognition of all kinds of bullying – in 2009 something that Physical Education New Zealand conference attendees dismissed as not happening here – has recently become a hot topic for Aotearoa New Zealand researchers (e.g., Raskauskas, Gregory, Harvey, Rifshana, & Evans, 2010; O'Driscoll, Cooper-Thomas, Bentley, Catley, Gardner, & Trenberth, 2011; Green, Harcourt, Mattioni, & Prior, 2013). There is a growing cultural recognition that some tenets of male culture in themselves are problematic, which mirrors such programmes in the United States as Sut Jhally, Jackson Katz, and Jeremy Earp's work on masculine identity construction and what Katz terms 'gender violence prevention' (2006, p. 37).

Premises and limits

Autoethnography, by definition, is limited to a first-person point of view. Auto-ethnography across cultures, then, is a butting up of first-person points of view – but paradoxically told from one subject position, in storied form. Difficult at best, the *doing* of it reveals many potential difficulties.

Among these difficulties are how good stories work best: they focus on the particular, on the idiosyncratic (Rinehart, 1998). The unfettered use of fiction or faction for autoethnographic 'tale telling' clearly has limitations, simply because the values and requirements for a good story can sometimes butt up against this concomitant generality: inductively, our autoethnographic tales are meant to point readers to larger truths.

Working against particularity is the notion of generalization. Denzin (1990) warned us about the modernist project of Mills, particularly in *The Sociological Imagination*:

> his 'nowadays' sentence reflects either what he imagines men (and women) nowadays feel about their lives, or what others have written about men nowadays. It cannot be that he writes of his own sense of being trapped and without meaning, for Mills the intellectual craftsman finds meaning in his theorizing about these lives his texts neither touch nor allow to speak.
>
> *(p. 4)*

The cautionary for all projects of this nature is that over-generalization may lead to stereotyping. Denzin's 1990 answer was to create theoretically minimalist social texts.

Nowhere is the idea of over-generalizing leading to easy stereotyping more evident than in my relating my experience(s) in relation to other men, classifying them as 'Kiwi blokes' or 'American bros', in writing up such experiences as if they are some sort of yardstick or norm for these hugely diverse cultures, sexualities, generations, ethnicities, and so on. Denzin (1990) terms this (speaking of Mills) a 'manipulation of me, flesh-and-blood reader, to his own ends, [which] erases my trust' (p. 4). The same, I realize, could be said of my (and many autoethnographers') manipulations of texts – using singularities as metonymic for universality.

I re-discovered this *caveat* regarding autoethnography when I attempted to construct a story about two bi-sexual Kiwi 'blokes' who happened to play rugby. Just as with every story, there are no generalizations for this tale. There are only specificities that either reinforce what Denzin terms 'verisimilitude' (1994) – and Banks and Banks (2000) distinguish from veridicality: 'Veridicality is the accurate representation of a reality or fact; verisimilitude conveys the appearance or feeling of reality in a text' (p. 237) – or ring false. If everything is a story, an interpretation, then calling into question how closely a text aligns with lived experience (or a sense of the reality of lived experience) remains one of the fundamental criteria for judging effective autoethnography.

However, what if the 'origin' of the story is itself derivative? In the suggested (and aborted) tale of the two bi-sexual rugby mates, my 'experience' is observational, not from direct experience. The heart of my tale of these two blokes was a simulacrum based upon a simulacrum: derived from talking with people, from popular culture, from readings both academic and popular. While crafting the story, I gradually felt that I could not tell the story in the detail I wanted (for verisimilitude), with the background confidence of coming close to 'knowing' the experience.

I could have 'member checked' it for how it resonated with a selected group of informants (bi-sexual, gay, Pakeha, Māori, Pacific Islander, veteran, novice, world-class, regional-class), but I came to realize that, on balance, I was constructing a stereotypical tale. Nothing I wrote would be 'representative' of 'bloke culture', unless I resorted to cultural stereotypes. The form (fictionalized autoethnography) belied the function.

So: lesson (re)learned. Autoethnographic stories, based on real particular truths, have their limitations for broadening out to *how it works*. We can likely amend the reach of our autoethnographic truths to *how it sometimes can work*. Further than that, we may link our own personal troubles to public issues, as C. Wright Mills advises (1959). But Denzin's caution – that C. Wright Mills is never speaking of real people in real situations – is a haunting reminder of running away with theory without remembering human agency.

With the single life we each have, there is a recognition that, to experience the ebb and flow of life itself, our own lives have to be lived. We can never truly live the life of another person. Reading about other's lives points us in certain ways. But we cannot put so much stock in it that we subsume our own lives. Thus, the cautionary regarding individual experience: though a story may affect us deeply,

116 Robert E. Rinehart

inspire us, anger us, create empathetic passion in us, we must take the time to let it simmer, brew. We must learn to mull, to savour, and to put these singular tales into a larger perspective. In a so-called 'post-truth' world, the ability to hold back and mindfully assess (historically, contextually, culturally, for example) is becoming more and more critical to finding a balanced way forward.

Oddly, then, fictionalized or factionalized autoethnography does have lessons to teach us. These are, oddly, paradoxical lessons. Autoethnography can teach us to interrogate stories – not as mistrusted for the ways the teller somehow 'remembered it' happening – in the way that we, as readers, become involved in them, in the world of them. We have to 'suspend disbelief' while remaining sceptical; we have to swallow every single detail as something that 'could have happened', while wondering in counterposed dialogue with the autoethnographer if there could have been other ways of seeing it, other ways of dealing with it. We have to remain mindful, and 'fact check' just as assiduously as some critics when a 'false' story is put on social media. As autoethnographers, we must rely upon our own intellect, sense of justice, and ability to engage with the other. Our sources of knowledge have not changed: we still apprehend the world as humans have always done, through our cognitive abilities, our senses, and so on. In the final analysis, we should attempt to live lives that use our own experience(s) and relational skills to approach, but never assume, the other.

Notes

1 Given different names – 'Bro,' 'Bloke,' 'Mate,' 'Dude,' 'Lad' – these roughly equivalent terms describe young (usually white) males who are embattled with the task of attracting friends while simultaneously repelling any hints of difference (see, e.g., Wheaton, 2000).
2 In New Zealand, almost everyone conflates the terms 'American' with 'person from the United States'. I spent many years trying to correct this misconception, pointing out that Canada, the USA, and Mexico comprised *North* America, so all were 'Americans'. This, of course, was not even to mention those deriving from Central or South America: *latinamerican* has become a bit of a pushback to the stereotyping of Americans throughout the world.
3 One of the interesting, albeit alarming, facets of the Trump presidency has been, for that safe middle-class white American, the crumbling of surety in their own unexamined sense of safety.

References

Banks, S. P., & Banks, A. (2000). Reading 'the critical life': Autoethnography as pedagogy. *Communication Education* 49(3): 233–238.

Bell, L. (2006). Auckland's centerpiece: Unsettled identities, unstable monuments. In A. E. Coombes (Ed.), *Rethinking settler colonialism: History and memory Australia, Canada, Aotearoa New Zealand and South Africa* (pp. 100–120). Manchester, UK: Manchester University Press.

Ben W. (2012). The 10 Best Hunting Rifles: The Browning BAR .30–06. Off The Grid News, http://www.offthegridnews.com/self-defense/guns-ammo/the-10-best-hunting-rifles-the-browning-bar-30–06/ (accessed 13 August 2017).

Coombes, A. E. (2006). Introduction: Memory and history in settler colonialism. In A. E. Coombes (Ed.), *Rethinking settler colonialism: History and memory Australia, Canada, Aotearoa New Zealand and South Africa* (pp. 1–12). Manchester, UK: Manchester University Press.

Denzin, N. K. (1990). Presidential Address on *The Sociological Imagination* revisited. *The Sociological Quarterly 31*(1): 1–22.

Denzin, N. K. (1994). Evaluating qualitative research in the poststructural moment: The lessons James Joyce teaches us. *Qualitative Studies in Education 7*(4): 295–308.

Denzin, N. K. (2014). *Interpretive autoethnography* (2nd Ed.). Los Angeles: Sage.

Green, V. A., Harcourt, S., Mattioni, L., & Prior, T. (2013). *Bullying in New Zealand schools: A final report.* Wellington: Victoria University of Wellington, School of Educational Psychology and Pedagogy.

Jhally, S. (1999). *Tough guise: Violence, media, and the crisis in masculinity.* Northampton, MA: Media Education Foundation.

Katz, J. (2006). *Macho paradox: Why some men hurt women and how all men can help.* Naperville, IL: Sourcebooks, Inc.

Majors, R., & Billson, J. M. (1993). *Cool pose: The dilemmas of Black manhood in America.* New York: Touchstone.

Mills, C. W. (1959). *The sociological imagination.* Oxford: Oxford University Press.

O'Driscoll, M. P., Cooper-Thomas, H. D., Bentley, T., Catley, B. E., Gardner, D. H., & Trenberth, L. (2011). Workplace bullying in New Zealand: A survey of employee perceptions and attitudes. *Asia Pacific Journal of Human Resources 49*(4): 390–408.

Raskauskas, J. L., Gregory, J., Harvey, S. T., Rifshana, F., & Evans, I. M. (2010). Bullying among primary school children in New Zealand: Relationships with prosocial behaviour and classroom climate. *Educational Research 52*(1): 1–13.

Rata, E. (2011). Discursive strategies of the Maori tribal elite. *Critique of Anthropology 31*(4): 359–380.

Rinehart, R. (1998). Fictional methods in ethnography: Believability, specks of glass, and Chekhov. *Qualitative Inquiry 4*(2), 200–224.

Smith, L. T. (1999). *Decolonizing methodologies: Research and indigenous peoples.* London: Zed Books, Inc.

Springwood, C. F. (Ed.). (2007). *Open fire: Understanding global gun cultures.* Oxford: Berg Publishers.

Statistics New Zealand. (2015). '2013 census: Major ethnic groups in New Zealand.' http://www.stats.govt.nz/Census/2013-census/profile-and-summary-reports/infographic-culture-identity.aspx

Tapsell, P. (2006). *Taonga, marae, whenua* – negotiating custodianship: A Maori tribal response to Te Papa: The Museum of New Zealand. In A. E. Coombes (Ed.), *Rethinking settler colonialism: History and memory Australia, Canada, Aotearoa New Zealand and South Africa* (pp. 86–99). Manchester, UK: Manchester University Press.

Wheaton, B. (2000). 'New lads'? Masculinities and the 'new sport' participant. *Men and Masculinities 2*(4): 434–456.

11

IN WHICH I AM SUNG TO, CRY, AND OTHER SUCHLIKE

Reflections on research in and with Tibetan refugees in India

Harmony Siganporia

COMMUNICATION AREA, MICA, INDIA

This chapter explores the experiences and reflexive identity positionings appropriated by and attributed to an Indian ethnomusicologist, me, currently researching among the Tibetan refugee community in and around Dharamsala, India. My work in this context examines the role of music(s) in the articulation of identity and place-making and, in particular, the making and performing of identities through cultural practices in exile settings. The *performance* of identities is key, because Tibetan identities are no more homogenous or fixed-in-time than 'Indian' identities – or any other too-large, broad-brush-strokes, nation-based identity label. Indeed, in all culturework, including ethnomusicology, there is a risk of ossification of cultural practices: in a bid to preserve 'culture', researchers risk creating museum-pieces that cease to be live practices and, at best, represent what *was* rather than what *is*. In addition, of course, there is the insider/outsider question. I am not Tibetan, and not trying to hold onto my culture amidst the tumult of an enormous, complex country that is not my own. How am I to navigate this reflexivity as I work from/in the margins? I am also a practising musician. This brings me in – an insider identity – *and* sets me apart all over again. This chapter is therefore a meditation on the identity work and place-making that both my participants and I do, in different ways, through the medium of music/s. I discuss the interplay of 'self' and 'other' in the research setting, and the positionality of a researcher who is, in turns, both insider and outsider. While cultural practices like music can tell researchers a lot about the society that creates them, it is also necessary to reflect on how the researcher's own voice may harmonise – or not – with the voices of 'the researched'.

Introduction

> Jamyang: 'Wait: you're Indian?' (Bursting into full-throated song:) *'Chandni! O meri Chandni! Rang bhare baadal se, tere naino ke kaajal se; maine iss dil pe likh liya tera naam – Chandni! O meri Chandni!'* (Chandni! oh my very own, Chandni! From the many hues of the clouds; from the sooty liner around your eyes, I've etched your name across my heart – Chandni! Oh, my very own, Chandni!)

The year is 2012. We are in the beginning of winter in the beautiful Himalayan town of Dharamsala, and the setting for this impromptu serenade is a set of rooms at the Om Hotel, in the heart of McLeod Ganj.

This was my second visit to Dharamsala/McLeod Ganj, and my first as more than a tourist. By this, I mean it was the first time I was introduced to the inner life of the place by locals who took me into their homes, gave me rum and other hot beverages to drink, and momos to eat, and sang to me constantly. It was the first time I met Jamyang, who I was to later learn was one third of the 'JJI Brothers', one of the best known contemporary Tibetan musical acts in the exile community today. Jamyang wasn't the only one to sing me (dated) Bollywood songs that night; a number of others who have since gone on to become dear friends, to the point where I no longer remember a time when they were not a part of my life, also decided that singing old Hindi film songs to me was par for the course, given that I was 'Indian'. Introduced into this celebratory setting (Ingcel, the 'I' in JJI who now lives abroad, was home for a visit, and this night was turned over to revelry in his honour: friends from Vietnam and France rubbed shoulders with Tibetan 'locals' and two Indians, of which I was one), my night was a delicious one, where these Hindi film songs (everything from old 1950s classics such as 'Mera Joota Hai Japani, Ye Patloon Englistani, Sar Pe Laal Topi Russi, Phir bhi Dil hai Hindustani', which loosely translates to 'my shoes are Japanese; my pants from England; the red hat on my head is Russian, but my heart is Indian for all that', to the 90s ode to that hapless woman named 'Chandni' I started this piece with) kept punctuating fascinating conversations with Gaphel, for example, on his childhood years as part of the travelling convoy of Tibetan sweater sellers who set up shop across the length and breadth of India every winter, or speaking to Kunkey, who had just completed her education and was moving back to Dharamsala, about what was to come next for her.

The reason I was in Dharamsala at all, was to invite poet-activist Tenzin Tsundue to a winter school on the life and thought of Gandhi I was a part of which was running not too far from where they were based, but more on that later. This visit pretty much decided my mind: I had completed writing my PhD thesis earlier that year, and was casting about for a project I felt passionate enough about to immerse myself in. There was something special, surreal even, about being sung Hindi songs to by a group of Tibetan exiles all night. It brought home to me the role of music in the bridging of cultural boundaries; Bollywood songs, I later realised, were a vital entry point into the very idea of India as far as a lot of Tibetan exiles were concerned. Apart from serving as a medium that allowed for linguistic crossing and the acquisition of Hindi (a useful thing, if one is to negotiate India), it also serves as a space – a shared discursive field which draws on the same popular cultural references – which enables or allows the possibility of dialogue when it comes to interacting with Indians (a necessary part of living in exile in India, you will appreciate). It was interesting also that, as one of the two Indians in the room that night, and the only one who was 'new' to the group, there was the assumption that we did indeed share the code 'Bollywood' in common, even though I had to later confess to Jamyang, Gaphel and Anto that they knew far, far more Hindi songs than I did.

I've lately taken to describing myself as an academic mongrel, wandering as mongrels do, between Literature and Culture Studies ('home' during my Master's degree) and Social History (in which discipline I have a PhD). My current research – and I've been working on this project formally since 2013, but I believe I began living with the idea from the night of this meeting described above in late 2012 – is among the Tibetan refugee community living in and around the Himalayan town of Dharamsala/McLeod Ganj in India's northern state of Himachal Pradesh.

The project began as an exploration of the role of music as a set of practices and cultural artefacts aiding in the articulation of identity and place-making and, in particular, the making and performing of identities in exile. As with most cultural artefacts and the practices which produce them, there is a risk of ossification: in a bid to preserve 'culture', practitioners as well as researchers such as myself risk creating museum-pieces that cease to be live practices and, at best, represent what *was* rather than what *is*. An example of this is to be found in the discourse around Ache Lhamo (Tibetan Opera) today. To put things into perspective, there exist a handful of canonical pieces of Ache Lhamo (Norbu 2015). Borrowing from Benedict Anderson's (1983) description of the mechanisms which allow imagined communities to cohere, this is the corpus of a community's stories in common, known intimately by all three generations living in exile today. Efforts to create new pieces are often met with resistance from the community at large. Here's an example to illustrate my point: 2015 saw a massive celebration of Ache Lhamo in Dharamsala, marking the 20th anniversary of the 'Shoton' ('yogurt') festival in exile. This meant ten days of Tibetan Opera, with performances from troupes representing myriad Tibetan Settlements from across India and Nepal (there are some 39 major and minor 'Settlements' in India alone, home to over 90,000 Tibetan refugees[1]). The highlight of this festival was meant to be a 'new' piece created by the Tibetan Institute of Performing Arts (TIPA) based in Dharamsala itself, outlining the major events in the life of the Buddha.[2] This production was saved for the last day of the festival, and things were heating up in Dharamsala prior to it: I was privy to much speculation about TIPA's use of a recorded backing track – a first for Lhamo – and their elaborate costumes and stage settings. There was excitement and hesitation in almost equal parts, leading up to the performance. Eventually, as with most things which mark a departure from the known – even where the piece in question

ILLUSTRATION 3 Members of the Tibetan refugee community engaged in a spontaneous group dance at the end of the Shoton Festival at TIPA, Dharamsala, April 2015 (© Harmony Siganporia)

hearkens back to stories held in common – the crowd appeared somewhat listless in the face of what they witnessed that day, eschewing the 'newness' of that performance for the familiarity and comfort of the spontaneous group dancing which followed it (see Illustration 3), something I read as a site which allowed full expression of what it meant to be Tibetan in India today; and this was true equally for all three generations in exile. Amalas (mothers) and Palas (fathers) danced in abandon with their children and their children, till the sun set slowly – almost unwillingly – across the Himalayan sky. In this, the site continued to remain relevant to the youth who were not necessarily schooled in the idiom of Lhamo, had neither been born in, nor so much as ever seen Tibet, and did not know these stories as intimately as did their parents and grand-parents. This is how the generation that only inherits the idea of Tibet learns to inhabit it symbolically, taking ownership of what is a category in a constant state of negotiation' (Siganporia, 2018a).

Emic? Etic? Er, emetic, please?

I find I constantly have to contend with the insider/outsider question, or what ethnography would call the juxtaposition of 'emic' and 'etic' perspectives. As Kottak defines it, 'The emic approach investigates how local people think'; how people

122 Harmony Siganporia

organise and make sense of their world, their codified rules, how they make meaning, and perpetuate it. The assumption here is that cultures are best described from the inside out – one's location within the group in question is a pre-requisite if one is to be able to not merely record but analyse and decode the meaning-making apparatuses which combine to create complex identities. On the other hand,

> the etic (scientist-oriented) approach shifts the focus from local observations, categories, explanations, and interpretations to those of the anthropologist (or 'specialist'). The etic approach realizes that members of a culture often are too involved in what they are doing to interpret their cultures impartially. When using the etic approach, the ethnographer emphasizes what he or she considers important.'
>
> *(Kottak 2006, p. 47)*

The implication here is that ethnographic work may be undertaken from the outside in; that in some ways, not being part of the community one works in and with allows for a more dispassionate perspective/reading of it. This is a dialectic I'm aware I, at different moments and wearing different identities, find I have to inhabit on either side. I am not Tibetan, do not live in exile, and am not trying to hold on to my 'culture' – were such a thing possible – amidst the tumult of an enormous, complex nation-state which is not my own; I am nowhere near as marginal as the Tibetan refugees I work with. This places me along the etic axis; in this respect, I am an outsider to the society I attempt to work with.

But an 'Indian' researcher among Tibetan refugees is not my only identity. 'Indian' is as much a catch-all term as is any other large, contested, and polyphonic identity-marker. I am Indian, but I am also Parsi – a minority community within the Indian mainstream. In numbers alone, Parsis form a group smaller than the Tibetan exile population living in India today – we number a mere 69,000 inhabitants in India (0.006 per cent of the population, just to put things into perspective). It could be argued that this minority identity would render me marginal. However, two more disparate minorities (Parsis and Tibetan refugees) one could not find: my lived experience is anything but marginal, given the long history of Parsis in India (it is held that, possibly escaping religious persecution in then-Persia, the Parsis migrated to Indian shores anywhere between the 8th and 10th centuries CE[3]). This tiny community is known to have some of the highest literacy rates in India, and includes some of India's wealthiest industrial players (including the Tata, Wadia, and Godrej families) in its ranks. However, the privileges – socio-economic class and (lack of, since it isn't a widespread structuring principle for Parsis) caste – afforded to me as a Parsi Indian researcher are counter-weighed somewhat by the fact that I am also a woman attempting to negotiate her way through one of the world's most strident patriarchal societies.

Apart from this, I am also a practising musician. This brings me in – conferring on me an emic or insider identity – even as it sets me apart all over again, because my study is not one premised on researching Tibetan musicians alone; if anything,

Reflections on research with Tibetan refugees in India **123**

I try and follow musical productions through the cultural circuit they navigate from their inception to their consumption by an exile community which exists in what Judith Butler identifies as a permanent state of 'precarity' (2009).

Inhabiting this dichotomy, my method, such as it is, has largely been an exercise in narrative ethnography, which, as Carolyn Ellis puts it, is a mode in which the narrative encompasses 'stories that incorporate the ethnographer's experiences into the ethnographic descriptions and analysis of others. Here, the emphasis is on the ethnographic study of others . . . accomplished partly by attending to encounters between the narrator and members of the groups being studied' (Ellis *et al.* 2011).

Building on this premise, my account is a meditation on the identity work that both my participants and I engage in, in different ways. It corresponds loosely to, as I outline above, narrative ethnography, but with elements of reflexive ethnography built into it, because I seek to find room for the many 'ways in which the interviewer (myself) may have been changed by the process of interviewing' (Ellis 2004, p. 18) those I write and work among and with. In this kind of research, 'even though the researcher's experience isn't the main focus, personal reflection adds context and layers to the story being told about participants' (ibid.).

(Re)Introduction (because who said anything about time being linear?)

In the interest of establishing further context, I must go back somewhat further than the beginnings of my project proper, so this part of my story begins in 2008, with an experience I have never quite managed to make sense of. I have gone back to it in my head so many times in the interim, it seems to me almost ridiculous. Drawn to Art Bochner and Carolyn Ellis's idea that autoethnography can be therapeutic; that a number of researchers come to their areas of interest owing to certain events in their lives or family histories, suggesting that the impetus behind the research can be the desire to better understand something that moved them, and/or because they seek 'social justice for others and themselves' (2016, p. 246), the following passage can be read as my attempt to confront an incident I have struggled with in more ways than I can here enumerate. There was a festival of non-violence in my city (Ahmedabad, Gujarat) in January 2008, and the Dalai Lama was its keynote speaker. I was a journalist then, covering the 'culture beat' for a national newspaper, when word came in that His Holiness would grant a chosen handful of us a personal interview. This announcement filled me with as much dread as it did excitement: I knew a little about the history of Tibet and its on-going occupation by Chinese forces, but this interview meant I would have to amp up this information several times over before I felt able to ask His Holiness anything even remotely meaningful.

We met in his hotel room, which had been more or less fortified by his security detail and the bevy of officers and translators who accompany the Dalai Lama everywhere he goes. We were, if memory serves me correctly, five or six journalists – one each from the city's leading print newspapers. He greeted each one of us individually, as we were introduced to him. I folded my hands into a *namaste*, only to have this venerable monk laugh in my face and call me a *buddhiya* – an old woman. The man was clearly an imp with a delicious sense of humour – something that came ever clearer into view as the hour I spent with him wore on.[4]

What I did not put into my article is what happened after the interview had finished. I am avowedly atheist, and have been for as long as I can remember. And while I've always been interested in Buddhism as a philosophy, I've also been extremely uncomfortable with its ritualisation into what looks and feels very much like any other 'form'-al religion. At the end of the interview, people were posing for photographs with the Dalai Lama. When it was my turn to have a moment with him, I told him I had a question for him instead: one that was for myself, not the interview we had just completed. He held my hand as we spoke, and I proceeded to ask him when Buddhism, which as I understood it, was conceived as an invitation to navigate one's own path through life, the world, and one's place in it, had turned into a codified, ritualised set of practices to be followed unquestioningly. I do not remember his answer, although I know he gave me one, because almost before I could finish my question, I began to sob. Not whimper. Not tear up quietly. I began to sob. It was visceral: a sob that began from deep within my gut and demanded to make itself heard. Embarrassed by something I did not then – and do not now – understand, I bid him goodbye and hot-footed it out of that room, and the hotel, as quickly as I could. I have since thought about this occasionally, but have been unable to decode it in any meaningful way. I left the newspaper soon after this event, and began work on my PhD. It was with some – but only some – surprise therefore, that I found myself flinging headlong into working on hearing and reconstructing identity through the sounds of Tibetan exile a few years later, once I had completed my degree. It felt oddly, dare I say it, preordained.

Dubious though I may be of neat little origin stories, this feels like a good one, and while I am tempted to keep it – and I do not for a moment doubt it is one, in some ways – it certainly isn't one that has made my life as a researcher particularly easy. Early into my research I became aware of a schism within the exile community, and it was one which runs deep. From the mid-80s onward, the Dalai Lama and Central Tibetan Administration (known locally as the Government in Exile) have espoused the *Umey Lam* or 'Middle-Way' policy, which seeks meaningful autonomy for Tibet within the Chinese Republic. This puts them at odds with many in the community who seek *Rangzen* or 'full independence' instead. Given that the Dalai Lama was, till he devolved political authority in 2011, the sacred as well as secular head of Tibetan Buddhism (and Tibetans) world over, countering his position is a task fraught with all kinds of difficulties. The 'Independence' activists are sometimes shunned within their community, and ostracised for having gone against the wishes of the Dalai Lama, despite the fact that he has been an outspoken advocate for an open and robust democracy; one which is polyphonic and can accommodate many voices. The most recent example of such intolerance comes in the form of the attack on Lukar Jam Atsok's car in Dharamsala on

March 22, 2017. Lukar is a writer, former political prisoner and outspoken *Rang-zen* activist who contested last year's elections for Prime Minister of the Central Tibetan Administration on the 'Independence' platform – the first candidate to ever do so in the exile community.[5]

Another such outspoken 'Independence' activist is my friend, poet/activist Tenzin Tsundue. He precipitated what has turned into this present project, in many ways. Tsundue was on a speaking tour in late 2012, and lectured at my campus that November. Tibetans were self-immolating in huge numbers during this period, protesting Chinese oppression and what they viewed as the Chinese Communist Party's (CCP) efforts to eradicate Tibetan language, religion, and in sum, what is thought of as Tibetan culture.[6] It was this phenomenon that Tsundue was travelling India apprising people about. Having long worked on Gandhi and Gandhian frameworks of non-violent direct action and civil resistance, when we first met, Tsundue and I argued over whether violence unto one's self qualified as violence or not (I was of the opinion it did, but Gandhi was on Tsundue's side on this one). I was to be at a winter school on Gandhian thought at the Indian Institute of Advanced Studies (IIAS, Simla) soon after we met, and invited the poet to join us so that we could explore whether this radical old man and the challenge he posed to the very foundations of the modern nation-state were not ideas that could also help Tsundue and his compatriots imagine a future Free Tibet that did not necessarily look like anything which had come before it.

These conversations continued over the following months, and I knew then that I too had to talk Tibet before audiences I could reach, in the language I knew best: the captive audience afforded by academia. So, thank you for listening.

Conclusion

What followed was constant shuttling between Ahmedabad and Dharamsala, a full day and night's journeying away – all while keeping up the back-breaking teaching load which is the lot of most young(ish) academics who occupy precarious spaces in universities and institutions of higher learning which are part of the neoliberal order. Four years, several visits and exchanges later, I cannot in good faith call the people I attempt to write about 'respondents': they have opened their homes, tables, and lives to me, as I have, to them. This is precisely what has made me cast about for more inclusive methods of 'doing research', and it is this I continue to struggle with most. Ellis writes that,

> interactive interviews usually consist of multiple interview sessions, and, unlike traditional one-on-one interviews with strangers, are situated within the context of emerging and well-established relationships among partici-pants and interviewers . . . The emphasis in these research contexts is on what can be learned from interaction within the interview setting as well as on the stories that each person brings to the research encounter . . . We do not . . . regard them as impersonal 'subjects' only to be mined for data.

126 Harmony Siganporia

> Consequently, ethical issues affiliated with friendship become an important part of the research process and product.
>
> *(2011, p. 8)*

Read in this light, the differences of opinion between the middle way and independence cohorts I referred to earlier (and their exploration/representation in my research) are an area fraught with pragmatic ethical considerations. Specifically, because of the precarity of exile, any such tensions within the community are viewed by the larger group as dangerous, because they might weaken or take away from their ability to speak in one unified voice: something seen as essential to the tending of the 'cause' for their homeland. Dissent might not be disallowed, but it isn't necessarily seen as having a constructive role to play in the shaping of a plural and heterogeneous public culture. As a researcher, how am I supposed to treat this discursive strand? I may have the consent of those who let me in on their deliberations about 'events' which might have caused strife within the community, but how am I to work through that material without doing disservice to the larger aspirations of a group attempting to negotiate its new tryst with democracy? Are those my stories to tell at all? I don't have an answer to this question, but I mean to remain 'present' and keep searching.

It is these 'relational' concerns that remain of paramount importance, long after projects have been completed. These are friendships and relationships which go beyond projects, oozing into my life and theirs: I am delighted each time Tsundue sends me a short story or poem to edit (typically at very short notice), and have thought it the most natural thing in the world to write press releases and the like for the TCHRD (Tibetan Centre for Human Rights and Democracy) when I am in Dharamsala and they need something done, or to organise sessions with my students for visiting activist friends from Students for a Free Tibet (SFT), for example. It goes without saying that all the pieces I write are immediately sent to the Dharamsala residents who figure in them – the ones who've helped me understand what exile looks and sounds and tastes and smells like – and I hope to goodness they know the work we've thusly produced is an ode to their lives, our time together, and the closest that I come to 'prayer'.

But because there is no such thing as unmediated re-presentation, I struggle to negotiate the baggage of my, for example, distrust of the construct 'nation' and its corollary nationalism, and the obvious yearning for it which animates the very struggle for a Free Tibet: what happens when my post-nationalist self encounters the burning desire for a nation that is the Tibetan movement? With what standing, and in what language am I to discuss the post-nationalism of Benjamin Zachariah's *Playing the Nation Game* (2011) with Tsundue and other Tibetan activist friends? I want to walk and talk about a future Free Tibet with them, but I teach an ever more fractious and splintered India in my classroom; about how the construct 'nation' has perhaps outlived its usefulness as a principle of societal organisation.

I waltz into Dharamsala with my postmodern sensibilities and healthy distrust of meta-narratives only to rub up against practices such as the exquisite, if

Reflections on research with Tibetan refugees in India **127**

unarguably canonical, Ache Lhamo, and cultural texts which attempt to 'anchor' not 'relay', in a Barthesian sense (1977), identity and meaning-making. Tsundue will tell me that it is vital Tibetans marry and have children only with other Tibetans living in exile; I tell him that this impinges upon agency and choice and sounds too forced – too didactic and essentialising – to work. His response is that it is the need of the hour if the exile community is to survive at all, which brings us back to the question at the heart of any study which seeks to engage with the precarity of life in exile: what does it mean to be Tibetan today? Who gets to lay claim to this identity marker? Those in Tibet? Those who, like so many of my friends in Dharamsala, have never seen Tibet because they were born in India, where they've always been marginal to the imagination that animates this nation-state? This is when I have to own my otherness – and my significant privilege – and it remains an on-going challenge to work through it, and still be able to, well, work at all.

These tensions are real, and they force me to attempt to understand arguments my instinct as a postcolonial, post-nationalist scholar would be to contradict sharply or seek to deconstruct. These negotiations are not easy, but it is from these engagements that the richest, most exhilarating melodies come. Sometimes, we manage to harmonise. Sometimes, it takes more doing than we have life and time enough for. But why should cacophony be shunned? Perhaps it is merely an opportunity to create a new musical lexicon.

Notes

1 A survey by the Planning Commission of the Central Tibetan Administration in India, titled 'Demographic Survey of Tibetans in Exile–2009' cites the total number of Tibetans living outside Tibet as being 1,27,935. Of this number, 94,203 people live in India. For details, see this *Hindustan Times* article. Accessed on October 4, 2016: http://www.hindustantimes.com/india/127935-tibetans-living-outside-tibet-tibetan-survey/story-ELAHRcCZQ8NFNxTdCbWoMM.html

2 Sections of this performance can be watched on the CTA portal. Accessed on October 4, 2016: http://tibet.net/2015/04/shoton-2015-life-of-buddha-tonpae-zenam-by-tipa-part-1/#/?playlistId=0&videoId=0

3 See 'Memories of/and Mobility: Parsi Diasporas in South East Asia' by Siganporia (2018a) for more details about the Parsis, what distinguishes them from Zoroastrians, and how this ethnic group – despite its tiny numbers – has long been a driver of social change in India.

4 The full interview can be read here: http://www.tibet.ca/tibet/en/library/wtn/712 (Accessed on: March 27, 2017)

5 This article references the incident in question holistically, locating the back story which led up to the present moment, as well as outlining why Lukar has been accused time and again of going against the wishes of the Dalai Lama: http://www.phayul.com/news/article.aspx?id=38833&article=Lukar%27s+car+vandalized%2C+says+his+family+feel+%27threatened+by+anti-social+elements%27#.WNQDQsMcQxE.facebook (Accessed on: March 27, 2017)

6 Over 140 people are known to have set themselves on fire inside Tibet to protest their repressive Chinese occupation since 2009. These protests peaked in 2012, when more than 80 such self-immolations took place. Though now much fewer in number, they are still very much a feature of Tibetan resistance. For more, see: https://www.freetibet.org/about/self-immolation-protests (Accessed on: March 27, 2017)

References

Anderson, B. (1983). *Imagined communities: Reflections on the origin and spread of nationalism.* London: Verso.

Barthes, R. (1977). Rhetoric of the image. In Stephen Heath (Trans.) *Image-music-text.* London: Fontana Press (pp. 32–51).

Bochner, A. & Ellis, C. (2016*). Evocative autoethnography: Writing lives and telling stories.* New York: Routledge.

Butler, J. (2009). Performativity, precarity and sexual politics. *AIBR Antropologia IberoAmericana,* 4(3): 1–13.

Ellis, C. (2004). *The ethnographic I: A methodological novel about autoethnography.* Walnut Creek, CA: Altamira Press.

Ellis, C., Adams, T., & Bochner, A.P. (2011). Autoethnography: An overview. *Forum: Qualitative Research,* 12(1): 1–18.

Kottak, C. (2006). *Mirror for humanity.* New York: McGraw-Hill.

Norbu, J. (2015). The wandering Goddess: Reviving and sustaining the spirit of Ache Lhamo in exile. *Shadow Tibet* blog, April 3. Accessed on October 4, 2016 from: http://www.jamyangnorbu.com/blog/2015/04/03/the-wandering-goddess/

Siganporia, H. (2018a). Memories of/and mobility: Parsi diasporas in South East Asia. In J. Daboo & J. Sinthuphan (Eds.) *Mapping migration: performing identity and culture in the Indian diasporas of South East Asia and the UK.* Newcastle upon Tyne: Cambridge Scholars Publishing.

Zachariah, B. (2011). *Playing the nation game: The ambiguities of nationalism in India.* New Delhi: Yoda Press.

12

WALKING TO HEAL OR WALKING TO HEEL?

Contesting cultural narratives about fat women who hike and camp alone

Phiona Stanley

SCHOOL OF EDUCATION, UNSW SYDNEY, AUSTRALIA

Obesity discourses portray fat bodies as failures of individual ir/responsibility. But such discourses, this chapter shows, have come to transcend their epidemiological origins, informing social imaginaries of obesity and its associated moral opprobrium. Fatness as a social semiotic informs the ways in which human beings are judged and categorized. However, against such a constructed discourse, resistance is fertile. This paper explores the 'fat girls hiking' sub-culture, in which fat-identified women stray not from the trail but from the social script. This is framed with Connell's gender order theory and with reference to a Foucauldian model of self-monitoring in the face of social surveillance. In terms of methods and contribution, the paper uses evocative autoethnography through on-trail streams of consciousness and suggests a queering of mainstream discourses about obesity and about the questionable wisdom (or badass temerity?) of women who hike and camp alone.

The bus driver

I'm the only person on a bus heading to a trailhead, so I'm sitting up front, chatting to the driver. He asks about my plan and I tell him about my hike. In response to my description – eight days' hiking and camping solo on the Larapinta Trail – he responds with: 'Yeah, one guy I was talking to said he lost ten kilos walking the trail. And then, when you get home, it's kind of a kick start.' This comes apropos of no mention whatsoever of weight loss as my rationale for hiking.

The body-positivity activist

I'm in the city, on a Sunday morning, going to a 'body positive' women's adventure and outdoors event. I'm excited: I've been reading about body positivity for a long time now, and here it is, coming to Sydney. It's springtime and sunny, and I set off early to walk an hour across town to the event. I'm wearing longish denim shorts and a cotton vest top. My hair is straight and newly cut. I'm very much in city mode: neither at work nor on the trails, where denim and cotton are useless.

I arrive at the expo, find the events stage where the speeches are taking place, and then I'm smiling and nodding along with the presenters. They are trotting out a well-worn but very welcome mantra of wellness and body positivity, 'You go girl!' This stuff is all over *Instagram*, but I rarely find it in real life. This feels good. Perhaps, though, my smiling and nodding are misread. Does it appear, from the outside, as if I'm having a transformative experience? Might my inviting facial expressions be read as naivety? Do I look like just another fat, mumsy, middle-aged woman in city clothes who would dearly like to become a little bit adventurous and outdoorsy and who hasn't, until this point, dared set foot in a national park? Charitably, I'm hoping this is the reason for what happens next.

After the presentations are over and everyone is milling around, one of the speakers comes directly to me, and smiles, and tells me, 'Don't let this' – she looks me up and down, indicating with a sweep of her eyes that by 'this' she means my

ILLUSTRATION 4 Fat girl hiking: Blue Mountains, NSW, Australia (Photo: © Matthew Crompton)

body – 'get in the way of adventure! Don't let *anyone* say you can't do cool, amazing stuff! Just don't *worry* about it. Get *out* there and give it a go!'

I am not often speechless. Indeed, it's a cliché to say, 'I was speechless'. But I *was* speechless. I was silenced. I was un-speeched. The polite me mumbles, 'Uh huh, thank you'. The activist me screams, 'Seriously?! What the actual *fuck*? I have just been fat-shamed by a *body positivity activist*!' The academic me critiques the irony: this woman peddles an oppressive body-hatred even as she spouts her half-baked 'wellness' slogans. The social me rushes to meet my friend Kirsty, telling the story, laughing, embarrassed, unbelieving, recounting. Turning it into shared hilarity even as it hurts. The guilty, overwhelmed, shamed me looks at my feet and wonders just how many others also looked, and judged, because if even the *body positivity activist* assumed I must be sedentary and unadventurous, then perhaps I do need to try to lose weight again, if only to get this albatross of people's judgement off my back.

The fishermen

Click, clack. Click, clack. My walking poles mark my walking rhythm. Click. Clack. I walk up, over, towards the plateau. Some steps up, and I'm out onto the rocky platform and the view, oh the view. But I can't linger. It's early spring, and the light is short. I've driven four hours from home and it's already almost lunchtime. It'll be dark by five thirty. And so, although the sun is high, I'm conscious of the walk ahead and what might be tricky navigation. Click. Clack. Click. Clack. I'm fairly confident with a compass and I've got some decent maps. But there's a number of ridges and I need to find just one in particular, Gingra Ridge, to bring me down gently to the Kowmung River.

A shriek of black cockatoos flies up on thermals from the valley. Otherwise: silence. Searching, I find the fork in the indistinct trail that drops me down to a saddle, through trees. A short cliff-break scramble then delivers me to a cave-like overhang. There's water here, and although my bottles are full, I'm glad to see it. I get through a lot of water when I hike, more than most. That's OK. Water's good. But on some hikes, on dry stretches, it's a question of planning, organising, knowing to carry enough. Mostly I'm pretty good at figuring it out. I don't often run out.

The trail drops down again, bends around another rocky wall, and, looking at the map contours, I know I'm on track. Yellow wattle is in bloom and I pause, noting how much calmer my mind is whenever I step into a forest.

Walking alone, in silence, is infinitely preferable to imported chatter. I have a couple of good, reliable walking buddies who know how to rein in the rush and the movement, but they're not available this weekend and I am. So I'm going anyway because the only alternative is not to go. Is it weird to camp and walk alone, especially as a woman? But nature doesn't care. Thus, I don't care. Or: I try not to care. I'm pretty safe: I have maps, a Personal Locator Beacon, a smart head on my shoulders. Walking in groups is no safer. There's only the illusion of safety.

I wouldn't walk with those who wouldn't walk alone. (This wisdom also applies to life, of course.)

I keep going, uphill a while, and then I'm resting on a fallen tree when two young guys appear. I'm not really scared of humans this far out onto a trail. Car parks and road-accessible camping areas are much scarier. If someone can be bothered to walk all this way, with no guarantee of running into anyone, they're probably not looking for trouble. We chat, briefly. They're going fishing.

No snide comments, or innocent comments or, seemingly protective comments, or comments of surprise are made. Nothing is said this time about my weight, my fitness, my femaleness, my aloneness, or my preparedness. This time: nothing. But I realise how attuned to on-trail, gendered fat-shaming I have become. I anticipate it, always prepared to defend my legitimacy even as my body says that I must be sedentary, unfit, unadventurous, and my gender says that I don't belong out here alone. Fat women's bodies have social meanings, and 'badass solo hiker' is not usually one of them. I feel I have to prove something, and I consciously and constantly perform the role of 'experienced bushwalker' and 'competent outdoorswoman'. Years ago, I was body-normative (slender, fit and athletic), and I know from that time that this on-edge anticipation of never-far-away body shaming was the last thing on my mind. Now, it is the burden that I carry along with my backpack.

I keep going and, walking, I drift off, mediative, all the while keeping an eye out for the turnoff to Roots Ridge. The trail notes say it's a right turn from a 'small clearing', and I'm wondering, 'how small?' Every clearing could be the right clearing. I re-check the bearing, the ridge, the contours. It should be around here. I poke around in some bushes, and there, carved onto a tree is 'Roots Ridge', with an arrow off to the right. Ah, 'thank you', I say out loud, to no one. There are no trail blazes to guide me. Thank you.

Roots Ridge is undulating, with a couple of little summits. But then the trail is getting faint. I keep losing track, backtracking, taking stock, backing up. I can see the river now, but there doesn't seem to be a trail anymore. What I should do is go back, find the trail, follow it to where it goes gently down to the river. What I actually do is bushwhack, setting out steeply down to the river, which I can see in the distance. It's not that far.

My steps down are ridiculous. Each step down is like coming downstairs, but the loose topsoil brings me sliding down much further with each step. I'm skiing. It's fast, fun, and my walking poles are no longer clicking and clacking but are holding me, balancing me. It's slightly reckless, I know, to be off trail and so steep and sliding, but it's also fun and, before long, these crazy steps bring me to the river. But where exactly am I? I look again at the map and although I'm at the right river, I'm quite far from the bend where there's flat, dry ground with easy water access. This is not that. This is boggy, marshy, and full of close-packed trees. I need to bushwhack some more to get to a decent camping spot. There's still some light and I'm next to the river, so it's all good. If I had to, I could stay somewhere here. I've got this. I self soothe with logic and chocolate.

And so, I bushwhack along the riverside. This isn't nearly so much fun. It's sweaty and frustrating, and I scramble up and down soggy, boggy earth piled over loose rocks, clutching at clumps of weeds. My right hand tingles from clutching at nettles. I swear a bit. There's what looks like an established track along the other side of the river but it's winter and the river is high: chest-deep, I'd guess. There's no way of crossing, certainly not alone and off trail. I throw in a stick to test the flow and the current outwalks me. It is too fast to ford. Plus, there's the very real possibility that what looks like an easy trail on the other side of the big river is nothing of the sort. The grass is greener. The trail is easier. The moon is bigger. These are life lessons: be glad even of the most nettle-strewn trails because the other side of the river is no easier, and you'd also have to get there. (This is another lesson that also applies to life more generally.) So I stay on this side and spend a slow, frustrating hour pulling myself along, hand over hand, with loose footing and snatched foliage, towards the ridge that I should have descended.

But I'm making good progress, and I'm almost around the bend when I meet one of the fishermen from before. He's standing up to his thighs, in waders, in the cold river, and seems surprised to see me, my hair wild from bushwhacking, coming the wrong way, as if from nowhere.

- Hey, how ya goin'? Catching anything?
- Yeah, nah. Just started.
- How much further along did you guys come down? The trail, I mean, how far along is it from here?
- Oh, you know. Maybe ten minutes?
- Cool, so I'm about there? I couldn't find the track, so I bushwhacked down to the river.
- Yeah, the trail's not that clear back up there, eh? Pretty hard. There were ribbons and that on some of the trees. Bit hard to see.
- Ah yeah? Didn't see those. Would'a been easier. Well, happy fishing, hope you catch something.
- Yeah, have a good one. You camping?
- Yep. You?
- Yep, along at the clearing.
- Alrighty, have fun.
- Yeah, you too.

Again, relief. Are you, the reader, waiting for the fat-shaming now, too? Do you *see* what it is like? Imagine the held breath and the too-careful listening of anticipation, on every trail, in every encounter, in every conversation in or about the outdoors. Am I too sensitive? Or am I simply inured? Even as I fill my social media with 'body positivity' and my academic days with critical readings that problematise obesity alarmism, I tense as I wait for the combative commentary. This time, though, it doesn't come.

134 Phiona Stanley

I carry on for another five minutes, pulling up at the perfect campsite: a flat patch of earth a couple of metres above and about 20 metres back from the swollen river. Close enough to hear it and accessible to refill my water bottles, but I'm out of harm's way if it rises. My campsite has an armchair-shaped sitting rock, on which I enthrone myself, getting organised, setting up my tent, making soup. It's cold: five degrees Celsius, according to the thermometer on my pack's zipper. My sleeping bag awaits and in it are the possum-wool bed-socks that I now fetch and put on. I contemplate the river and my awesome luck to be out here, absolutely alone. I'm a heady combination of proud of myself but also not really thinking about anything bigger than the immediate here and now. I'm by a river, sipping whisky from a pewter hipflask. The water rushes by. I think about where it will meet the sea, how far it still has to go, and all the places it will see, the others who will see it. I don't think about defending my right to be here anymore. I'm just here. Here and now.

The solo hiker

I've walked with people whose pace differs from mine. Some are too fast, and I'm panting, feeling emotionally and physically wrecked, and not having any fun as I'm feeling I'm holding them back. These experiences pack the *hauntology* (Derrida, in Buse & Scott, 1999, pp. 11–12) of competitive sports at school and the shame and sting of bullying manifested as a 'team effort'. In contrast, some hikers I've walked with are *So. Damn. Slow.* Inspecting every damn tree and every damn bird when, really, I just want to get some rhythm going and feel like I'm walking. It is not easy to find the right hiking buddy. No, it isn't.

Walking clubs are also not my scene. When I've camped at organised campsites on trails, such as on the Overland Track and the Thorsborne Trail, I been surrounded by the yip and natter of carping, competitive hiking-club groups whose 'conversations' seem to consist of comparing gear and establishing trail status (after Sorensen's 'road status', 2003) by bragging about other, harder hikes they have done. Nor is this the company I seek.

My friend Miko and I walk well together: when I'm fit, we walk in sync. When I'm less fit, we each walk alone and I'll round a corner and find him waiting for me, sitting on a rock, reading a novel. My other walking buddy, Matthew, is a keen photographer. Where he slows to compose a shot, I'll slow because I'm slow. And so we walk mostly in sync, too. With Miko and with Matthew, I feel no pressure to prove anything. However, neither one lives in Sydney. And so, my tripartite choice is this: I go with someone whose company does not add to my experience. Or I do not hike and camp at all. Or I hike and camp alone. Faced with this choice, obviously, I go alone.

Hiking and camping are 'flow' activities (Csikszentmihalyi, 1990). The mind calms and the clatter and clutter of life become quieter, further away. It is like putting day-to-day worries into a smaller font. Connection with nature is foregrounded.

But is it safe? Well, no, not entirely. (I also cross roads in cities, which is manifestly unsafe, too. Silly me.) Arguably, in some ways, it is safer to hike alone, because in a group it is easy to assume that someone else has the know-how or the map. And also: being perfectly alone in nature is, quite simply, a thrill. Like an addict, I return for the 'high'. While solo, wild camping, I wrote:

> It is dusk. I've been walking all day. It is still warm. The swimming hole [in the river, by my wild campsite] is perfectly calm and inviting. I go down to the water's edge to collect water and realise I want to swim. So I strip down and I swim. There is no-one else around. I float on my back, looking up at the bats and the tree tops and think: I am lucky. I am grateful.
>
> *(Trail Notes, Megalong Valley, 2015).*

The theorists

At a scholarly level, how are we to make sense of the discourses in the above scenes? This section teases out the various ways in which these narratives contest cultural scripts. First, there is the discord between 'hiking with a buddy' and 'sleeping alone in the woods'. Then, there is the question of gender and the 'marked' status of women in the outdoors. Finally, there are the symbolic interactionist (mis)readings of fatness. Importantly, these are inseparable strands of one felted, fabric. I am a woman, hiking and camping alone, and I am fat. (I am also over 40, and white, and middle class, and educated, and able-bodied. While ageism, racism, classism, and able-ism also all push powerful narratives that adversely affect diversity on hiking trails, I do not deal with these identity markers here.)

The question of hiking alone is perhaps least controversial: Coble, Selin and Erickson (2003) found solo hiking offered autonomy, reflection, communion with nature, and a chance to experience 'flow', which Mills and Butler (2005) identify as most often experienced when walking alone. In part, the benefits of lone hiking may be attributable to the spiritual dimensions of the experience, and Fox (1997; cited in Heintzman, 2010) reports that going alone is particularly important for women as it provides peace, tranquillity, an 'inner journey', and space for reflection.

But while its benefits are manifest, hiking alone is a gendered pursuit, of which Trimble (1994, p.60) writes: 'Cultural barriers and fears keep many of our daughters away from the woods . . . women may crave solitude but many fear being alone on the landscape.' Fear causes women to be underrepresented among solo hikers, and Chasteen (1994) found that almost all her women participants would never hike alone because of feelings of vulnerability and isolation. Specifically, they were worried about being attacked by men.

But it is not just about fear. McNeil, Harris and Fondren (2012) analysed representations of women in wilderness advertisements, finding that as well as being underrepresented, women are also represented in very particular ways: in limited and passive roles, being instructed or guided by men, or lounging passively in nature rather than engaging in active pursuits. Importantly, also, women are rarely depicted as spending time alone in nature. Whereas men are taught from a young

136 Phiona Stanley

age 'to use their bodies in skilled, forceful ways, which allows them to successfully perform masculinity' (p. 42) women's gendered performances seem to be threatened by association with this kind of 'rugged individualism'. For this reason, even where professional women athletes are depicted in outdoors advertising, their images are often accompanied by back stories that safely 'feminize them' (p. 49) for the benefit of the normative gaze.

Connell's gender order theory (2005) provides a toolkit with which to unpack these issues. Hegemonic masculinity critiques the configuration and modalities of practice that legitimise men's dominant position in society and which work to justify and normalise women's subordination. Accordingly, a woman who exhibits normative ways of performing femininity is an acceptable foil to masculinity, even as she is irreducibly constructed as other, as lesser. However, in a social script based on hegemonic masculinity, there is little conceptual leeway for women to undertake idealised 'masculine' pursuits and ways of being. These might include traits like strength, toughness, independence, adventurousness, and self-sufficiency: a Man-Versus-Wild-type taming of and survival in/against the forest, and a conscious swallowing of fear in order to behave agentically in pursuit of one's own chosen path (literally as well as metaphorically, here). For women who hike and wild camp alone, there is necessarily an explicit pushing back against the machinations of power that inscribe how women *are supposed to behave*. For these reasons, outdoorswomen (including those who are fat and those who go alone) disrupt normative cultural discourses:

> What is an unlikely hiker? It's ironic, tongue-in-cheek, reclamatory. There is nothing *unlikely* about wanting to enjoy and explore nature. It's one of the most natural things any of us can want to do. Yes, the outdoors and public lands belong to all of us and sure, no one is getting a handwritten invitation to our National Parks and trailheads, but exclusion isn't always verbal. A lot of the time, it's about representation. Representation matters! Who is being targeted for outdoor recreation? Who has a seemingly natural sense of access? I was so tired of seeing the same kind of person on seemingly every social media based hiking community. The *image* of the outdoor adventurer is white, thin, 'fit' and straight-looking. Often, moneyed (read: top of the line gear). Often, a man. The typical woman featured fits an even narrower set of guidelines. . . . *Unlikely Hiker* encompasses anyone who doesn't fit that image. Bigger body types, people of color, queer, trans, gender nonconforming folks, differently-abled people and so on. The people you don't see in the outdoorsy ads.
>
> *(Bruso*, Unlikely Hiker, *n.d.)*

Countercultural pushback, like this, finds support in efforts to 'diversify outdoors', both in terms of gender and fatness but also along other identity axes. Queering the trail online are activists such as *Fat Girls Hiking* (2015), *She Explores* (2014–17), *and Jenny Bruso's Unlikely Hikers* (2012–17).

Contesting cultural narratives about fat women hiking **137**

But challenging normative discourses also necessarily entails a more generalised challenging of mainstream constructions of fatness. The 'conversation' about obesity, between epidemiologist-led public health officials and media (the 'obesity alarmists') and countercultural obesity 'sceptics' (Gard, 2011), is one in which fatness stereotypes are either re-inscribed or contested. On one side, Australian media discourses portray fat bodies as: '[P]hysical manifestations of individual (ir)responsibility and psychological dysfunction, [which] contributes to the ongoing stigmatisation of obesity' (Monson, Donaghue & Gill, 2016, p. 524). As a result, fat people are pitied and patronised, ridiculed and reduced (Monaghan, Colls & Evans, 2013), often in what Gard (2011, p. 38) calls a 'shame-led public health agenda'. Largely unfettered by critical scrutiny, media tropes of fatness include headless fatties, face-stuffing fatties, sofa-bound fatties, self-loathing fatties, in-denial fatties, and poor, dumb fatties. There are also 'good' fatties, such as those who submit to *Biggest Loser*-style bullying (Monson *et al.*, 2016). In this vein, medical discourses pathologise 'overweight'. But 'overweight' relies on a sense of 'normal' (otherwise, it begs the questions: over what weight? And why that?) And then there is the statistic that 63 per cent of Australians are 'overweight' (Australian Bureau of Statistics, 2015). So, what does 'normal' mean, if most people are not 'normal', according to normality's own norm? In fact, 'normal' is less a *norm* than a *normativity*. That is, 'normality' is an aspirational 'should' rather than a descriptive 'is'.

This counter position, which Gard (2011) calls that of the 'obesity sceptics', critiques this mainstream 'obesity crisis' narrative. Positions here vary hugely, from the libertarian pushback against the nannying state to empirical sceptics pointing to the dearth of evidence that overweight *in and of itself* is deleterious to health. There are also feminist critiques of body shaming as the 'extension of patriarchal science's centuries old persecution of women' (p. 44), and critiques of the obesity panic as a coded morality, produced 'in an attempt to discipline people's desires, behaviours, relationships and subjectivities' (p. 43).

Drawing on these latter discourses, the body positivity strand of the 'diversify outdoors' movement regards fatness neither as something to be battled ('trails not scales!' says *Fat Girls Hiking*) nor as something to be uncritically celebrated. It is still the case that fat people experience multiple, interconnected negative outcomes in areas of life including mental health and a lowering of socioeconomic status (Fikkan & Rothblum, 2012). Fat bodies also experience specific challenges, including the frustration of sourcing plus-size outdoors clothing (e.g. *The Heavy Hiker*, 2016) and fat-phobic comments from mainstream commentators, including other hikers (e.g. Summer & Lezley, 2017). There are also physical challenges: breathlessness and foot pain, for instance (e.g. Fleming, 2015). These are real challenges, and although they may affect other body types too, the reality of hiking while fat is that it is harder for fat bodies than for non-fat bodies: carrying a 20kg (44lbs) pack is tough. Carrying a 20kg pack *and* 30kg (66lbs), or 50kg (110lbs), or more of extra bodyweight is tougher.

But, crucially, rather than telling fat people simply not to hike, thereby confirming and compounding the reduction of fat identities to an aesthetically distasteful,

138 Phiona Stanley

confirmatory, slothful stereotype, the fat-positive 'small' culture (Holliday, 2013) helps fat hikers find ways around potential issues. Because hiking in nature lowers stress, lowers pulse rate, and lowers blood pressure, enhances mood, promotes self-esteem, and combats mental fatigue (Barton, Hine & Pretty, 2009; Park, Tsunetsugu, Kasetani, Kagawa, & Miyazaki, 2010). Given hiking's myriad health benefits and its comparative accessibility by people of all levels of fitness and fatness, the erasure of all but young, white, heterosexual men from social imaginaries of hiking is counter-productive.

This 'obesity sceptic' discourse is therefore subversive: it questions and rejects stigmatising, limiting, surveillance discourses of *what fat bodies can do*. Instead of reinscribing reductive, homogenising, and deterministic narratives of what fatness *means*, this discourse allows for the possibility of fat people who are adventurous, physical, and, indeed, happy. This is empowering. Fatness, in body-positive discourses, is not something that needs to change before real life begins. Rather than self-loathing, the message is one of self-acceptance.

But why not just diet? Isn't it irresponsible to 'encourage' obesity? Why should we 'glorify' fat? To those bored and lonely people who seek to set strangers 'right' on the internet, the equation may appear simple: *eat less, move more*. As if fat people were stupid. As if this was all there was to it. As if solving the global obesity 'epidemic' – a discourse of contagion – were as simple as awareness raising and individual self-determination (Lupton, 2014). It isn't.

While sustained caloric restriction, through diet and/or exercise, inexorably produces fat loss, for the previously fat, maintaining a bodyweight significantly below the previous, 'obese' weight is significantly more difficult than it is for the never-dieted body (Mann *et al.*, 2007). Specifically: if yours is a body that has been obese, and if you have successfully lost weight, you can eat and exercise exactly the same as a never-fat person, whose body composition is exactly the same as yours, and yours, the dieted body, will retain significantly more weight (Fothergill *et al.*, 2016). Thinning a fat body is therefore a near futile exercise in hyper vigilance, because relaxing into 'normal' eating patterns is to slide back to fatness (Mann *et al.*, 2007). This is before eating disorders, hormonal imbalances, and other psycho-social and socio-economic weight-gain contributors are factored in.

For this reason, weight loss through calorie restriction and exercise is almost entirely futile. Citing a longitudinal, 25,000-people-strong cohort study, Adams (2011) reports that 'only 10% [of dieters] manage to lose a significant amount of weight. Of those that do, most will put it back on within a year'. In addition, and more importantly, the much-vaunted linking of obesity with ill health is less causal than the 'obesity crisis' rhetoric suggests:

> 'Success' in dieting interventions has traditionally been defined as weight loss. It is implicit in this definition that losing weight will lead to improved health, and yet health outcomes are not routinely included in studies of diets. . . . We examine[d] whether weight-loss diets led to improved

cholesterol, triglycerides, . . . blood pressure, and fasting blood glucose, and test[ed] whether the amount of weight lost is predictive of these health outcomes. Across all studies, there were minimal improvements in these health outcomes, and none of these correlated with weight change.

(*Tomiyama, Ahlstrom & Mann, 2013, p. 861*)

Just as problematically for the panicked fat-phobic 'obesity crisis' discourse, a 35-year, 100,000-participant Danish study (Afzal, Tybjaerg-Hansen, Jensen & Nordestgaard, 2016) found that 'overweight' adults actually lived *longer* than those in the 'healthy' category, and that those categorised as 'obese' had *no more risk of premature death* than those categorised as 'normal' weight, even controlling for variables of age, gender, family medical history, socio-economic status, and smoking. It appears, therefore, that the alarmist obesity discourse is more to do with aesthetics and demonising a constructed 'other' than it is about public health.

These discourses, then, of obesity alarmism, of gender conformity, and also of the perils of hiking alone, together form a larger assemblage of social control (Deleuze & Guattari, 1993). Much like Foucault's panopticon (1977, pp. 195–228), in which prisoners come to self-monitor lest they be caught out by official surveillance, these norms work together to get individuals to knuckle down and follow the social rules. However, as these norms are constructed, they can also be contested. When hiking as a lone, fat woman I stray as much from the script as I do from the trail.

Mother Nature and Pablo Neruda

The route up looks vertical.//Once I get up there, there won't be water, so do I have enough now, or should I fill up one more bottle here? Nah, I'm OK.//Pause. Breathe.//My sunscreen is melting, running from the creases at the sides of my eyes down my cheek. It looks like tears, and isn't.//I concentrate.//I am totally in this moment.//I wipe my face with a bandana until it feels red, raw. But I cannot see the colour of my face: it is sunburn or abrasion? Maybe both. I won't see a mirror for another few days. By then I'll be nut brown, so who cares?// The cliff *is* kind of vertical.//Now, though, I notice handholds and, looking closely, there are also rock platforms. It would suck to fall here, but it wouldn't be fatal.// Pause. Breathe.//Look out over the valley.// Galahs swoop in formation, their red bellies catching the light.//Back to it. Handhold. Pause. Foot secure? Pause. Handhold. Pause. Long reach, foot, in the gap, made it. Handhold.//Breathe. Pause. //Move foot. Handhold. Getting there.//Hey, this is easier than it looks.//Don't look down.// Pause. Breathe.// I am completely in this moment.//It's hot.// I feel so freakin' capable.//Almost there.//Pause. Breathe.//Scramble. A few more steps.//Top! Ahh! Pack off. Swig water. Look around.

It's my 43rd birthday and I'm on top of a hill in outback Australia. I'm perfectly alone, hiking for a week straight, carrying everything, camping. Maybe twice a day I run into another hiker and we exchange pleasantries, but mostly I'm alone.

140 Phiona Stanley

I prove to myself I am capable. I am strong. I may be fat, but also I am quite fit. I am determined. I can keep going. I push through foot pain, the fear of falling, the fear of failing. Here, it is just the landscape and me. Mother Nature doesn't care. Mainstream culture is a cacophony of voices telling me hateful things about my body. But out here those voices are so much quieter, so much further away, quietened by the wind. On the hilltop, I pause, and look around, and read a Neruda poem aloud to myself from my notebook. Poetry is as necessary as water here.

The poet's words fill the air. They fill me. Like the wind, they hold back the critiques, the hatred, the scorn. Instead of the self-loathing of hating my fatness, my body, my*self*, I am choosing to find wonder and calm and beauty in nature. My body is the interface, the only one I have, and it lets me walk in forests. Here I am, embodied, reading aloud to myself on a hilltop because the sun is shining, and because I can.

References

Adams, S. (2011). Losing weight on a diet? It won't last. *The Telegraph* (UK). Accessed 18/02/2017 from: http://www.telegraph.co.uk/news/health/news/8657825/Losing-weight-on-the-diet-It-wont-last.html

Afzal, S., Tybjaerg-Hansen, A., Jensen, G.B., & Nordestgaard, B.G. (2016). Change in body mass index associated with lowest mortality in Denmark, 1976–2013. *Journal of the American Medical Association 315*/18: 1989–1996.

Australian Bureau of Statistics (2015). *National health survey: First results, 2014–2015.* Accessed 14/06/2017 from: http://www.abs.gov.au/ausstats/abs@.nsf/Lookup/by%20Subject/4364.0.55.001~2014–15~Main%20Features~Overweight%20and%20obesity~22

Barton, J., Hine, R., & Pretty, J. (2009). The health benefits of walking in green spaces of high natural and heritage value. *Journal of Integrative Environmental Sciences 6*/4: 261–278.

Bruso, J. (2012–2017). *Unlikely hikers.* Accessed 05/06/2017 from: https://jennybruso.com/unlikelyhikers/

Buse, P. & Scott, A. (1999). A future for haunting. In Buse, P. & Stott, A. (Eds.) *Ghosts: Deconstruction, psychoanalysis, history* (pp. 1–20). Basingstoke: Palgrave Macmillan.

Chasteen, A. (1994). The world around me: The environment and single women. *Sex Roles 31*/5–6: 309–328.

Coble, T.G., Selin, S.W., & Erickson, B.B. (2003). Hiking alone: Understanding fear, negotiation strategies, and leisure experience. *Journal of Leisure Research 35*/1: 1–22.

Connell, R. (2005). Masculinities (2nd Ed). Sydney: Allen & Unwin.

Csikszentmihalyi, M. (1990). *Flow: The psychology of optimal experience.* New York: Harper and Row.

Deleuze, G. & Guattari, F. (1993). A thousand plateaus. Minneapolis: University of Minnesota Press.

Fat Girls Hiking (2015). *Fat girls hiking: Trails not scales.* Accessed 05/06/2017 from: https://fatgirlshiking.com/

Fikkan, J.L. & Rothblum, E.D. (2012). Is fat a feminist issue? Exploring the gendered nature of weight bias. *Sex Roles 66*/9: 575–592.

Fleming, L.M. (2015). Tips for fat hikers and others who don't look like the REI commercials. *Huffington Post.* Accessed 05/06/2017 http://www.huffingtonpost.com/lauren-marie-fleming/7-tips-for-fat-hikers-and_b_7646190.html

Fothergill, E., Guo, J., Kerns, J.C., Knuth, N.D., Brychta, R., Chen, K.Y., Skarulis, M.C., Walter, M., Walter, P.J., & Hall, K.D. (2016). Persistent metabolic adaptation six years after 'The Biggest Loser' competition. *Obesity 24*/8: 1612–1619.

Foucault, M. (1977). *Discipline and punish: The birth of the prison*. New York: Vintage Books.

Gard, M. (2011). Truth, belief and the cultural politics of obesity scholarship and public health policy. *Critical Public Health 21*/1: 37–48.

Heintzman, P. (2010). Nature-based recreation and spirituality: A complex relationship. *Leisure Sciences 32*: 72–89.

Holliday, A. (2013). *Understanding intercultural communication: Negotiating a grammar of culture*. Abingdon: Routledge.

Lupton, D. (2014). 'How do you measure up?' Assumptions about 'obesity' and health-related behaviors and beliefs in two Australian 'obesity' prevention campaigns. *Fat Studies 3*/1: 32–44.

Mann, T., Tomiyama, A.J., Westling, E., Lew, A., Samuels, B., & Chatman, J. (2007). Medicare's search for effective obesity treatments: Diets are not the answer. *American Psychologist, 62*/3: 220–233.

McNeil, J.N., Harris, D.A., & Fondren, K.M. (2012). Women in the wild: Gender socialization in wilderness recreation advertising. *Gender Issues 29*: 39–55.

Mills, A.S. & Butler, T.S. (2005). 'Flow' experience among Appalachian Trail thru-hikers. *Proceedings of the Northeastern Recreation Research Symposium*. Accessed 04/08/2017 from: http://www.americantrails.org/resources/benefits/flowexperAT.html

Monaghan, L.F., Colls, R., & Evans, B. (2013). Obesity discourse and fat politics: research, critique and interventions. *Critical Public Health 23*/3: 249–262.

Monson, O., Donaghue, N., & Gill, R. (2016). Working hard on the outside: a multimodal critical discourse analysis of 'The Biggest Loser Australia'. *Social Semiotics 26*/5: 524–540.

Park, B.J., Tsunetsugu, Y., Kasetani, T., Kagawa, T., & Miyazaki, Y. (2010). The physiological effects of Shinrin-yoku: Evidence from 24 forests across Japan. *Environmental Health and Preventative Medicine 15*/1: 18.

She Explores (2014–2017*). She Explores: Podcast*. Accessed 05/06/2017 from: http://she-explores.com/podcast

Sorensen, A. (2003). Backpacker ethnography. *Annals of Tourism Research, 30*/4: 847–867.

Summer & Lezley (2017) Fat Girls Hiking wants you to love your body – and take it outside. *Outside Magazine*. Accessed 05/06/2017 from: https://www.outsideonline.com/2162451/trails-not-scales-guide-self-and-body-love-nature.

The Heavy Hiker (2016) Plus-size hiking apparel as common as unicorn tears. Accessed 05/06/2017 from: http://theheavyhiker.com.au/2016/08/30/plus-size-hiking-apparel-as-common-as-unicorn-tears/

Tomiyama, A.J., Ahlstrom, B., & Mann, T. (2013). Long-term effects of dieting: Is weight loss related to health? *Social and Personality Psychology Compass 7*/12: 861–877.

Trimble, S. (1994). A land of one's own. In G.P. Nabhan & S. Trimble (Eds.) *The geography of childhood* (pp. 55–75). Boston: Beacon Press.

13

READING SHIVA NAIPAUL

A reflection on Brownness and leading an experiential learning project in Malawi

C. Darius Stonebanks

SCHOOL OF EDUCATION, BISHOP'S UNIVERSITY, CANADA

This chapter proposes to advance the seldom heard voice of the (South Asian/ West Asian/Middle-Eastern) Brown experience within Western university experiential learning programs (ELP) abroad. Often caught between Western multiculturalism's understanding of a dichotomy/binary of "Black and White", Brownness is often recognized in regard to such realities of racial profiling in airport securities, but invisible, misunderstood or even purposefully misconstrued in the academic setting. For over eight years, the author has led a university project in sub-Sahara Africa which seeks to facilitate local creation of an Education, Health and Development emancipatory-based knowledge transfer campus and has incorporated university undergraduates and graduates as part of the process. As students primarily come from White backgrounds and attempt to develop intercultural competencies while navigating culture shock, the inclusion of anything else besides White and Black relationships are rarely, if ever, part of the discussion or consideration. During a recent ELP based trip with students to Malawi, the author read Shiva Naipaul's (1978) *North of South*, and reflected on his own shared attempts to make sense of the kinds of liberatory movements that have and still take place in the sub-Sahara, and the often-ignored perspectives outside of the predominantly White voice.

> "We are nonpersons," Ashraf said. "They only see us when they want to hate us."
>
> (Naipaul, 1978, p. 109)

I often feel as though I do not exist, or as "Ashraf", a non-fictional character in Shiva Naipaul's (1978) travelogue autoethnography book, *North of South: An African Journey*, describes the sensation; that I am a 'nonperson'. Being Brown in Canada is to be outside of the White/Black[1] dichotomy Western multiculturalism both teaches against, yet reinforces. It is an experience of being Brown at the Canada/US border when we are travelling to attend conferences on diversity, but an inconvenient minority, at best, when we arrive. Racially profiled by police, Homeland Security, border guards, CSIS, cashiers at shopping mall stores, airports and elsewhere, but not a race. "A problem" Bayoumi (2009) reminds us through our daily existence growing up in the Global North (GN[2]) as students in schools, but as we move further into academia, often not recognized as a group that faces discrimination among faculties claiming to value inclusiveness (Tehranian, 2009). Drawing from personal life experiences, we can be called an Eye-ranian, terrorist, Paki, brown-piece-of-shit, Ay-rab, sand-nigger and a myriad of other racial slurs while playing sports, at school or in public spaces, but then have race erased (Jiwani, 1999) in higher education, leaving us out of anti-racism conversations. Often referred to, in a tight paragraph or two in passing, by the White majority in academia through their publications when they want to draw examples of the dangers of subjects like neo-liberalism's new world orders and global conflicts, but then out of sight in their deductions of racism in America or Canada. "Seen", Ashraf mourns, when we are hated, but obscured when we try to make space in a fabric of racial identity and culture that is so heavily constructed through the global domination of Whiteness in its construction of self and others (Allen, 2001). *Racially profiled, but not a race.*

I have become accustomed to this experience of being a nonperson within an educational system of higher education that is infused with the dominance of Whiteness (Smith, 2010). I am *accustomed,* but ever resentful and increasingly angered. Always mindful, however, that anger in the GN from a Brown Muslim man with Middle-Eastern heritage must be kept in check as it can quickly become an "orange threat", that when you are profiled and stereotyped are paradoxically told has nothing to do with racism. In the GN, Brown lives with the image of oneself being controlled by the same White dominant groups for the stories we see, hear and read that validates you are indeed a danger (Dabashi, 2011), yet can also state does not exist. It seems almost a purposeful intention to be spoken about so problematically by the dominant group, but kept voiceless. And nowhere does this masterful dominance of White in defining and manipulating Brown seem more purposeful than in academia, where our autoethnographic narratives, our lived realities are so tightly controlled, often by the very people who consider themselves champions of words like social justice, equity, multiculturalism and solidarity. As a child of an Iranian mother, and a half Italian half English father who was born and raised in Egypt, I am well accustomed to my mind and body being a source of scrutiny by the White power bloc, well before 9/11. Brought to Canada as an infant in the late 1960s and growing up in a White cultural context that far too often felt at liberty to commit violent verbal and physical acts with impunity, and then entering academia where the further I moved from student to professor, those lived experiences would be increasingly shaped by non-Brown, as if we were nonpersons. In this chapter I examine the challenges to find voice and space within the imposed multiplicity of being both Brown, yet nothing, and the baffling existence of being the Other (Said, 1978) in the "good versus bad" binary to the GN

144 C. Darius Stonebanks

power bloc (Apple, 1996), while not fitting into the USA's highly persuasive and highly problematic way of seeing race solely through their other binary of Black/White in which "other" groups are not a part of the racial discourse (Perea, 1997). This nonpersoness is explored through the position in which Brown is relegated while supervising university students in the sub-Saharan country of Malawi, most of whom fit the White, female, middle-class profile described by Heron (2014) of Canadian development workers, and contemplate this personal cultural experience in relation to a chance reading of Shiva Naipaul's travel book, *North of South*, as autoethnography.

Brown as nonperson

Naipaul a self-described Brown author of Indian origin, has been both acclaimed for his craft, while also receiving criticism of writing with imperial eyes and the traveler's gaze (Nixon, 1991, 1992; Odhiambo, 2004). Although those critiques are not to be overlooked, the main focus of this chapter are his perspectives on the reality of Brown outside of the strict Black/White binary, which in itself has been largely ignored among his critics. Naipaul's writing challenges my imposed identity at home and in travel, because even though there is much to disagree with, there is so much that he describes in relation to being a nonperson that echoes in personal experience. In reading Naipaul, I began to reflect on the condition of being both judged and omitted, a condition that I would argue is familiar to many in the Brown community in Canada and the GN. However, whereas Naipaul speaks on the experience of being Brown in the late 1970s as being either hated or nonexistent, the manner in which this non-existence (or nonpersoness) has been modified in the current GN is to silence Brown by including us in Whiteness as a new means of control, despite Whiteness never being a part of our lived experience.

Tehranian refers to the reality of being a Brown Middle-Easterner in the streets with all its negative stereotypes and baggage, but uses the example of being excluded from any possible benefits of being a minority in academia as a "Catch-22". The contradiction of living as a visible minority throughout one's life, and then having race and/or ethnicity either whitewashed (to borrow a phrase from Tehranian), acknowledged, co-opted, thrust upon, ignored or vilified in the GN academia, has resulted in a call to examine its impact on mental health (Tehranian, 2009). To have Brown identity further manipulated and controlled moving from the ivory towers of the GN, to the university experiential learning sites in the Global South (GS) compounds the crisis. It is in this travel-oriented academic space that I attempt to make sense of yet another location where Naipaul reflects "we", Brown, are nonpersons and White prescriptions of race become more pronounced in their comfort of dominance in all narratives with locals, while consigning others as inconvenient interlopers, or as Naipaul observes as being relegated as a "complicating factor" (p. 109). Too complicated to acknowledge, we become voiceless background figures, reflecting the same conditions of the GN where formal and non-formal locations of education reinforce allowable narratives of experience.

When we popularly exist in autoethnographic genres, we do so through stories, such as Nasifi's *Reading Lolita in Tehran* (2003), that typically affirm White intellectual and moral superiority over Brown (Dabashi, 2011) and as an ongoing means of domination that acts as "a genre in service of empire" (Akhavan, Bashi, Mana, & Shakhsar, 2007), manufacturing just cause to military actions. Ignored or vilified, Brown exists as something to be classified by White in the GN, with that authority preserved as we travel as nonperson members of the GN in sub-Sahara Africa (sSA),[3] silencing voice and controlling cultural interaction. While reminding us that "race" is a social construct and not biological, Apple (1996) challenges hegemonic powers by asking why White dominant culture continues to dictate which non-White "stories of the past, present, or future are 'legitimate' and bestow 'official imprimatur?'" (p. 17). Despite Apple's wisdom, this is exactly where Brown finds itself; judged and shaped by White dominant culture acting as the gatekeeper to defining (amongst others) race, ethnicity and experience, even as we travel in our capacity as members of our GN institutions.

Pratt's (1992) work is predicated on the reality of "imperial eyes" of travel writing, and begins her preface by acknowledging a "legacy of Euroimperialism, androcentrism and white supremacy in education and official culture" (p. xi). In consideration of Pratt's perspective with Apple's critique that autobiographical models in qualitative research has, despite its original call for the historical voiceless to have a voice, resulted in becoming yet another forum for "privileging the white, middle class woman's or man's need for *self-display*" (1996, p. xiv), I question the place, both control of and omission, of Brown as it relates to academic efforts abroad. But, to understand what being Brown Canadian or American means as a traveler in the sSA, we first must understand what it represents in the GN.

Brown

Iconic comedian, George Carlin, raged that despite the USA's job prospects, healthcare and education being moribund, they were excelling in one area: "bomb(ing) the shit out of your country (. . .) *Especially if your country is full of brown people*" (Urbisci, 1992). Carlin's comedic tirade against racism reveals the malleable, yet imposed characterization of Brown in the GN to include a wide variety of peoples from Latin America to the Middle-East, and is meant to indicate what others think about such classifications, not his own. This malleability, mostly shaped by outside and not within, necessitates a definition of Brown for the context of this writing. Recognizing a wide variety of meanings, in this chapter Brown refers to those from North Africa, the Middle-East, West Asia and South Asia whose roots are wrapped in colonialism, imperialism, the 'war on terror', and who predominantly exist outside of the GN's Black/White paradigm of discussing racism. For over 20 years and largely speaking to the Latina/Latino experience, Perea (1997) argues that the prevailing paradigm of a Black/White binary has taught the US how to view race and racism solely among two groups, consequently omitting outsiders to participate in racial discourse and revealing

146 C. Darius Stonebanks

racism, and I would argue that their assumptions permeate throughout Canada as well. Because of this, the ever increasing 'racial profiling' environment of the post 9/11 context's so-called 'war on terror', those of us who are Brown are targeted and discriminated against, yet our voices are absent from the racism discourse. The recent 2017 murder of Srinivas Kuchibhotla and injuring of Alok Madasani,[4] two Indian nationals shot in a Kansas bar who were killed by an assailant who attacked them because he thought they were Iranians, reveals the fusing of Brown in the GN. This tragedy pressed authorities to investigate the killing as "racially motivated" (Schmidt, 2017, ¶1), prompting news channels to debate "whether the United States was now a danger zone for those with brown skin", asking "Is this the new normal?" (¶10). The Kansas bar shooting reinforces another example of a perceived interchangeability of, for example, Arab, Afghani, Iranian, Pakistani and Indian when it comes to racism in the GN (Stonebanks, 2004), providing a racial reality for Brown that is both largely unrecognized or denied ("*they* are not a race" in academia) but enforced ("*they* must be racially profiled in airports"). These acts of racism also beg the question as to how on the one hand, members of Brown, such as Iranians and Arabs, are legally classified White in the USA (Tehranian, 2009), but are nevertheless targeted because they are non-White? Although Canada's definition of visible minorities includes, for example, Iranians and Arabs, the USA's distinguishing of race and anti-racism narratives persuades heavily across the GN. The increased level of media-reported violence and discrimination against Brown as the "new normal" has given rise to the idea that "Brown is the new Black", advanced by some members of the Brown community (Bayoumi, 2009; Dabashi, 2011). Although well intentioned in that it is an attempt to confront racism through an analogy, it is problematic for a number of reasons, two of which I will briefly forward. The first being that racism towards Brown is not "new" since 9/11, as noted by Said who stated that his motivation for the book *Orientalism* (1978), stemmed from the *experience* of being an Arab and the West's *representation* of Arabs as overwhelmingly negative (Said, 1978). The second is that, as Brownness grapples for space and autonomous voice, it should never be done in a manner that assumes to fully understand another's struggle against racism, as this counters the conviction of the rights of self and/or group representation. In Perea's undertaking to create space, he cautions that his "goal is not to take away anything from the study of White racism against Blacks. Rather, it is to identify some limitations of this study (. . .) and understand White racism in all its forms" (p. 169). In keeping with Perea's intent, it is the relationship between the privilege of Whiteness constructing and imposing meaning of Brownness that is of paramount interest, and not an analysis of Black in comparison or in relation to Brown.

Historically, Brown has been racially classified apart from White by Western pseudoscience of the 17th to 19th centuries, with the 20th century creating Otherness through US and British military strategic thought, making the Middle-East and its people "a malleable geopolitical construct" (Tehranian, p. 66). Moving from geopolitical considerations to academia, who shapes the malleable construct of racial and ethnic identity, I would argue, is still in the hands of White dominant culture who are now reticent to allow space at *their* table, even the social justice, anti-racism, or multiculturalism tables where they sit at the head. Better, it appears, to provide limited space for Brown than risk losing control of the table (so to speak). The table is simply more manageable with less people talking, less expertise, less experience, and less stories. Recognition of Brown in academic contexts becomes a threat to comfortable control of spaces of authority, even while in travel as a professor working with Canadian university students in the GS on an emancipatory-based project in the rural region of Malawi called, Transformative Praxis: Malawi (TPM).

The project and the travelers

TPM is primarily an action-research-based project, whose philosophies draw heavily on the works of Freire's (c2000) liberatory theories in unison with the decolonizing scholarship of intellectuals like Fanon (2004) to attempt new modes of collaborative engagement with local community members in the rural region of Kasungu, Malawi. TPM makes great efforts to actualize that all participants are members, with our undergraduate students in the early stages of their careers, engaging primarily though experiential learning. This approach has resulted in the local community calling for the creation of a campus dedicated to Education, Health and Development initiatives. Despite massive poverty, local Malawian TPM members continue to challenge thoughts of hopelessness and see their communities as locations of possibility (Stonebanks, Sheerin, Bennett-Stonebanks, & Nyirenda, 2017), and the campus has done much to foster this hope with tangible outcomes, such as a "Learning Lab", a community center, women's farming cooperative, teacher professional development programs, a radio station, community health teams, experimental farming, a communal water pump, and a new effort to build an elementary school that will act as a pedagogical research space for Malawian teachers to develop and share new modes of teaching and learning.

TPM's relative success is not without struggles, and one of our earliest challenges was navigating "old habits" (Stonebanks, 2014) of what GN 'engagement' in the GS meant. Since we began our project, we have worked with over 150 students, the vast majority of which fit the description given by Heron (2014) for the Canadian student involved with development abroad, as predominantly White, upper middle-class women, with genuine motives to "do good", which often become mixed with simply "feeling good". Being a university project with its initial roots in an administrative recommendation to simply "re-engage" Canadian students in sSA, and to "do good" by providing opportunity through travel-based experiential learning, the endeavour unsurprisingly suffered from all the predictions Illich forewarned at a Conference in 1968 where he told GN university students wanting to work among the impoverished in Mexico, "to hell with good intentions". Illich challenged volunteers on their uselessness to local communities and strongly suggested they would better serve in the role as simple tourists, providing income to

148 C. Darius Stonebanks

locals while sightseeing rather than pretending their mere presence alone, or their short-term relationships would change anything.

The 'special relationship'

With full knowledge of Illich's declaration, over time our students were asked to read not only his works, but that of the likes of Freire, Fanon (2004), Tuhiwai Smith (1999), Scott (1985) and Memmi (2003). However, despite these readings and the multiplicity of authors' positioning and geographical variances of decolonizing struggles, I could not help but notice that many GN students, wonderful as they really are, viewed their special relationship with sSA as something intimate, enduring and natural between White and Black that would solve all problems. On this connection, Naipaul wrote:

> The assumption has always been that it is only the relationship between black and white that really matters. The African was taught – and eventually came to believe – that his destiny was inextricably linked with the destiny of the white man. Marginality was thrust upon the Asian. Both black and white could regard him as an outsider intruding into *their* special relationship.
>
> (Naipaul, 1978, p. 109)

Ultimately, their "special relationship" alone would endure, and all others simply an inconvenience. In reading Naipaul, comparing my Brown experience abroad to his, it became an insubordinate act towards the imposed bonds and definitions that dominant White culture tells me is the whole story; the one true narrative of relationships and place. In an effort to make sense of this, three years ago I came across Naipaul's book to try and find presence in an environment overwhelmed by White narratives. Born in 1945 in Trinidad and Tobago and descended from Indian indentured farm labourers, Naipaul died far too young at the age of 40 in 1985. An award-winning novelist and journalist, he is (unfortunately) best known as being the younger brother of the Nobel Peace Prize recipient, author V.S. Naipaul. Naipaul's *North of South* can be described as a scathing, pessimistic, sometimes unkindly and often cringe-worthy humorous critique of, what he would judge to be so-called, post-colonial societies, the manner in which words like "socialism" and "liberation" were being lived, and their ongoing relationships of dependency and sometimes imitation of the very Western/GN forces from which they struggled to free themselves. In reading Naipaul, although there was much in which to disagree, I discovered a perspective and voice that surprised me in its parallel of at least one prominent experience while abroad in sSA almost 40 years later, that of being the eternal outsider between Black and White, perpetuated by echoes of colonialism unwittingly reinforced by GN students.

Typically (but by no means exclusively), the White undergraduate student is reluctant to make space for any of their Brown Canadian co-travelers (be it professor or peer) and in similarity to the academic space, when vilification or nonperson-ness fails, will assimilate them into Whiteness, effectively silencing their experience in the GN as a group that faces daily discrimination. In this situation, Brown is told "you are Canadian, and Canadian means White". On one occasion, a Brown student was publicly told by a White peer that she never experienced racism as a Canadian, I suspect because to admit that would be to relinquish complete control over dominating the conversation of systemic oppression in Malawi caused by colonialism. Naipaul concludes that the sub-Saharan African desire to make Brown disappear currently stems from the differences between European/White travelers' and locally residing Browns' narratives. One of which creates the illusion of acceptance through Europeanization or Americanization, and the other of inaccessibility through the closed society of Brown, making them "the eternal 'other'" (p. 121). The narrative that Canadians 'do good', that good is White, means Canadians are White, forcing all non-White Canadians to represent White. Otherwise, they are apart of the solidarity that is being sought as we cross borders. Naipaul writes that in pursuit of doing good and of "racial harmony" in sSA, Brown (Naipaul refers to Indians, Arabs and Persians as Brown or Asian) "do not enter this happy picture. (. . .) It is as if they did not exist; had never existed" (p. 113). Crashing their happy picture as Brown, and not embodying White, means doing so as an uninvited guest.

The uninvited guest

Whole books have been written about race relations in Kenya that neglect – except as a more or less complicating factor – the Asian population (Naipaul, 1978, p. 109). Naipaul dedicates an entire chapter to Brown-ness in *North of South*, titled "Between Master and Slave". Largely ignored by many book reviewers, the action of omission in many ways validates Naipaul's assertion that the dominant narrative of racial relationships in sSA has relegated Brown in the "most shadowy of presences. They are just *there* – like a natural outgrowth of the soil" (p. 110). Although critics of Naipaul, like Maja-Pearce (1985), are accurate in their assessments that he portrays nearly everyone he encounters in a negative light, it is impossible to avoid Naipaul's anger at the racism and dependency he deems is perpetuated by White, and Black's acceptance of this relationship. Naipaul is cynical of everyone in his travel autoethnography, and portrays himself like an uninvited person at a members-only social event. Watch any GN movie located in the sSA where the lead is White, and Black co-stars. Scan the background scenery and you will find the silent Brown, disengaged from the main story. In his movie, Naipaul is the scene crasher that walks out into the foreground and asks uncomfortable questions. In some ways, Naipaul is reminiscent of the Indian character Hrundi V. Bakshi, performed by Peter Sellers, in *The Party* (1968), unwittingly crashing a private Hollywood gathering where the understanding is simply that the absurdity of his very presence equates comedy. In such a context, Brown simply does not belong. However, unlike Sellers, Naipaul is not in Brownface, nor is he a bumbling, quaint and naïve stereotype, yet he still creates chaos and makes people uncomfortable.

150 C. Darius Stonebanks

He makes the reader writhe or cheer by referencing Fanon's "settler's town" (pp. 66–69) and contrasting it to what he saw as the new space of a "tourist town" where Fanon's native and foreigner relationship has now become fueled by travel fantasies. Naipaul is clearly stating that the relationship is still one-sided, oppressive and filled with the colonized "dreams of possession" (Fanon, 2004, p. 5). Brown-ness is never absent from his writing, and I wonder if it is this positioning that causes irritation and offence in his descriptions as he is not part of this "special relationship", therefore, not allowed to experience, assess and/or speak. As I read his work, I realized very quickly that he was writing from a perspective that was indeed subversive of the travel genre, as it did not come from the usual sources of Whiteness, nor did it fall into the category of writer as the comprador intellectual (Dabashi, 2011) fueling fantasies of Kipling's (1899) "White Man's Burden". He is not writing as White or Black, and therefore risks being a nonperson.

Forty years after its publication, I am amazed that such dynamics of inequity and privilege along with exclusion are still intact and described with disturbing accuracy by Naipaul. From witnessing the predatory sex-trade tourism on the beachfronts of Lake Malawi by White travelers cloaked in words like "solidarity", "liberation" and "social justice", to the combined distrust that Black and White share of Brown, much of what Naipaul describes of that special relationship is all too familiar. In regard to the distrust of Brown, although as I walk past Brown (referred to as "Amwenye" in Chichewa) shop owners in Malawi, who are quick to greet me and ask from what part of South/West Asia or the Middle-East I originate, some of the Malawians I work with almost regard this question indicating Brown connectedness as an insult. Pressing one of our Malawian colleagues on his apparent disfavour with the question, I asked why it would bother him if I was Amwenye. He responded, "Not here. In Malawi, you are Azungu."[5] Pushed further, he said, "If you dressed like them (wearing a kurta shalwar) or owned a shop, people would say you were Amwenye. But everyone here knows you are doing good things, so they say you are Azungu." Although sometimes Brown Canadians have been referred to as "coloured", "half-caste" and even Black, Brown participants in TPM are rarely called Amwenye by local community when they move in spaces that are connected with Canadians "doing good".

Before I had even read Naipaul's account, I had experienced the White equaled good, Brown equaled bad position in this "special relationship" play. To be clear, many other Malawians had no issue with how people self-identify and judged good or bad on actions, somewhat diffusing Naipaul's feeling that "I was not an individual any more. In the twinkling of an eye I have been transformed into a spokesman for my race: one more specimen for a dangerous breed" (p. 98). Still, the majority understood the complexity of racial designations in Malawi, with the ever-present history of colonization and a top-down relationship with Whiteness that excludes or remains oblivious to all others, creating an illusion of GN (White) as giver and GS (Black) as receiver. Talking to both Black and White, others, like Brown, simply did not really exist or matter, or when they did, it was in the role of historic "Arab slave trader" or the more recent "greedy Asian/South Asian", reinforcing Naipaul's (1978) observation that Brown "is the eternal 'other'" (p. 121). Whereas GN students self-cast White with qualities such as liberators and do-gooders, and stereotype Black as appreciative long-lost friends and quaint wisdom givers, the eternal others were simply not a part of *their* play. "Other" personal experiences were not present and not important; *we* were not and are not present, not important. Rather, if we push for our own space we become the interloper, the outsider, the inconvenient, the uninvited, the unallied, the dismissed, the villain, the unsympathetic, the selfish, the scheming and ultimately the Other. To be good cannot relate to Brown, therefore for many, race must be erased. Brown must be omitted and replaced, or vilified. Always, however, Brown's relationship with Black in this Malawian context must be filtered, shaped and defined through White. White stands between ethnicities and defines relationships even outside of the GN, with that stance sometimes being physical through a scenario I forward to illuminate this nonperson othering which has become far too common.

A common scene

The scene plays out typically during the third week of the students' time in Malawi where their culture shock takes a turn from celebrating everything new, to self-blame, despondency, to anger at others (Pedersen, 1995). A knock on the door of the small professors' house on our campus, and as I open the door, I see the usual positioning of the university student, physically placing herself between myself and a Malawian TPM member. The student is always at the forefront, the Malawian always standing steps behind, blocked from view, as if her march to the professors' house left the local colleague in her wake. The body language of the student always seems so clear and the face so resolute, as if to say about the Malawian behind them, "I will protect this person, I will make demands on behalf of him/her, I will speak the truth about their lives to power, and I will show courage and speak for those who cannot." The words that follow echo and confirm the stance and *their role*. Impassioned and determined, the student will tell me what is to be changed and what is to be done. "We", meaning the student and the Malawian TPM member, I am usually told have discussed the matter thoroughly, but "he" or "she" is typically silent, and sometimes I am told (in the presence of the local TPM member) that they are too afraid to speak. The ultimatums are typically large, sweeping, well intentioned, but accusatory. Rarely is it a dialogue, more often than not it is a one-sided declaration. In such performances, in which White is so integrally tied to Black, Brown is at best a third wheel in this special relationship; at its worst, we exist to define White's goodness. In this piece, I know what role I am supposed to play; I have gone from nonperson to villain.

After the student speaks, I bend sideways to make eye contact with the person behind her, and they often bend to acknowledge both our presence. There is often a moment of uncomfortableness, as the original physical stance that has come to represent my part in this scene, filtered and shaped through Whiteness is now being challenged and changed. Speaking directly with the local TPM member

152 C. Darius Stonebanks

I ask questions regarding community established democratic processes, local consultation, risks, responsibilities, inclusion, sustainability and more. Our local TPM members have been in this situation before, and despite the fact that most of them are usually old enough to be the student's parent, this relationship between giver/receiver, White/Black has become an old habit. Through dialogue we can usually bring the core of the concern back into the realm of community agency and problem solving, but sometimes these encounters can leave students in tears, especially when we try to unpack privilege (McInstosh, 1990), made all the more emotional because, with all due respect to Illich, the vast majority really do have good intentions.

In the context of what Heron (2014) calls "the helping imperative", the necessity to "help" is, unknowingly or not, linked to the same desires of the legacy of Lady Bountiful's (Meiners, 2002) enterprises of old, that being to civilize the uncivilized. The helping imperative can be made even more complicated by those working with social justice and/or feminist lenses whose image of self is inherently antiracist, good and innocent, producing strong emotional responses to any question of examining discrimination (Srivastava, 2005). Naipaul (1978) wrote that the role of Brown had been caricatured in sSA, and so had the role of White "but in a contrary direction" (p. 111), representing care, progress and all things good. A young English woman he encounters yearns for the White European settler's life in 1930s British-ruled Kenya, and when he asks her how she imagined her relationship with indigenous Kenyans, she responds, "I would be very maternalistic to them (. . .) That was how it was in the old days" (p. 112). Forty years later, this romantic notion is still very much alive and played out on my doorstep with roles set and unchanged.

Words, words, words

Naipaul's early death leaves his writing in stasis, a snapshot of *his* moment, yet not fully realized and open to valid and unanswered criticism, sadly, leaving us with no idea how he would have re-examined his narrative. However, Naipaul's examination of Brown as a marginalized experience resonates today with those who are questioning the limitations of the prevailing Black/White anti-racism paradigm. Scrutinizing the "special relationship" constructed by Whiteness at the expense of Brown, Desai (2016) writes, "(f)or Naipaul, the racial predicament of East Africa's Asians can only be explained by what is popularly known as the 'divide and rule' strategy of colonial politics" (p. 74), summarizing Naipaul's criticism of ongoing pursuits of empire. Also, examining the apartness of Brown from White and Black through Naipaul's work as well, Dubin (2013) explains in South Africa how this conglomerated group has remained "uncomfortably betwixt and between'" (p. 48). Utilizing Naipaul, Cao (2003) writes, "(a)lthough the United States is increasingly diverse ethnically, ethnic relations in the country are framed primarily in terms of blacks and whites" (p. 1536). Quoting Naipaul's assessment of the "special relationship" he states "it is similarly so in the United States", thereby moving the context of being unseen or hated from the GS, back to the GN. It is, after all, in the GN where these ideas take root, influencing students who in turn dictate either a vilification, whitewashing or nonpersoning of Brown, effectively contributing to the silencing of voice. In doing so, those words of social justice, equity and anti-racism become just words.

Smith reveals a culture of risk of being branded a "tattle tale" (2010, p. 37) for communicating stories about racism in Canadian academia. I work with wonderful people, most of whom completely understand the systemic nature of racism in higher education. However, and at risk of tattling, that realization does not put an end to the regular discriminations *all* minorities face in academia, including Brown. The existing Black/White paradigm being enforced by White does little to end discrimination against Black (and all others), because by its very nature it condones marginalization of some and a complete control of the minority experience and voice. In this paradigm, there is no doubt who remains privileged. Yet, I still remind myself that the students I work with abroad are truly wonderful and filled with good intentions. To hell with good intentions indeed, but those good intentions draw many GN students into spaces where, when challenged on their assumptions, can lead some to expanded perspectives on anti-discrimination and liberation work beyond the dominant narratives. In largely discounting any real effect of the liberation movements for the masses in Tanzania, Naipaul wrote, "Words, words, words . . . They can, when handled promiscuously, gradually begin to take the place of reality. They can, in the course of time, become complete substitutes for it" (1978, p. 284). It may be tattling when I repeat the same sentiments when I am told that universities in the GN are spaces of equity, social justice and anti-discrimination/racism where *all* voices are respected; "Words, words, words." Naipaul's work has allowed me to re-think my place with students and commit to a narrative autoethnography of Brown both at home and abroad, challenging presumptions of roles and words that risk losing meaning.

Notes

1 I use White/Black and Black/White interchangeably.
2 In this chapter, the GN countries primarily examined are Canada and the USA.
3 Although Naipaul discusses the problem with generic geographical terminology in *An Unfinished Journey* (1987), this chapter will use sSA for the sake of brevity.
4 Ian Grillot was also shot and injured in a heroic attempt to intervene.
5 Chichewa word for White, and although plural of Mzungu, Azungu is commonly used.

References

Akhavan, N., Bashi, G., Mana, K., & Shakhsar, S. (2007, 2 1). *A Genre in the Service of Empire: An Iranian Feminist Critique of Diasporic Memoirs.* Retrieved from Payvand: http://payvand.com/news/07/feb/1007.html

Allen, R. L. (2001). The Globalization of White Supremacy: Toward a Critical Discourse on the Racialization of the World. *Educational Theory*, 51, 467–485.

Apple, M. W. (1996). *Cultural Politics and Education.* New York: Teachers College Press.

Bayoumi, M. (2009). *How Does It Feel to Be a Problem?: Being Young and Arab in America*. New York: Penguin Press.

Cao, L. (2003). The Diaspora of Ethnic Economies: Beyond the Pale? *William and Mary Law R*, 44(4), 1521–1625.

Dabashi, H. (2011). *Brown Skin, White Mask*. New York: Pluto Press.

Desai, G. (2016). *Commerce with the Universe: Africa, India, and the Afrasian*. New York: Columbia University Press.

Dubin, S. C. (2013). *Spearheading Debate: Culture Wars & Uneasy Truces*. Johannesburg: Jacana Media.

Fanon, F. (2004). *The Wretched of the Earth*. New York: Grove Press.

Freire, P. (c2000). *Pedagogy of the Oppressed*, 30th Anniversary Edition. New York: Bloomsbury Academic.

Heron, B. (2014). *Desire for Development: Whiteness, Gender and the Helping Imperative*. Waterloo: Wilfred Laurier Press.

Jiwani, Y. (1999). Erasing Race: The Story of Reena Virk. *Canadian Woman Studies*, 19(3), 178–184.

Kipling, R. (1899, February 1). The White Man's Burden. *McClure's Magazine*.

Maja-Pearce, A. (1985). The Naipauls on Africa: An African View. *Journal of Commonwealth Literature*, 20(1), 111–117.

McInstosh, P. (1990, Winter). White privilege: Unpacking the invisible knapsack. *Independent School*, 49(2), 31–35.

Meiners, E. R. (2002). Disengaging from the Legacy of Lady Bountiful in Teacher Education Classrooms. *Gender & Education*, 14(1), 85–94.

Memmi, A. (2003). *The Colonizer and the Colonized*. UK: Earthscan.

Naipaul, S. (1978). *North of South: An African Journey*. London: Peguin Books.

Naipaul, S. (1987). *An Unfinished Journey*. New York: Viking Penguin Inc.

Nasifi, A. (2003). *Reading Lolita in Tehran: A Memoir in Books*. New York: Random House.

Nixon, R. (1991). Preparations for Travel: The Naipaul Brothers' Conradian Atavism. *Research in African Literature*, 22(2), 177–190.

Nixon, R. (1992). *London Calling: V.S. Naipaul, Postcolonial Mandarin*. New York: Oxford University Press.

Odhiambo, T. (2004). Holding the Traveller's Gaze Accountable in Shiva Naipaul's North of South: An African Journey. *Social Dynamics*, 30(1), 51–68.

Pedersen, P. (1995). *The Five Stages of Culture Shock: Critical Incidents Around the World*. Westport: Greenwood Press.

Perea, J. F. (1997). The Black/White Binary Paradigm of Race: The 'Normal Science' of American Racial Thought. *California Law Review*, 85(5), 127–172.

Pratt, M. L. (1992*). Imperial Eyes: Travel Writing and Transculturation*. New York: Routledge.

Said, E. (1978). *Orientalism*. New York: Pantheon.

Schmidt, S. (2017, February 28). Suspect in Kansas bar shooting of Indians apparently thought they were Iranians. Retrieved March 3, 2017, from *The Washington Post*: https://www.washingtonpost.com/news/morning-mix/wp/2017/02/28/suspect-in-kansas-bar-shooting-of-indians-apparently-thought-they-were-iranians/?utm_term=.c0a64240c5a0

Scott, J. C. (1985). *Weapons of the Weak: Everyday Forms of Peasant Resistance*. New Haven: Yale University Press.

Smith, L. T. (1999). *Decolonizing Methodologies: Research and Indigenous Peoples*. New York: Zed Books.

Smith, M. S. (2010). Gender, whiteness, and 'other Others' in the academy. In M. S. Sheren Razack, *States of Race: Critical Race Feminism for the 21st Century* (pp. 37–58). Toronto: Between the Lines.

Srivastava, S. (2005). 'You're calling me a racist?' The Moral and Emotional Regulation of Antiracism and Feminism. *Signs*, 31(1), 29–62.

Stonebanks, C. D. (2004). Consequences of Perceived Ethnic Identities. In J. L. *Kincheloe* & S. R. Steinberg, *The Miseducation of the West: The Hidden Curriculum of Western-Muslim Relations* (pp. 87–102). New York: Greenwood Press.

Stonebanks, C. D. (2014). Confronting Old Habits Overseas: An Analysis of Reciprocity between Malawian Stakeholders and a Canadian University. In N. D. Giardina, *Qualitative Inquiry Outside of the Academy* (pp. 107–127). Walnut Creek: Left Coast Press.

Stonebanks, C. D., Sheerin, F., Bennett-Stonebanks, M., & Nyirenda, J. (2017). Just Give the Money to the Women: Overly Simplified Advice that Works in International Education, Health, and Development Initiatives. In T. N. Normore, *Racially and Ethnically Diverse Women Leading Education: A World View* (pp. 255–277). Bingley: Emerald Group Publishing.

Talreja, S. (Producer), & Jhally, S. (Director). (1998). Edward Said On Orientalism [Motion Picture].

Tehranian, J. (2009). *Whitewashed: America's Invisible Middle Eastern Minority*. New York: New York University Press.

Urbisci, R. (Director). (1992). *George Carlin: Jammin' in New York* [Motion Picture]. USA.

14

UNTANGLING ME

Complexifying cultural identity

Gresilda A. Tilley-Lubbs

FACULTY OF TEACHING AND LEARNING, VIRGINIA TECH, USA

In the past few years, several events and situations have occurred that have destroyed my notion of who I am, what I believe about myself, and how others perceive me. In 2011, when I wrote a poem called "The coal miner's daughter gets a PhD," I firmly situated myself as an Appalachian woman, not to be confused with a "Southern woman" (Smith, 2016). In a later poem, "Reconciling two selves in one body," I referenced my family's childhood stories about my dad's Cherokee grandfather. I referred to another Tilley family story that our ancestors were named "Tellez," the last name of the Spanish sailor who shipwrecked with the Spanish Armada on the coast of Ireland in the 1500s, never to return to Spain. In that same poem, I talked about being bilingual, deconstructing a friend/colleague's comment that I was a different person depending on whether I spoke English, which is my mother tongue, or Spanish, my acquired language. This is a perception that I question now. I thought I had figured out my cultural identity. In my graduate course on diversity, for years I have used myself as an example of someone who to all appearances is white, middle class, and so on, but who has indigenous and Spanish heritage. But I am someone whose cultural memberships are within the categories normed as having power and privilege. The conundrum I will explore in this chapter is: how do I reconcile my perception of who I am and what I believe about myself with new information I recently discovered about my family and my way of navigating the world?

I look at my first-grade picture, and memories flood into my mind. 'No, no, no!' I scream and cry as our neighbor Marie cuts my hair. I twist and turn, creating short spots all over my head as Marie snips. "I want long hair like Carol's."

Mom stands at the stove, stirring a big pot of fudge. "You can't have your hair long like your friend Carol's. It's too hard to comb. You've got your dad's thick, straight, stubborn Indian hair, and you won't cooperate to get it combed."

She keeps stirring, and the thought of her rich, chocolatey fudge poured over a graham cracker while still hot and runny calms my hysteria.

"I just don't want kids to laugh at me and call me four eyes. Then they make fun of my hair because it's so short and straight."

"You should be proud of your hair," Mom replies. "You look just like your daddy and his people. It's all from their Indian granddaddy – that would be your great-granddaddy. Thick, straight hair. Turned down mouth. High cheekbones. They're all good-looking, just like you. If you could have ever seen your great aunt Drucilla, you wouldn't ever doubt that you're pretty. She looked just like an Indian princess. I always thought she must have looked just like Pocahontas. Don't you ever let people make you forget. You have a heritage to be proud of and a daddy that loves you more than anything in the world."

My attention shifts as I watch the smooth, creamy chocolate sauce spill over the edges of graham crackers laid on the turquoise Melmac plate. The glow of being as beautiful as an Indian princess helps me to sit straight so Marie can finish cutting my hair. I guess it's not so bad to have short, thick, straight Indian hair after all.

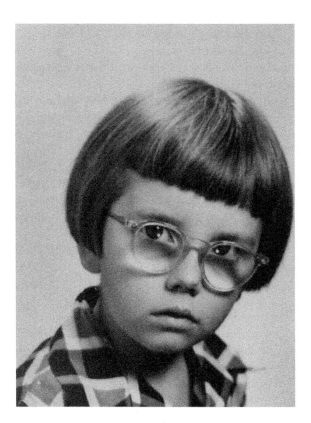

ILLUSTRATION 5 Me at six (Photo: Fayetteville Elementary School, 1952)

158   Gresilda A. Tilley-Lubbs

Now, 65 years later, I sit here trying to make sense of the DNA report I received in June, telling me I have no Native American heritage. I'm still trying to untangle, but now it's Self, not hair.

What about the other narratives that shaped my life? I wonder how identity is constructed. Did I create my Self, based on the narratives that surrounded me? Did my experiences shape the trajectory of my life? Why does it matter?

Another picture fills my mind. Mom, Daddy, my grandmother, and I drive through the curvy, narrow mountain roads that lead us out of Hinton, West Virginia, located in the region defined by the Appalachian Mountains, now referred to as Appalachia, not only because of mountains, but also because of its distinct cultural characteristics. Like most of southern West Virginia, great tall mountains overshadow the roads on either side, winding along beside the New River. We follow the road until Daddy pulls into a dirt yard in front of a log cabin. Two people sit in rocking chairs on the front porch, wizened older people who remind me of carved apple heads I used to see on Appalachian dolls. The man wears overalls and a plaid flannel shirt. The woman has on a full gathered long skirt, covered by an apron, a corncob pipe hanging out of her mouth. Both are barefoot. As I grow up, Mom reminds me from time to time of that visit to Grandma's parents when I was about five years old. She always refers to my great-grandfather as Cherokee Indian. The memory of seeing them on that porch is vivid, but it's a still, not a movie. I never know how much is true memory, and how much is what Mom told me, or how much comes from some picture I saw of Appalachian folks. After my DNA report, I now wonder whether my memories are complicit in my stereotyping a culture and co-opting identity.

The stories continue through the years, but always with my Cherokee heritage front and center. I hear about Pocahontas having been my great-great-great-to-infinity grandmother, a family legend corroborated by a chef in California. As he slices the prime rib, I notice his nametag and exclaim, "Al Tilley! That's my dad's name."

Without taking his eyes away from the meat, he says, "Then we're related. My sister is into all this genealogy stuff, and she tells me that everyone with the last name 'Tilley' or 'Tilly' is related. She says we all descended from Pocahontas. She also told me a story about how we're descended from a sailor in the Spanish Armada who crashed on the banks of Ireland in 1588. The poor guy couldn't make it back home, so he stayed in Ireland. His name was Tellez, but it became Tilley, probably because no one could pronounce it."

"I've heard the Pocahontas story all my life, but never the Spanish sailor one. Interesting."

I consider this latest information. In high school, I learned Spanish without effort. I skipped a year of Spanish in high school. I majored in Spanish as an undergraduate, and in Spanish literature as a master's student, never struggling with language. This story of ancient heritage from Spain reinforces the mystical notions I have always held about Spanish and Spain. I wrote a poem called "Reconciling Two Selves in One Body," published in English and in Spanish (2016a, 2016b),

Untangling me: Complexifying cultural identity **159**

where I examine a comment from a Mexican friend that I am a different person when I speak Spanish than I am when I speak English.

At the time, I didn't know about co-opting identity or about colonialism, nor had I begun the search for the name Tilley in the Cherokee register. I didn't realize until years later that the Cherokee connection was on my paternal grandmother's, not grandfather's, side. My grandmother shared the last name Bolling with her sister Drucilla, to whom my mother always pointed as the idealized image of what an Indian princess would look like, and Bolling, or Boling, appears on the Cherokee websites that list last names of Pocahontas' descendants.

Soon after meeting the chef, we move to Virginia, a state that borders West Virginia, the state where I was born. In a random conversation with a clerk in a store, she notices a dark gray spot in the lower outer corner of each eye. "You must have Cherokee heritage," she says as if stating a fact. I add that to the identity narratives that shape my sense of Self. My annual visit to the ophthalmologist occurs, and I ask Dr. Strelow about the gray spots in my eyes, explaining the reason I want to know. He examines both eyes, and says, "They aren't gray spots. They're pigment changes in the sclera. The name escapes me, but I'll look it up and send you the name. Not everyone has them, but I have never heard that they're more predominant in any ethnic or racial group."

"May I quote you in my chapter?" I ask.

He smiles, and says, "Sure. That will be fine."

That same afternoon, I receive an email confirming that I have Cogan's scleral plaques in the white of my eyes, a condition found in about 10 percent of folks over age 60. Not as romantic and exotic as the story that they are Cherokee markers! Another chink in the Cherokee heritage narrative!

These narratives informed how I performed life. I never questioned the veracity of heritage narratives that traced a path through my life. Whenever anyone asked, I said I was Native American, English, Scots, and Irish. I even applied for a Native American scholarship at the insistence of my advisor who had heard my narrative while I was working on my doctorate. Also at her suggestion, I applied for one for Hispanic students, based on the Tellez/Tilley story. Of course, I was rejected for both, much to my relief, since I would have felt like an impostor. I had never experienced discrimination or minority status of either group. I grew up as a white person with great privilege based on my skin color.

My memories shift back to two years ago, as I work to finish the book manuscript I have been working on for the last year. My husband Dan comes into the study and finds me staring at the computer screen.

"How's the writing coming?" he inquires as he sets a cup of cappuccino in front of me.

"I'm stuck!" I turn to face him as I pick up the steaming cup.

"How are you stuck?" he asks.

"It's not making sense to me," I state. "I can't figure out where I fit in critical pedagogy or in critical autoethnography. The more I write, the more I doubt."

160 Gresilda A. Tilley-Lubbs

"We need to take a trip to West Virginia so you can reconnect with your roots, and understand why you are who you are," he states.

We arrange a trip to West Virginia where I reconnect with buried memories. The trip leads me to question another aspect of my identity in a chapter titled "Am I Really an Appalachian Coal Miner's Daughter?" in the book, *Re-Assembly Required: Critical Autoethnography and Spiritual Discovery* (2017). I had written a poem called "The Coal Miner's Daughter Gets a PhD" (2011), about growing up in West Virginia until I was 12 years old, at which time my dad accepted an offer to leave the coal mines and move to the Chicago area to be a carpenter in my cousin's housing development. As I write the book, I question whether I have co-opted identity, both as an Appalachian woman, and as a coal miner's daughter. I spent so many of my formative years in the Chicago area, and at the University of Illinois in Champaign-Urbana, that when I think of home, I think of Illinois at least as often as I think of West Virginia. I seldom think of identifying with Virginia, where we have lived since 1980. My dad had moved far away from being a coal miner, and I had moved even farther from being a coal miner's daughter.

Soon after we return from the trip, I receive an email with the results from the DNA test Dan gave me for my birthday. I mention the lack of Native American heritage in that same chapter, but after I submit the book manuscript, the questions brew in my mind.

When Dan gave me the DNA test for my birthday, I was certain the results would reflect the heritage narratives that had shaped my life for as long as I could remember. When the email arrives, I click to see these regions and percentages listed under "Ethnicity Estimate": Great Britain, 44%; Western Europe, 19%; Ireland, 15%; Eastern Europe, 8%; Scandinavia, 6%. Under the heading "Low confidence," I see Iberian Peninsula, 5%; Finland and Northwestern Russia, 2%. Scrolling down, I see all the other regions listed as 0%. Under America, I see Native American, 0% (https://www.ancestry.com). I spend several hours clicking around the website, certain there is a mistake. The Great Britain and Ireland percentages make perfect sense, because my mom always told me that her family was Scots-Irish, and my Dad's was English and Cherokee. The Iberian Peninsula piece fits in with my identity construction from speaking Spanish and loving Hispanic culture. But no Native American? Impossible!

When I go to campus after receiving my results, I see my friend Betti. We eat lunch, chatting as we chew.

"Dan gave me a DNA test with Ancestry.com for my birthday in June. I got the results last week. I have no Native American DNA!"

Betti and I co-teach a class called Diversity and Multicultural Education. She has witnessed my leading the students through an activity on the Public Broadcasting System interactive website, *Race: The Power of an Illusion* (http://www.pbs.org/race/000_General/000_00-Home.htm). Students place photos of people into four race/ethnicity categories used by the US Census Bureau (https://www.census.gov/). Out of 24 photos, students might place two to four in correct categories, providing evidence that socially constructed categories of ethnicity and race can't be determined by appearance. I then inform them of my Native American heritage, contrary to my pale whiteness, which leads to several activities about race and ethnicity.

"I read that those tests don't prove anything," replies Betti. "If your mom told you your great-grandfather was Cherokee, then he probably was."

"Dan's convinced DNA tests aren't accurate. Years ago, my mom ordered a coat-of-arms plaque for the Tilley family from an ad she saw in the back of a magazine. She gave it to my dad for his birthday, but she also wanted it so that his descendants would have it to know where they came from. This was from my mom who always scorned any kind of pride in heritage. We all thought the plaque was fun, but we figured it was made up. I think Dan equates DNA tests with that plaque."

Betti smiles as she stirs her heated-up leftover casserole.

"Eowyn's first reaction was, 'You don't suppose Gramma messed around, do you?'"

Betti laughs since she knows how mischievous our younger daughter is. "If your mom is as much like my mom as she sounds, that's pretty unlikely!"

Later that week, a doctoral student comes by my office. I had told the students in my Critical Autoethnography class about my DNA test. By now, I feel like an impostor, because of all the times I have used myself as an example of how it's impossible to judge ethnic heritage by appearance. Melissa says, "I heard something about DNA tests. So few Native Americans do DNA tests there's no reliable database of their DNA. So you may have Native American heritage after all."

An internet search of Cherokee and DNA informs me regarding the complexity of the indigenous people who settled in southern Appalachia, suggesting origins as diverse as the Middle East and the lost tribes of Israel. The more I read, the less I believe. My inherent disbelief of "scientific evidence" increases as I search, creating tension with my desire to "prove" my Native American heritage.

I mull over the results of my DNA test until I question my obsession. What does it matter? How does any of this affect who I am? Why do I care if I have Native American or Spanish heritage? What difference does it make if I am Appalachian or if I am a coal miner's daughter? How will this affect the way I perform my life? For that matter, why did I even want to have a DNA test? I write as inquiry (Richardson & St. Pierre, 2005), trying to understand why my DNA test results have disrupted my entire sense of world understanding.

If I were worried about a genetic disease that I might pass to unborn children, then genetic heritage could matter. If I discovered Jewish heritage, I might want to watch for symptoms of Tay-Sachs, or if I had African American heritage, I could be vigilant about symptoms of sickle cell anemia. However, I'm not plagued with these worries. I'm not concerned with my descendants exhibiting signs of a devastating disease germane to a specific ethnic group.

Membership in certain groups can lead to unconscionable discrimination, but that doesn't figure into this narrative. Some of the genetic groups in which I have claimed and do claim membership aren't considered among the powerful or privileged in the dominant society I inhabit, and to whose values I realize I refer. In

162 Gresilda A. Tilley-Lubbs

fact, Native Americans and Appalachian natives are often among the vulnerable populations who often suffer great discrimination in one aspect or another of their lives. For example, Dan, who was born and raised in Illinois, reminds me of his inherent perspective as a Midwesterner, or a person who lives in the states in the middle of the United States, including Illinois and the surrounding states. He jokes, 'When Midwesterners hear West Virginians talk, they often deduct 50 points from their IQs.' I remember how my parents and I practiced reverse discrimination when we moved to Illinois and regarded Midwesterners as pretentious and snobbish. His observation parallels what happened to me when my mom enrolled me in junior high school when we first moved from West Virginia to Illinois (2011). The guidance counselor tried to put me back a grade because I was from West Virginia and she knew the education was inferior. I ponder whether Midwesterners decide about West Virginians' intelligence before or after they name them "hillbilly," which also happened to me the first year or two after we moved. For many years I suffered jokes about "barefoot hillbillies" who "married their cousins."

That's not Appalachian heritage as I know it. Appalachian refers to cultural features that shape character and worldview. My mom never talked about being Appalachian. She was a West Virginian through and through. After we moved to Illinois, during the summers, she worked at the ticket office for the summer theater. One evening she returned home, her eyes flashing and her voice sharp. "A man who came to pick up his tickets asked if I was from Texas. He said I sounded like a Texan. Can you imagine? A Texan! I told him I'm a West Virginian!" Texas has a different culture from West Virginia.

I still speak slowly, like a West Virginian, with a slight Midwestern accent, which I worked hard to acquire so I could fit in. Nonetheless, when I talk to my family on the phone, all these years later, Dan says he still hears West Virginia. Our son now works at the University of Texas, and when we go to visit him in Austin, I do hear traces of the speech I grew up hearing. I suspect that my mother's aversion to being called "Texan" had more to do with West Virginia pride and homesickness than disregard for Texans. I imagine her reaction was similar to mine when anyone refers to me as a Southerner. In my West Virginia history class, I was taught that West Virginia separated from the rest of Virginia during the Civil War in 1863, protesting Virginia's support of slavery and its secession from the rest of the United States. Therefore, West Virginians aren't Southerners.

I drift between emotional construction of Self and desire to construct a physical sense of Self, based on someone testing my spit and determining my ancestors. I examine the contradictory nature of the binaries I construct, realizing I can't make them work. Today when people ask where I am from, I may give them the whole story – born in West Virginia, moved to Illinois at age 12, married and moved to California, settling in Virginia in 1980. Most often, I say I'm from West Virginia or Illinois, but never from Virginia. What do our subconscious words say about us?

My heart feels a strong affiliation with Spanish language and with two countries where I often travel to teach, conduct research, and spend vacation days, Spain and

Mexico. I advocate for immigrant rights and for reform of immigration law in solidarity with my Mexican friends and colleagues. I am neither Spanish nor Mexican, and as I think about co-opting identity, I question the poem I wrote exploring my affinity with Spanish-speaking places and people.

I base my writing on critical autoethnography, which relates the personal to the political (Ellis, 2004; Bochner & Ellis, 2016), and on the examination of one's own power and privilege in relation to vulnerable communities where we work or conduct research. So why am I so bothered to learn that my identity as one-eighth Cherokee has no genetic basis? Questioning my heritage and DNA exemplify the great privilege I have. The academic world grants certain prestige to being a member of a diverse group, and I wonder if my obsession has to do with wanting to be considered diverse rather than average middle-class white university professor! Have I created "inverse symbolic capital" in an attempt to "legitimi[ze] 'disadvantage'" (personal communication, Phiona Stanley, May 10, 2017)? Alternatively, am I simply disappointed on a personal level as I question the identity my mother created for me through the years?

The majority of college students has always socialized with people similar to themselves, and they continue to do so, even after they go to college (Wildman & Davis, 2000). That has never described my pattern of choosing friends. Since I was in high school and to the present day, I have always sought friends with different backgrounds. In high school, I sought Catholic friends in contrast to my protestant upbringing. In university, my best friends included Jewish and Latin American students who seemed far more interesting than my middle-class white protestant friends. Was I seeking an exotic identity, proved by a "scientific" DNA test showing my Native American heritage?

The central question revolves around what identity is in terms of how we construct and perform identity/Self. For many years, I performed being English, Scots, Irish, and Cherokee. I grew up in a family shaped by stories. My mother was close to her sisters, and when we lived in West Virginia, we spent many hours together. My dad worked night shift in the mines, so my aunt and uncle picked us up every evening to go to another aunt's house. I followed the aunts to the bedroom. As they talked and smoked cigarettes, they talked and told stories for several hours every evening. I heard all the family gossip, which shaped my ideas about proper behavior.

The stories informed my construction of Self. "Storytelling is fundamental to human experience. Through narration, we make meaning out of experience" (Jago, 1996, p. 495). I was an only child, and tended to relate better to adults than to peers. I always managed to find a spot on the bed where I read – or pretended to read – all the while with one ear cocked to hear the stories. Sometimes I asked where Mom's family came from. I knew so much about my dad's "Indian blood," but I never heard much about Mom's family. The standard answer was, "We don't know anything about them. They were probably horse thieves." Past the stories about Grandma's "having the Irish sight," and Aunt Luly communing with spirits and making tables talk, I never knew much about Mom's side of the family.

164 Gresilda A. Tilley-Lubbs

I reflect on the irony. I often heard about my Cherokee heritage, which wasn't found in my DNA test. I never heard much about the English-Scots-Irish heritage, and that showed up as 59 percent of my genetic make-up. I identify strongly with Spanish, and the Iberian Peninsula is a questionable 5 percent. I look back through the writing I have produced in the last 15 years, and the theme of Spanish language and culture is present throughout. Was that identity formed by the six years I spent at the University of Illinois studying Spanish, or by the time I have spent in the Spanish-speaking community since 1970, or the multiple trips we have made to Spanish-speaking culture? Or does it just seem exotic and romantic to feel a connection with that world?

Does my strong identification with all things Appalachian come from the time I lived in West Virginia until I was 12 or the time I have lived in Virginia since 1980? I submitted a manuscript to the Appalachian Writers Workshop in hopes of beginning the process of reinventing myself as a writer outside academia. Nevertheless, what did I submit? A young adult novel about a 12-year-old girl who emigrated with her parents from Oaxaca, Mexico, to Roanoke, Virginia, a story based on interviews I conducted with women who emigrated from Mexico. The text is sprinkled with Spanish, and the theme is integrated with Mexican culture, but I am bringing the protagonist to Roanoke, which sits on the edge of the area designated as Appalachia. No matter how I try to set up binaries and separate cultures, they always come out blended, just as happens in my construction of Self.

While working in Spain and Mexico, I have realized that "Appalachia" and "Appalachian" are meaningless outside our region. I explain that I live in the *Montes Apalaches,* and people smile and nod, but I can sense that means nothing to them in terms of the culture and emotion included in either word. Even people who live in the United States, but not in Appalachia, pronounce the word as "Appa-LAY-shuh" instead of "Appa-LATCH-uh," letting every Appalachian know they are not part of the culture.

So what is Appalachian, and what does it mean to be Appalachian? The Appalachian Regional Commission (ARC) defines Appalachia as including "all of West Virginia and parts of Alabama, Georgia, Kentucky, Maryland, Mississippi, New York, North Carolina, Ohio, Pennsylvania, South Carolina, Tennessee, and Virginia . . . home to more than 25 million people . . . [covering] almost 205,000 square miles" (https://www.arc.gov/).

As an agency of the federal government, the information on the webpage focuses on a changing economy, due to the decline of coal mining, the forestry industry, and chemical factories, and the resultant rising poverty level. None of this encompasses what it means to be Appalachian.

Another webpage is from the Urban Appalachian Council (http://www.uacvoice.org/) in Cincinnati, Ohio. Sharing a border with West Virginia, Cincinnati is a city to which many people migrated following World War II in search of employment. The UAC asks, "How do you know if you're Appalachian?" They suggest criteria including Scots, Irish, English, and Welsh heritage, from some of North America's earliest non-Native American settlers. They characterize

Appalachians as independent, with an "intense desire for freedom," which describes my family. They also talk about a group of people who "kept outsiders out and insiders in," also descriptive of my family. The webpage talks about people who "brought their traditions, values, and beliefs with them" when they settled the region, although they also declined to belong to institutions, religious or otherwise. There's my family again. But it's not only my family. All of these characteristics describe me as well. Puzzle pieces start to fall into place as I realize that the culture and customs of the Appalachian Mountains must run deep in my veins. The UAC states that it's "important for people to know their roots, to pass their heritage on to their children, to celebrate in ways that are their own."

Roots! That's what I seek – a sense of belonging.

I receive an email update from Ancestry.com telling me that a new feature, Genetic Communities, is available, so I click to "learn more." I open the page, and find that I belong to one Genetic Community: Settlers of Southern West Virginia, where I have my roots. A sense of belonging and familiarity come over me. I start receiving emails from people who tell me we are a DNA match, and I share this information with Dan.

"It's not about blood or DNA," I tell him. "It's about connections and understanding how I fit into the world I live in. I can feel a connection to Mexico and Spain, and to Spanish-speaking people, but I doubt it is related to my possible 5 percent Iberian Peninsula DNA. I can feel nostalgia for the lost Cherokee heritage I never had, but who knows, maybe I do have it, and there is just no established database. But knowing I am Appalachian explains a lot about why I am who I am, and why I believe what I do, and why I behave the way I do."

I think a minute.

"You know, your birthday is in just over a week. I'm going to give you a DNA test. Now that you're retired, you can start searching for your connections."

Dan looks at me. "I'd rather have a computer," he states. But I can tell he's interested.

I go upstairs to write at the desk overlooking the mountains that surround us, the Blue Ridge of the Appalachian Mountains. I feel peace. I feel home. I conclude that my sense of Self has been constructed by all the experiences I have had, the books I have read, the places I have visited, the family that has loved me, the friends who have spent time with me, the sunsets I have watched, the oceans I have waded in, and the list goes on. Depending on which way I turn the prism, and how the light enters, I am the embodiment of all that went before on the path that has become my life, regardless of my DNA results.

My roots are as tangled as my hair.

References

Ancestry DNA. https://www.ancestry.com/

Appalachian Regional Commission. https://www.arc.gov/index.asp

Bochner, A., & Ellis, C. (2016). *Evocative autoethnography: Writing lives and telling stories.* New York: Routledge.

Ellis, C. (2004). *The ethnographic I: A methodological novel about autoethnography.* Walnut Creek, CA: AltaMira Press.

Jago, B. J. (1996). Postcards, ghosts, and fathers: Revising family stories. *Qualitative Inquiry, 2*(4), 495–516.

Race: The power of an illusion. Public Broadcasting System. http://www.pbs.org/race/000_General/000_00-Home.htm

Richardson, L. & St. Pierre, E. A. (2005). Writing: A method of inquiry. In N. K. Denzin & Y. S. Lincoln (Eds.), *The Sage handbook of qualitative research* (3rd ed.), pp. 959–978. Thousand Oaks, CA: Sage.

Smith, L. (2016). *Dimestore: A writer's life.* Chapel Hill, NC: Algonquin Books.

Tilley-Lubbs, G. A. (2017). *Re-assembly required: Critical autoethnography and spiritual discovery.* New York: Peter Lang.

Tilley-Lubbs, G. A. (2016a). Reconciliar dos naturalezas en el mismo cuerpo. *Revista CES Psicología, 9*(1).

Tilley-Lubbs, G. A. (2016b). Reconciling two selves in the same body. In Tilley-Lubbs, G. A., & Bénard Calva, S. (Eds.). *Retelling our stories: Critical autoethnographic narratives,* pp. 245–258. Boston, MA: Sense.

Tilley-Lubbs, G. A. (2011). The coal miner's daughter gets a Ph.D. *Qualitative Inquiry, 17*(9). doi: 10.1177/1077800411420669

United States Census Bureau. https://www.census.gov/

Urban Appalachian Council. http://uacvoice.org/

Wildman, S. M. & Davis, A. D. (2000). Language and silence: Making systems of privilege visible. In M. Adams, W. J. Blumenfeld, R. Castañeda, H. W. Hackman, M. L. Peters, & X. Zúñiga (Eds.), *Readings for social diversity and social justice: An anthology on racism, anti-Semitism, sexism, heterosexism, ableism, and classism,* (pp. 50–60). New York: Routledge.

15

WHOSE STORY IS IT ANYWAY?

Reflecting on a collaborative research project with/in an educational community

Greg Vass, Michelle Bishop, Katherine Thompson, Pauline Beller, Calita Murray, Jane Tovey and Maxine Ryan

SCHOOL OF EDUCATION, UNSW SYDNEY

In this chapter, we present a collection of short vignettes about the *Culture, Community and Curriculum Project*. This is an action research study that is designed to establish and support collaborations between people from the local Aboriginal community and classroom teachers. The stories from the various contributors serve to illustrate that our personal histories and current location within the project result in seeing and thinking about the study that differ in thought-provoking ways. Central to the concerns underpinning this chapter then, are questions about what sorts of stories can and should be told about the project. As such, rather than attempting to bring these differences together to offer a cohesive account, or to compare them in potentially problematic ways, the approach to co-constructing the chapter has adopted 'refusal' as an analytic practice. In this way, we hope to highlight how and why it is worth pursuing efforts that interrupt dominant knowledge-making practices.

About the authors

Michelle is a *Gamilaroi* woman, with family connections to Western New South Wales and kin connections all over. She grew up and lives on the lands of the Dharawal Peoples. After starting out as a primary school teacher, she spent five years coordinating a state-wide academic enrichment program for Indigenous high school students. Wanting to find ways to disrupt dominant discourses for the benefit of all students, and in particular, for Indigenous students, she joined the Culture, Community and Curriculum Project (CCCP) research team because it seemed to have integrity in what it is trying to achieve and how it is going about this.

168 Greg Vass et al.

Pauline is an Aboriginal Education Officer (AEO) and is currently President of the local Aboriginal Education Consultative Group (AECG). She left school in Year 10 to work because she hated school, but eventually got involved in education. Having completed her qualifications and worked in other childcare settings, she started volunteering at her children's schools. Pauline has worked in most of the public schools in the area to support the Koori kids in the local community. She wants them to be able to go somewhere in life, feel like they're someone, and know that they are capable of doing things, in ways she was never made to feel at school.

Katherine is the coordinator of a partnership between the university and the local learning community, the UNSW Matraville Education Partnership (MEP). While occupying a non-academic position, her role in the processes of building this partnership and facilitating the activities is considerable and often high-stakes. Usually the first point of contact, Katherine has for several years been cultivating relationships to try to build mutual trust and understanding. The blurring of the personal and the professional are challenging in this sense, as she may 'represent' the university, but many of the relationships have become quite personal. Once a high school teacher, she is a white, queer woman from the American South.

Jane was born in England and has lived in Australia for 40 years. She is 47 and has two children. She has been a primary school teacher for 21 years and has advised schools as a behavioural consultant in primary, secondary and juvenile rehabilitation settings in the UK as a part of her practice. She has been involved in Aboriginal Education at a school and district level, and lectures for *Yarn Up Aboriginal Public Speaking for Primary Schools*, working with the Aboriginal Education Team in Arncliffe.

Calita is an AEO in a local primary school, and a member of the AECG. Originally from the south coast of New South Wales, she never really liked school, so now finds it ironic that she works in one. In school, she didn't have a voice and was not allowed to learn about Aboriginal culture. A bad experience with a teacher in year 9 was the end of high school for her. While not initially introducing her children to books because 'our stories' are told orally, she started volunteering as a reading mum in school when they were young, and eventually ended up working in schools to promote the importance of education in her community.

Greg is an education researcher, and hence is involved with the formal dimensions of the study, which sit uncomfortably, as he feels like more of a learner. White and in his forties, involvement in Indigenous education initially arose from his experiences as a History high school teacher concerned with race-based discrimination. His formative years were spent on the lands of the Quandamooka Peoples in Queensland. He now lives and works in the Eastern suburbs of Sydney as a lecturer of initial teacher education.

Aunty Maxine is a well-respected Aboriginal Elder from the La Perouse community of Botany Bay, New South Wales. She belongs to the Dharawal People. She has spent many years working in education and health settings and is an accomplished artist.

Foreword: A note on positioning

Cultural protocols for many First Nations Peoples entail exchanging details about connections to places and people, with the practice becoming more recognised and accepted in locations such as Australia. Taking this up here, we would like to acknowledge that the research connected with this chapter is/was undertaken on Aboriginal Country, on the lands of the *Bidjigal* Peoples, with inequities and injustices impacting on Indigenous communities as central to the reasons for the study.[1] The *Culture, Community, and Curriculum Project (CCCP)* is financially supported by a philanthropic not-for-profit organisation, and is designed as a collaboration that is reliant on the efforts and energies of members of the local community, teachers and school leaders, and those from the research team. The chapter draws on the voices of people involved in the project, all of whom come into the research from different trajectories, are participating in ways that differ significantly, and as such all experience and negotiate varying obligations, accountabilities and expectations in connection with our contribution and ownership of the study. Given that the study is framed and reliant on these collaborative relationships, there are ethical and methodological reasons for finding ways that enable a range of voices involved in the project to contribute to written representations of what has transpired. But what stories should be told? Why? And whose stories are they really? It is our aspiration in this chapter to reflect on these lines of questioning.

The chapter is organised to move in and out of a collection of vignettes that have been written by each of the contributors. This is, then, more akin to what Bessarab and Ng'andu (2010) might refer to as 'collaborative yarning' in research, which can be more focused as it is set up to explore concepts, bounce ideas around, and work towards new or different ways of shared understanding. However, it should be noted that this is, of course, not a genuine yarn as we did not literally sit together as a group for the purposes of writing, hence the decision-making connected with the micro-practices of collaborative writing are fraught in the context of this sort of discussion. What does it even mean to write collaboratively, particularly when some of the stories were constructed in isolation? How do you ensure everybody's voice is equally heard? Then there are issues with the collective pronoun, raising questions about the possibilities of the assembled 'we' that Holman Jones (2017) brings to mind; if 'we' is accepted as a speech act that is performative more than descriptive, what does 'we' *really* do and mean in this chapter?

In terms of how we approached constructing this text, each of the authors was asked to contribute a short story that provides the reader with a snapshot of their perspective on an event or experience in connection with the CCCP. While this has been loosely coordinated by the research team, there was minimal advice in terms of what to focus on or why. And, while Greg attempted to encourage focusing on just one encounter or 'moment' in time, this has been interpreted in various ways. This is, perhaps, quite telling in itself. This chapter raises further questions; what are the possibilities of telling different sorts of research stories, what should they look like, and who is the writing for?

170 Greg Vass et al.

Michelle's story

It had been years since I had entered the grounds of a primary school. So distinct from the concrete high schools I had been visiting across NSW, Victoria and Queensland for the past five years; here the walls burst colour. Yet, a deep sadness and despair creeps in, as it always does, when I find the entry point through the tall, ominous gates, the sign reading 'Close the gate for the safety of our children'. Hmmm . . . 'there's too much going on in my head with this sign, too much to unpack regarding how Aboriginal people may interpret this'. Schools have gained such significant status in their Protector role, and we are all implicated in enforcing this. I sigh, thinking how every day we lock 'our' young people up.

Here was a space I was familiar with, the front office. These nooks are the same in schools all over. Always with plaques boasting the names of past captains. The same glass divide. The same low, vinyl seats. The same framed 'Sorry' speech. It was my first meeting with some of the schools involved in the Project.

I had joined the research team a month prior and I felt nervous. I'd never been a 'researcher' before, what does that even mean? I reflected on what I perceived my role to be: a liaison with the community members; someone to hold the process to account; an Aboriginal person to automatically add 'creditability' to the research? The insecurities plague me and I'm reminded of being told I was a targeted graduate and would start my primary teaching career in a permanent position. That fear that everyone would look at me thinking, 'she only got the job because she's Aboriginal', followed immediately by, 'she doesn't even look Aboriginal'. Even if this wasn't the case in this job, even if I got the job on 'merit', I still perceive these thoughts to be happening in people's heads, I still embody the feeling that I'll never be good enough. I know where that comes from. I know the political and social rhetoric that has contributed to this feeling. Yet, I can't help but wonder whether I'm just the person hired to meet targets. I push those fears aside and give myself a talking to. Not just me; mum's voice, nan's, aunties and uncles all give me a talking to. You got this. *I think about the conversations I've had as part of the Project already. Introducing myself to community members and starting to set things up for the first workshops. It's going good. They are keen to get into schools.*

We were shown into the stuffy meeting room, the first to arrive, and sat down awaiting the arrival of the teachers and principals. It felt strange that the community members weren't involved in this meeting. It reminded me of all those times I had gone to school meetings and the student was asked to sit outside and wait while I was 'caught up' by the teacher or executive. How disrespectful this felt and how I would always advocate for the student to be in the room, to be part of the discussions that involved them and their future, to be better informed to make decisions by being part of the conversation – all of it. Why weren't the community members here? If part of their motivation for participating in the Project was based on an expectation to have shared power in planning and teaching a unit of work, what does this mean if they are not involved in the initial decisions being made about the structure of the Project? Are we kidding ourselves to think that power can really be shared? I had made my concerns known to the research team, but we were all in a tricky situation, trying to get this off the ground. To do this, we needed the schools. And schools are accustomed to dictating the terms.

The possibilities of coming to write collaborative autoethnography

> Today science stands at a crossroads. It has achieved an exalted status not radically different from other priesthoods of the past and, like all priesthoods, it is now subject to erosion and disgrace unless it finds a way to share its function with society and produce a qualitatively different society in the process.
>
> *(Deloria, 1980, p. 271)*

> Nothing is stranger than this business of humans observing other humans in order to write about them.
>
> *(Behar, 1996, p. 5)*

> While other research modes and practices are rightly and very capably interested in describing the world (a collective), our scholarship is – and should be – invested in gathering people together to create an us: one that brings about a plurality that is invested in one another.
>
> *(Holman Jones, 2017, p. 131)*

The opening vignette from Michelle steps us through the school gates, an account that speaks to the violence experienced by many Aboriginal learners, also gesturing then to the concerns underpinning the study. Concurrently, she raises questions about the equally violent contribution of research as a technology of (settler) colonialism that powerfully influences knowledge-producing practices (cf. Deloria, 1980; Nakata, 2007; Smith, 2012; Tuck & Yang, 2014). It is no understatement to note that the science-ing of knowledges about people has a problematic history that the various disciplines of the social sciences are yet to fully atone for. The use of 'science' as a verb is purposeful; it is an invitation to think about the practices that make 'scientific' knowledge, a thoroughly human undertaking, as an outcome with all of the fallibility and inconsistencies that remains concomitant with most human endeavours. In contexts where the process involves one group producing knowledge about a different group, particularly when there is an imbalance of power between the groups, there are well-established grounds for even further concerns to be raised. An example of this would be the all too familiar model of the White, English-speaking, often male researcher involved in studies that produce knowledge 'about' Indigenous peoples. The effects of this legacy have provoked reactions such as the oft-quoted comment from Smith (2012) regarding *research* being 'one of the dirtiest words' from the perspective of many Indigenous peoples, a succinct and pithy reminder of why it is objectionable to be turned into the object of research (also see Deloria, 1980).

The opening quote from Deloria (1980) draws attention to a prescient and foreboding warning regarding research and the work of researchers, and while not responding to him per se, the sorts of concerns he addresses were genuinely taken up by many. It is not our intention here to rehearse the debates that underpin one

172 Greg Vass et al.

such thread, the 'crisis of representation' of the 1980s–90s, as the various academic disciplines sought ways forward with somehow accounting for their problematic legacies, while also seeking to establish future trajectories for research practices. Illustrative of these efforts, however, in the case of Ellis (1995), are her experiences of returning to the site of earlier fieldwork in a fishing community. It became a highly emotional experience that provoked her questioning of research ethics, methodologies, and ultimately the ongoing relationship and responsibilities that researchers must address with care. It was these sorts of experiences that foregrounded her later efforts to establish autoethnography as an approach to sociological research that helps mitigate some of these concerns. In essence, this is a response that aimed to start taking seriously the responsibilities that come with conceding that the ethnographer's self 'cannot not be present' and there is 'no objective space' outside the practices of researching (Denzin, 2014, p. 26).

Moving in a similar direction, the opening quote from Behar gestures to the sort of introspection and self-reflection that anthropologists were asking of themselves. In *The Vulnerable Observer,* Behar (1996) also questions and challenges the traditional and dominant set of ideas and practices that underpin research. Namely, that the research process should entail the sort of objectivity that enables the researcher to not only observe, document and analyse in ways that account for bias and assumptions, but that the account of this should also reflect a level of detached distance that instils trust and confidence that rigorous, systematic, and, in some instances, repeatable, practices have been adhered to. In working towards interrupting this dominant approach to social science research, Behar (1996, p. 28) was seeking ways to bring the personal into the work we do, part of a broader fundamental shift away from viewing and trying to understand *difference* as a cornerstone of knowledge production, to instead focus on *identification* – in other words, what happens when we identify *with* the people involved in 'our' research?

This rethink about the subject and subjectivity in research emerged as an approach that sought to elaborate on and emphasise the relational dimensions of these practices. In particular, for Behar (1996), were concerns regarding the import of more effort and attention being directed towards fostering humanising encounters and representations in and of the field, and from this, with addressing the vulnerability of both the observed and the observer. The other quote that opens this section, from Holman Jones (2017), hints at the possibilities and trajectories researchers have subsequently pursued with their efforts in support of justice and ethics in work that is always (and already) political. This often entails a sense of 'precarity' that requires taking risks and getting outside of comfort zones (ibid., p. 134), something we are attempting here and connects well with the following vignettes that remind us of the blurriness of and (almost) irrelevance of traditional binary roles in the CCCP.

Pauline's story

Aunty Maxine has a close bond with the children, and the kids more or less fight over what class she's gonna go into, and they're always asking her for stuff and wanting to come into her

*class. And this is ALL of the students – even the non-Aboriginal students come up, saying
'Aunty Maxine, Aunty Maxine! Are you in our class?'*

*I was sitting in Jane's class when they were talking about the community, and the old
boatshed and that before it all blew over, and the kids were just amazed, like just to see the
expression on their faces was amazing. And they all sit there quiet, and they all listen, and
they all wanna ask a hundred questions. I think that's because of a bit of everything – it's
local knowledge, it's the relationship with Aunty Maxine, most of them have been out there,
and she's showing photos of what it looked like and how it looks today, and to a kid it's like,
wow, they just can't believe that it happened.*

*And the teachers too – it's good for them to get a bit of knowledge. You know how teach-
ers are, you don't have time, you've gotta do your structured thing, but then Aunty Maxine
takes over the class and the teacher is even asking questions. It's even having an effect on prac
teachers – like last week, a prac student got up and did a lesson on the Aboriginal flag and
the Australian flag, and videos of Aboriginal people speaking about the flag and stuff, and
the supervising teacher said, 'I didn't realise – I just never knew that. I'm really starting to
understand now.'*

Katherine's story

*It is impossible to see your whole self. In the mirror, looking down at your body – there are
parts of our own bodies that we may never see. I think about this when I think about culture.
How hard it is to examine your own culture from within the echo-chamber of itself. I grew
up digging arrowheads out of the creekbed on my parents' property, 120 acres of woodland
in rural Georgia. That land, undoubtedly, remembers its first custodians, remembers being
cleared and possibly farmed by enslaved persons, remembers being passed and passed and
passed through generations of white hands. I thought a lot about black-and-white race relations in America while I was growing up, but I never thought about colonisation. I was
simply never called upon to do so.*

*In Australia, schools open assemblies with Acknowledgements of Country. They fly
Aboriginal and Torres Strait Islander flags next to the Union Jack and Southern Cross.
They sport bush tucker gardens in their shady corners and Rainbow Serpent murals across
their concrete playgrounds. Policy documents task teachers with incorporating Indigenous
Perspectives into their lessons and reward schools for improving the outcomes of Aboriginal
students.*

*But still we face resistance when asking schools to embrace Aboriginal community mem-
bers joining classrooms on equal footing with teachers. We hear responses about time and
money and priorities. How much of each can be spent on 'Aboriginal programs'. There is
the syllabus to cover; there are colleagues to plan with, 'and we already do so much'. There
is some measure of goodwill, but its terms, though unspoken, are clear. As long as it runs
smoothly. As long as we don't have to do anything extra. As long as it doesn't cost anything.
As long as we can still get through the 'real' syllabus. As long as parents are happy. As
long as there's still time to prepare the kids for NAPLAN (the annual national literacy and
numeracy assessment). As long as we can feature it at the AECG meetings. It seems ironic.
The Aboriginal workers are the first to point out, with excitement and animation, the positive*

174 Greg Vass et al.

effects they see in the non-Aboriginal kids. How engaged they are, how excited, how eager to embrace Aboriginal culture, Aboriginal people. Some of the school staff though, seem to see only the effects on the Aboriginal kids, and never quite relax their grip to see the program as important for all students.

Jane's story

When the CCCP was announced at a staff meeting we were asked to register our interest to be involved. The details were sketchy, Aboriginal Perspectives were mentioned, so out of curiosity I put my hand up thinking, 'Another pair of hands could be helpful in the class-room.' Later, after meeting the community members and the research team, the 'Other pair of hands' contribution still seemed vague and unclear. I felt nervous as now I had agreed to participate in a project with no clear description of the roles and responsibilities of the community members.

The teachers and community members were put together in a planning session and I found myself being so uncomfortable thinking 'How am I supposed to put an Aboriginal perspective in every lesson?' and 'How can I not offend Aunty if I do not agree with her?' At the time, I was looking at the experience like one long Aboriginal lesson that I could tick off in my lesson sequence. I was so busy thinking about my own box-ticking prior to the experience that I was getting lost in my role of making it fit into my planning . . . What outcomes could be met? How could this be assessed? Is it going to be too Aboriginal in content? What if I can't handle the students' curiosity and it all becomes uncomfortable for everyone . . . well, me mostly.

Aunty Maxine and I agreed on a unit of work based on cooking, and during the first lesson I treated her as if she were a guest speaker. Aunty took the floor sharing narratives, connecting the students through mutual people they had in common. I was so overly polite that I thought I would explode. I let the students talk to her when-and-while she was talk-ing; to respect their obvious familiarity and ease (a relationship that was foreign to me). The students would gently and informally interrupt Aunty and she acknowledged every child with their questions and curiosity. I struggled to not control the whole room with my rigid 'hand up to speak' policy and thought how am I going to do this for 10 weeks?

As we started to plan and share what we observed about the students, I released my role as 'The Class Teacher' . . . it was too hard to maintain. I told myself to be a student, to let go and see what is going on here; the authentic relationships, no power struggles, no ultimatums, just instruction, guidance, and connecting though relationships.

As I allowed myself to be a student, Aunty's student, I learnt more than how to cook Johnny Cakes. I learnt how to listen to a personal history that I had been afraid to hear. I learnt about how an oppressed community felt, something that was never referenced in my own personal schooling. I learnt about how the environment can be read. I learnt about rela-tionships that were unconditional in both love and mourning. I learnt and learnt and learnt and I relocated my version of Aboriginal Perspectives away with the tokenistic box-ticking lesson plans.

I listened to the hushed 1970s version of Aboriginal history in myself. It was so quiet that it nearly didn't exist. I listened for the replicated themes that I had stenciled into my students' reality over the years, the intentional and unintentional teaching. The CCCP still does not have an adequate role and job description . . . I am not sure if it ever will!

Many voices

While the CCCP is designed broadly as a collaborative action research project in which the community members and teachers were framed as knowledge producers, there are a range of practical and ethical challenges to negotiate when trying to genuinely establish conditions for social change (Cahill, 2007). In essence, however, all involved with the project are viewed as co-researchers rather than participants, albeit contributing in very different ways depending on their location and role. Discussing the complexities of this as an overarching approach is beyond the scope of this chapter; however, some of our concerns do resonate through what we are trying to grapple with here – the methodological implications that impact on comfortably and fairly representing the story of our project. Despite this, our approach does fit well with Gobo and Marciniak's (2016) observation that there is growing attention being given to participatory, collaborative and critical qualitative studies. Central to many of these endeavours are efforts to undertake research 'through the consistent inclusion and participation of those being studied, local and native [sic] to the social setting' (p. 111). A further common feature in these projects is the 'ideologically driven' framing that aims to address 'inequalities and injustices' (ibid.). Collaboration can't just be something done 'in the field'; it has to extend beyond (Canagarajah & Stanley, 2015).

Also, picking up on this line of work, Ellis and colleagues (2011, p. 279) outline the developing profile of 'community autoethnographies' and 'co-constructed narratives', which also have relational dynamics and action as central elements of the research practices involved. As they note, this now also extends to efforts that include the reactions, responses or involvement of community members with constructing written accounts (Ellis *et al.*, 2011, p. 281). While agreeing with many of the difficulties touched on by Chang (2013) when discussing this sort of methodology, we also find much to merit in pursuing these efforts. The following story is a good illustration of this.

Calita's story

When we first started the project, one of the teachers was really anxious about it. She'd say, 'But I'm frightened of doing the wrong thing. What if I get it wrong?' And I'd say, it's okay if you make a mistake, you're only human, just so long as you learn from your mistakes. The teacher was anxious and worried about where this was going to lead, because she couldn't see the end goal, or how it would look. She was looking at it through Western education system eyes and not looking at it as just a journey with an Aboriginal person. Within the Western system, she's used to things needing to be really formal and structured. She needed to plan for her lessons and she needed to show results, gather data, make sure that she'd achieved what she's expected to do as a teacher, but she didn't understand that she could still achieve those

176 Greg Vass et al.

results using Aboriginal ways and processes. In the end, she started to come around and see the value, but it wasn't until further along on that journey that she could see it.

It was beautiful to watch the journey of one young Aboriginal student in that teacher's class. She had really struggled fitting into the Western education system, particularly with writing and literacy. For her to learn from an Aboriginal person, through oral interpretation of stories, built her confidence – it tapped into a talent for her, where she had always struggled before. She felt okay to take risks, and if she failed, she didn't feel as shamed. And at the end of the day, it actually complemented her skills and built on her learning style, because she connected a lot more with these stories and then felt comfortable to write two whole pages, as opposed to only two sentences like she might have done before. She didn't have that connection with other stories, books, the literacy activities she had been given before. So, the learning she accomplished helped her feel success in all the other learning.

If a school tried to do this kind of project by themselves, it wouldn't happen. It'd be so easy to use stumbling blocks as an excuse to give up, if the community member doesn't show up when they're supposed to or if the work in the classroom is challenging their way or their style of teaching. And a lot of people do not value Aboriginal culture the way they should. They expect Aboriginal people to come in and share their knowledge and skills for nothing, when they've got 40,000 years of knowledge that's been passed down. That's gotta be worth something – even in Western terms.

Listening to the stories

In many ways, the sentiments expressed by Calita could only have been framed from her (Aboriginal) standpoint. This is not to claim that the project is attempting to 'give voice' to the community, rather, it is to suggest that her trajectory into education, her current location and connection with the project, and her rhythm of communication are framed here in ways that could not have been (re)produced by anyone else. In other words, there is a power and authority that these narratives speak from and to that is independent of formal research practices, and that raises a bigger question: does the academic and broader community genuinely listen? In this sense, the vignettes are working from the sort of perspective put forward by Nakata (2007) when he explained that this approach accepts the lived experiences of people and provides a location and perspective from which to construct distinct knowledges of the world. Moreover, this offers much more than a perspective from the 'periphery', it is an 'Indigenous standpoint' that demonstrates reflexive and analytical awareness of experience, social location, and discursive practices (Nakata, 2007).

However, documenting or representing the project in some form is expected in addition to being a funding requirement. This is of course a key touchstone of 'research'; what is it that we are doing, if we don't write it up in some way and share it? As Greg began to think more seriously about how to approach communicating something about the CCCP, some of the questions and concerns raised across this chapter quickly came to the fore: which parts of the project should be focused on and shared, why, with whom, and what form/s should the representation take? Additionally, there was the line of thinking that from the outset the CCCP was conceptualised as something that was working towards a sense of shared ownership, not only with what was being undertaken in practical terms, but also, importantly, in regards to the knowledge/s being constructed. In this sense, the study was designed so that the participating teachers and community members were research collaborators, rather than objects of research. An event almost a year into the project still serves as a provocative reminder for Greg regarding the complexities of negotiating the interests and requirements of the numerous stakeholders connected with the project, which at times appear almost contradictory and competing with one another.

Greg's story

The hand of the man grasped my own, and as we exchanged introductions, the name was just as quickly gone. He was somebody from the university, carrying himself with a disposition that communicated a position of some status. I wasn't entirely sure of the department that he came from, but he moved on to chat with another senior member of the Faculty with a familiarity that confirmed my assumption. I wasn't entirely sure why they were here, but that was less important in the moment. The meeting was with the philanthropic organisation that was helping to fund the Project, and I was told it was a bit of a big deal that the CEO had made time in his busy schedule to come and meet with us. It was his interest in the 'grass-roots' nature of the study that he wanted to hear about first-hand, and in particular he wanted to be able to meet and hear from some of the local community members that were involved. So, two of the Aunties had kindly agreed to make time in their week to come in and chat with the people that were helping to put them in classrooms – to improve the learning experiences of Aboriginal children in the local area, and to localise the teaching of Aboriginal histories, knowledges and perspectives for all students.

There was a degree of anxiety that I suspect most of us in the research team were experiencing as we prepared for the meeting. It felt high-stakes. We only had an hour, the project was already behind in terms of the original timeline . . . and we were hoping to ask for a little additional funding. What did the CEO and his team really want to hear about? They could read about how the project was travelling in the short brief that had been written, so there was not much point in reproducing that information. Despite this, we put together a short presentation that touched on some of the key issues, including some quotes from participants and a few images to try and bring the Project to life. As it turned out though, I didn't even end up going past the first slide.

Following the introductions that went around the table, the Aunties were invited to start talking, and talk they did. Their stories about experiences of growing up in Australia across the twentieth century started filling the room. Moving back and forth across time and space, those listening were called on to reflect on the experiences of exclusion that the Aunties' parents' generation encountered, their own experiences of marginalisation and assimilatory violence, the hostility and disregard they later witnessed as workers in educational settings, the frustrations and concerns they felt as parents of children in the education system, and more recently the disappointment and despair they were unavoidably caught up in as grandparents

178 Greg Vass et al.

and older members of the local community. But they also spoke of looking forward, of hope, of aspirations . . . this is where they saw the potential of the CCCP . . . and their moving and confronting stories made it clear, to me at least, that this is why they were involved and had agreed to come along to chat on the day.

Drawing towards a conclusion, but refusing to draw conclusions

On the surface, the collection of vignettes across the chapter raises questions regarding the proximity of orbit to the university, in comparison to the lived experiences of being in and from the community, as potentially influencing the sorts of stories we are drawn to and how they are framed. If this seems a reasonable supposition, how do we account for the community members having a seemingly more positive and encouraging outlook? While this is affirming and rewarding in lots of ways, does it tell the whole story? Conversely, do the somewhat more critical concerns about power and authority raised by the university-based contributions, warrant being emphasised? To do so would seem to offer an equally problematic account, albeit for different reasons. We are left to consider that it is not entirely appropriate or helpful, in starting to draw this chapter to a close, to offer an account that attempts to legitimate or discredit any particular view.

Shared across the vignettes are concerns with the ongoing presence and effects of settler-colonialism, identity politics, and (questionable) efforts to interrupt dominant schooling (and/or research) practices. To discuss these would potentially reproduce yet another familiar narrative of binary relationships that negatively pathologises or unhelpfully romanticises issues, people and practices. As such, we have decided that there will be no recognisable analysis in the conventional sense of the term. This is a decision and act in the spirit evoked by Tuck and Yang (2014) when suggesting there are sound ethical and political reasons for adopting 'refusal as an analytic practice'. This is a research practice of resistance that works to avoid making someone or something a subject/object of the researcher's gaze, an approach that must 'precede, exceed, and intercede upon settler colonial knowledge production' (p. 812). As Tuck and Yang (2014, p. 814) encourage, this is more than simply refusal as saying no to traditional analysis, but rather it is a performative 'no'.

In adopting this sort of approach, in addition to the earlier story, Calita helped our thinking with a metaphor comparing differing approaches to teaching. However, we feel it is equally pertinent when considering research practices and knowledge production. As she explains it:

> The way I see the Western style of teaching is a box. The Aboriginal style of teaching is a circle. You know, where everyone's equal, it's continuous, never ending. No corners. In the box, the Aboriginal kids are hiding in the corners, or being put into them. And in the circle, there's a place for everybody, the non-Aboriginal kids too. There's nowhere to hide. Everyone's at

one level. If we're asking the Aboriginal kids to exist in that box, we should also ask non-Aboriginal kids to join the circle.

While Calita is calling here for a change in how teaching is understood and undertaken, this sort of sentiment seems to resonate with Tuck's (2009, p. 55) call for researchers to find new 'vantage points', what she describes as epistemological shifts that can be conceptualised as the 'inner angles of a circle rather than the opposing angles of a square'. The vantage points she speaks of, then, are 'intimately bound' together within the circle, designed to foster a sense of concomitantly engaging with and holding the complexities and interconnections within the space/s. Part of Tuck's (2009, p. 49) motivation for thinking her way through this was her growing realisation that dominant – Western – theories of change were inadequate, indeed that there is a 'paradox of reform versus revolution' that all too often permeates action research such as the CCCP. To help address these shortcomings, she outlines four vantage points; sovereignty, contention, balance, and relationships – vantage points that help us to reconsider what 'change' may mean and the courses of action that are pursued, and hence what the 'role of research can be' (Tuck, 2009, p. 64). We will finish this chapter with one final vignette that in many ways speaks from these vantage points. It is from Aunty Maxine, who championed and, in many respects, has led key elements of the project as it has unfolded across a number of the participating schools.

Aunty Maxine's story

The Elders that have passed away that were really into education would be over the moon about this (Project). This was something that they kept pushing, pushing, pushing for years but no-one was listening. It's a shame that a good handful have passed away, they were right into education and going into schools, volunteering, and putting Aboriginal stuff in schools, but no-one was listening, not like today. We're finally having a say. We're all here as one, and that's really important because these Elders that have passed away, they were the first push, so maybe they made us push, and maybe that's what it was all about, keep pushing, pushing, pushing till someone listens. This is what it's all about, education today. Education about Aboriginal ways. Which need to come back.

When I first arrived, I found it was going a bit slow. Everybody was learning, but once we went into the schools and got on board with the staff, things changed. Because you can talk about things, but when you work more hands-on, things are different. Especially with me, I know I work different to the other workers, I'm a hands-on worker. Taking children out of the classroom environment helps them learn too, and all staff were supportive when I got into the schools and started talking to them about it. So that's what we try and do, we try and do lessons outside if the weather's good. And the children, they learn a lot. They learn about the environment, they learn about the land, they learn about plants. We take the children into the school garden and they learn and do gardening. That's what we need, because these children are our generation coming up to look after the land as we looked after the land. We survived for thousands of years, now we can all get together and survive it as one.

180 Greg Vass et al.

It's so good how the staff are willing to learn more and more. Because I'm not a science person and if the teacher wants science, that's a hard thing for me. So I'd say, just because I'm Aboriginal doesn't mean that I know all my science, geography, history, whatever. We can both sit down and look it up. I'd say, like a maths teacher knows maths, they're not going to come over to art and know art, so I try to explain about that so they understand. Because they gotta feel that: when you get an Aboriginal worker into your school doesn't mean that they know everything, because that pushes the Aboriginal worker back, away, 'oh can't go there, I don't know it'. Whereas this (Project) has taught some of the teachers and the staff that we all don't know everything, just like they don't know everything.

I'm so happy that somebody has come along to our community, because there's a lot of stories, there's a lot of culture. And no-one's ever done anything this big. They say you gotta start from the bottom; you teach the children from the bottom so they learn all the way to the top.

Note

1 Engaging in depth with the politics and contestations regarding the power to name and the impacts on and for the identities of people is beyond the scope of this paper. However, it is important to note that the terms Aboriginal (and Torres Strait Islander) and Indigenous are recent constructs that have been ascribed to people and communities, hence they are sites of debate and disagreement. It is instructive then, that contributors to this chapter have chosen to self-identify in ways beyond these terms, yet this concurrently remains constrained as a text with an international readership, and connected to a policy context in which more familiar and established names are known and knowable, and hence are also used in this text.

References

Behar, R. (1996). *The vulnerable observer: Anthropology that breaks your heart*. Boston, MA: Beacon Press.

Bessarab, D. & Ng'andu, B. (2010). Yarning about yarning as a legitimate method in Indigenous research. *International Journal of Critical Indigenous Studies*, 3(1), 37–50.

Cahill, C. (2007). Repositioning ethical commitments: Participatory action research as a relational praxis of social change. *ACME: An International E-journal for Critical Geographies*, 6(3), 360–373.

Canagarajah, A.S. & Stanley, P. (2015). Working with linguistic minority populations: Ethical considerations. In F. Hult and D.C. Johnson (Eds.) *Research methods in language policy and planning* (pp. 33–44). Hoboken, NJ: Wiley-Blackwell.

Chang, H. (2013). Individual and collaborative autoethnography as method: A social scientist's perspective. In Holman Jones, S., Adams, T. & Ellis, C. (Eds.), *Handbook of autoethnography*. London: Routledge.

Deloria, V. (1980). Our new research society: For social scientists. *Social Problems*, 27(3), 265–272.

Denzin, N. (2014). *Interpretive autoethnography* (2nd Ed). Thousand Oaks, CA: Sage.

Ellis, C. (1995). Emotional and ethical quagmires in returning to the field. *Journal of Contemporary Ethnography*, 24(1), 68–98.

Ellis, C., Adams, T. & Bochner, A. (2011). Autoethnography: An overview. *Historical Social Research*, 36(4), 273–290.

Gobo, D. & Marciniak, L. (2016). What is ethnography? In D. Silverman (Ed.). *Qualitative research* (4th Ed.) (pp. 103–120). London: Sage.

Holman Jones, S. (2017). Assembling a 'we' in critical qualitative inquiry. In N. Denzin & M. Giardina (Eds.), *Qualitative inquiry in neoliberal times* (pp. 130–135). New York: Routledge.

Nakata, M. (2007). The cultural interface. *The Australian Journal of Indigenous Education, 36,* 7–14.

Smith, L. T. (2012). *Decolonizing methodologies: Research and Indigenous peoples* (2nd Ed). London: Zed Books.

Tuck, E. (2009). Re-visioning action: Participatory action research and Indigenous theories of change. *Urban Review, 41,* 47–65.

Tuck, E. & Yang, W. (2014). Unbecoming claims: Pedagogies of refusal in qualitative research. *Qualitative Inquiry, 20*(6), 811–818.

16

SIX TALES OF A VISIT TO CHILE

An autoethnographic reflection on 'questions of culture'

Esther Fitzpatrick

FACULTY OF EDUCATION, UNIVERSITY OF AUCKLAND, AOTEAROA/NEW ZEALAND

'Six tales of a visit to Chile' is my personal response, after being invited to read the pre-publication manuscript of *Questions of Culture in Autoethnography*: this book. And as noted in Chapter 15, 'Nothing is stranger than this business of humans observing other humans in order to write about them' (Behar, 1996, p. 5). Like several authors in this book, this personal response seeks 'ways to bring the personal into the work we do, part of a broader fundamental shift away from viewing and trying to understand *difference* as a cornerstone of knowledge production, to instead focus on *identification*. In other words, what happens when we identify with the people involved in "our" research?' (Greg Vass, Michelle Bishop, Katharine Thompson, Pauline Bellar, Calita Murray Jane Tovey & Maxine Ryan). However, in this piece I also ask, what happens when we identify with the personal stories gathered, written, and shared in this book. I now invite you, the reader, to 'mull, to savour, and to put these singular tales [I am about to share] into a larger perspective' (Robert Rinehart).

Tale one

I felt like a grandma.

Not that feeling like a grandma is a bad thing. It's just that when you are not a grandma, and people look at you and act like you should be one, well, it puts you into a particular category; expectations of what you do, think about, and feel are buzzing in the air. I am not quite there yet, although my daughter does send me photos of her puppy.

I had been fortunate to receive a grant to attend the 'U21 emerging researchers' workshop' in Chile, 2017. Participants were all invited to attend a welcome evening before the workshop. When Phiona Stanley talks about 'small cultures', here I was, like her, disturbing the traditional discourse. However, in my case the discourse was what an 'emerging researcher' should look like. Was it a type of 'ageism', the way the young (absolutely wonderful) other attendees looked at me the first night over canapés and *pisco sours*? Fortunately, I found another couple of attendees, Greg Vass and Angel Chan, who were similarly somewhat removed from the 'young' category that some speakers had ascribed us with. We three found a corner of the large reception room and discussed . . . well nerdy stuff. Which is what we/I like to do.

Questioning culture. My whole life has been about questioning culture. Both the big and the small. For some reason, I was the child that always asked questions. Which, unfortunately, was quite embarrassing for my mother. The reason I was in Chile at an emerging researchers' workshop after finishing my PhD at such a late age, 53, was because of the intersectionality of big and small cultures. As Gabrielle Piggin describes the different positionalities and complex nexuses of power in her experiences as an 'outsider' in Japan, I can reflect on how my different identities shaped the trajectory my life took. Those expectations thrust on me, and that haunted my becoming: female, low socio-economic status, uneducated parents, White rural colonial ancestors, extremely religious. I was repeatedly told I was gifted with 'child-bearing hips' and should aim high in life: a typist or a farmer's wife. And one of the difficulties in this whole story is my absolute love for my family and wanting to not disappoint them. Disappoint I did, but thankfully I have also brought delight.

Tale two

My first morning in Santiago was full of fear and adventure. As I wandered out of the safety of the hotel lobby, alone, the city was still waking up. The ground was wet from the rains in the night and there were no cars on the road. Instead, the road was full of policeman with guns. Walking up and down, speaking into their walkie-talkies. I stood still for a moment, undecided. Should I return to the safety of my room? There were small groups of people with large orange banners/flags standing clumped together. Were they protestors of some sort? Was this a political rally? Had there been unrest in the night? Was I caught up in another revolution? My friends from Chile, in New Zealand, had warned me to stay safe. I stood there in all my white skin, with my blonde hair piled on top of my head and a handbag tightly arranged on my front, unable to decipher any of the Spanish language surrounding me in the airwaves and on the billboards. I wondered if I was being stupid or adventurous. I chose the latter answer and began walking down the road. A 'badass solo' adventurer (I think, hopefully, a little like Phiona), disrupting the expected 'gendered performance' of a vulnerable older woman, isolated by language.

Packs of street dogs were running up and down the road, sniffing at the policeman and the 'protestors', barking and circling around. Adventurous, that is what I was being. I pulled my handbag closer, like a shield, breathed in deep and crossed the road, heading toward Bellavista, the shopping area I had discovered

184 Esther Fitzpatrick

the previous night, where I was certain I could find a café to hide in. I never imagined it would be closed on a Sunday morning, the tall wrought-iron gates topped with spikes denied me entrance. Inside, I could see the guards patrolling the alleyways and plaza. A young girl with long legs and deep red lipstick sat on the stone steps near the entrance, she looked up at me and asked, '¿café?', pointing to the large wooden door at the top of the steps. 'Coffee?' I queried. 'Sí', she replied, and unlocked the door for me. I followed her up the dark wooden stairway, curving around into a large room. Was I about to be abducted? Gosh, I wasn't worth much. But the allure of coffee, as well as my need for a curiosity fix, kept me walking up those stairs. Ten minutes later, I was sitting outside in the sun on the balcony looking out over the empty plaza, sitting on plush blue cushions and drinking a cappuccino (closest to a Kiwi flat white I could find). I wrote in my notebook:

> Privilege shouts loudly this morning.
> Security guards walk and check.
> Bellavista waits
> Beautiful cafés, souvenir shops,
> Freshly washed tiles.
> I sit comfortably up here
> Above it all.
> Slowly awakening.
> I drink my coffee.

Gabrielle Piggin writes of the 'unmarked marker' of white skin and the knotty problematic of privilege. I mull over these words, in such moments as this. Surely it would be difficult to stay unaware that the experience I was having of Santiago was so different than others were experiencing outside the large wooden door, in that same moment. In this 'nimble' city, a fragmentary whole, existing through intra-action with the fast-flowing river (David Bright). I think of the man who had shouted at me and the whole world, from the rushing riverside as I crossed the bridge, his arms punching the air, a revolution of his own. The pacing guards, locked doors, bolted gates: these were designed to keep some out and invite others in. I recognised this, sitting with my cappuccino, feeling slightly guilty yet also relieved that I was being treated as Other.

In all my visits to Bellavista I never saw a dog. The rest of Santiago seemed to welcome them as an important part of their society, providing the street dogs with shelter, food, medicine and the occasional doggie jacket. These things I came to know later: the love of dogs, and the closing of the road on Sunday mornings so the public could ride their bikes, run, walk, skateboard – there was never a political protest or any unrest. It had all been part of my reimaging of culture (Gabrielle Piggin) from those stories I had been told. From my reading of, and subsequent making of the Apillera (Fitzpatrick & Bell, 2016), in a faraway world. From my friends who had lived in another Chile, in another time, and not as a visitor.

Tale three

I was sitting in my hotel room, putting the final tweaks on the PowerPoint slides for the keynote I was to give the following day at a preparation symposium for the *Contemporary Ethnography Across the Disciplines* conference, to be held in Santiago in 2018. I was thinking about coffee. Another U21 workshop participant sent an email to the group, inviting anyone else who had arrived early to join in a bit of sightseeing. I emailed back and asked if he wanted to wander down to Bellavista for coffee. This was how I ended up spending an afternoon exploring the local haunts with Ed, a Colombian now working at Edinburgh University. Darius Stonebanks writes about the dominant discourse he experiences of the dichotomy/binary of black and white. I suppose to onlookers at first glance, my new friend Ed and I may have recalled such a binary, and the binary of young and old, male and female. These binaries are so easily used to categorise, to make sense of the 'others' in our immediate environment. However, as Ed so expertly explained, his experience was much more complex. With his immediate family, he was known as the 'darker' skinned child, a throwback to some previous ancestor now lost in the mists of forgotten stories. And yet his research participants in Colombia described him as 'pale'. The illusion of a black/white binary persists in discourse. I laughingly told Ed that I too was a throwback to some Viking ancestor, that when looking at me, my phenotypical features denied my Jewish heritage. Was I in this moment, as described by Gresilda Tilley-Lubbs, attempting to claim a type of prestige the academic world grants to being a member of a diverse group? Was I trying to make myself less *white*?

Autoethnography provides a place to write about the complexity of identity and disrupt the illusion of homogeneity of particular groups of people, including for myself the imagined homogeneity of white people. I, too, belong to a family shaped by stories (Gresilda Tilley-Lubbs). O'Loughlin (2009) and Maddison-MacFadyen (2013) describe how we are all haunted by our pasts and in particular 'our childhood touchstone stories, those stories that live deeply within us and inform our perspectives of the world' (op. cit., p. 4). Maddison-MacFadyen argues that by analysing our touchstone stories, which often provide a colonial meta-narrative, we engage with counter stories as an act of decolonisation. Society reifies particular stories that work to perpetuate the standard story through acts of 'remembering'. Those 'touchstone' stories, the *whakapapa* (ancestors) of my mind, are complicated and inform my forever becoming (Fitzpatrick, 2017b). And as David Bright describes, calling upon Nietzsche, we are forever incapable of 'being', and forever 'becoming'.

The term *whakapapa* refers to the layered Māori genealogy that includes spiritual, mythological and human stories (Taonui, 2013), including actual ancestors. In his essay 'Ancestors of the mind: A *Pākehā whakapapa*', Traue illustrated his *Pākehā* identity through using the Māori concept of *whakapapa* and recited his own genealogy. Traue's *whakapapa* included his ontological ancestors and making reference to the many different ideas of ancient and modern-day writers and thinkers. Metge, inspired by Traue's essay, went further to add to her European

186 Esther Fitzpatrick

'ancestors of the mind' significant Māori, who had also shaped her ideas, beliefs and values (Metge, 2010).

David Fa'avae's definition of *Pākehā* disturbed me. Whilst describing the complexity of his 'edgewalking' between Tongan and New Zealand culture, he (like others before him) simply describes *Pākehā* as 'people of European descent living in *Aotearoa*'. Here, again, he perpetuates the illusion of *Pākehā* as a homogenous group. In contrast, my experience as a fifth-generation *Pākehā* is more like his story, of an ethnically and culturally diverse range of ancestors, who experienced struggle, and a 'complexity of relational ties across social, cultural, spiritual, political and biological dimensions' (David Fa'avae). *Pākehā*, too, experience 'edgewalking', the intersectionality of our different identities, and different hauntings. The process of assimilation, however, has been both enforced and invited over many generations, where the broad-brush-stroke (Harmony Siganporia) of whiteness has whitewashed the colourful stories of my ancestors (Fitzpatrick, 2017b). These are the things I seek to disrupt.

Tale four

I am walking back to the hotel with a workshop participant and I jokingly share the story of another participant being confused with the Madonna statue at the top of the hill, thinking it should have been Jesus. Another participant had informed her that Jesus was in Brazil, 'unless he was now a "cross dresser"', and the statue in Santiago was of Mary. 'My father would not like that', she had replied to my story, 'he is a Methodist minister'. We then shared our different backgrounds with religion and agreed that Christian values still informed how we live. Silvia Bérnard Calva tells us about her Mexican family being haunted by their 'Lutheran' heritage. Although living in Mexico, they lived as an extended family in a rambling property with a chocolate factory and a large garden. Reflecting on her life through auto-ethnography has enabled her to speak with ghosts to make sense of her complicated childhood.

Derrida (1994) insists that it is at the 'edge of life', not through living, but through interaction with 'other', and with death, that we might learn to live (p. xvii). To learn to live, he suggests: first, you require knowledge of the ghost and to know the place it occupies; second, what marks the name of the ghost or place it occupies; and, last, how the ghost works, or transforms (Derrida, 2006, p. 9). For that purpose we follow a ghost, where the 'future, comes back in advance: from the past, from the back' (p. 10). To then deconstruct our past we need to take into 'account historical entanglement' (p. 16) where, our past, our inheritance is not 'at one' with itself (p. 18). Rather, in summoning the ghost

> one must filter, sift, criticize, one must sort out several different possibles that inhabit the same injunction . . . [we must] choose and decide from among what [we] inherit.
>
> *(p. 18)*

Furthermore, likening the researcher to Shakespeare's Hamlet, Derrida contends we are obligated to summon the ghost to find justice 'for a fault, a fault of time and of the times' (p. 23). Derrida reminds us that:

> If [we] love . . . justice at least, the 'scholar' of the future, the 'intellectual' of tomorrow should learn it and from the ghost. [We] should learn to live by learning not how to make conversation with the ghost but how to talk with him, with her, how to let them speak or how to give them back speech.
>
> *(Derrida, 1994, p. 221)*

Similarly, Fetaui Iosefo refers to the importance of haunting and learning to speak with the ghosts. Significantly, in her work, she draws attention to non-Western notions of *hauntology*, and draws us into the process of decolonisation (Fitzpatrick, 2017a) through focusing our attention on the *different* ways our ancestors can speak 'with' us. For Fetaui, this is through the vehicle of a dream, further critiquing how the 'unseen of colonisation could have crazily constipated [us]'. My childhood touchstone stories are full of dreamers and dream readers. The Madonna at the top of the hill in Chile, stretching her arms into the icy mist, is a long way from the *Ringatū* prophets of the misty Urewera I grew up listening to, yet is a reminder of the power of such stories. Founded by the prophet Te Kooti, *Ringatū* is an Indigenous Māori religion that incorporates aspects of traditional Māori practice with the Old Testament, and is closely aligned with Judaism (Binney, 1997, 2010; Elsmore, 2000).

Tale five

It is the first day of the three-day workshop. I am to present a three-minute synopsis of my research, as several participants will also be doing. I have not slept. My work is very different, using arts-based methods and autoethnography, and I am a little concerned. The other participants are all very encouraging, and as I tend to do, I put on my 'brave' shoes (Fitzpatrick, 2016). What I do notice is that although we are in Chile, where the dominant language is Spanish, the workshop is conducted in English. Spanish speakers, and other non-native English speakers, are all expected to speak in English. As I read Hyejeong Ahn's experience of English language, I can't help but wonder why and who made this decision. How is it that English, in this Spanish-speaking university, is the language of power and prestige? Again, I feel my privilege: there is no need for me to translate, no issue of being confused inside this space. Again, I have had the large wooden door opened for me and have been guided carefully up the stairs to safety.

Food has been a big topic of conversation on this trip. Jim asks if I have noticed the many Sushi restaurants in the city: even though there are not many Japanese immigrants, Sushi has become an important part of Chilean eating habits. There has been a push by some of us to experience authentic Chilean food. We have imagined turning a corner and suddenly coming upon the 'real' Chilean experience.

188 Esther Fitzpatrick

Authentic is such a problematic word when associated with culture. As Alice Cranney describes, we are looking nostalgically for the 'strange', and instead we are confronted by the liquidity of identities, shifting, fragmented and incomplete. A Peruvian restaurant also offers Chinese noodles. A group of us are sitting there, upstairs, dining on 'authentic' Peruvian food, on the night of the big qualifier for the Football World Cup between Chile and Ecuador. We are very conscious that our waiters want to watch the game, on the TV downstairs, so as a sign of our 'sympathy' we ask how the Chilean team are doing and shout with excitement anytime they score. After we leave, we discover our waiters were cheering for Ecuador! Our lack of Spanish, and our assumptions about who's who and what's what, has let us down again.

Tale six

It is my last afternoon in Chile. I have wandered back down to Bellavista and have found an outside table by the plaza to quietly eat my lunch and read through this manuscript. Suddenly I notice a scurrying of guards; they are trying not to draw attention to themselves, yet simultaneously they are darting up and down the alleyways, meeting up and hurriedly racing off again. I then notice how they keep grabbing something down by their waists: their guns. I had not noticed the guns before. I am now much more alert. Last year some colleagues and I wrote a response to the Orlando shootings, juxtaposing our differences through poetry. This was an extension of the method of duoethnography, as described by Ulrike Najar and Julie Choi on their work with immigrant and refugee women. Like Ulrike and Julie, wanting to give emotions and feelings space, duoethnography and poetry provided a way to share our embodied response (Fitzpatrick & Fitzpatrick, 2015, Fitzpatrick, Worrell, Alansari & Lee, 2017). Frank Worrell summed up his response:

> The equation is simple:
> Fewer guns in the hands of fewer people means fewer needless deaths.
> And although fewer guns may not have stopped this act of violence or the one before,
> It will stop some,
> And that is a start.
>
> *(Fitzpatrick et al., 2017)*

Gun culture in New Zealand is mostly limited to a few hunting rifles and random headlines of local gangs having illegal weapons. Bob Rinehart highlights the difference between the 'gun culture that is a prevalent sub-theme of white male acculturation within much of the US' and the absence of such a culture in New Zealand. Instead he describes a 'bloke' culture of Kiwi males. Carrying guns is a not a normal part of my experience. Earlier in the week, Ed had described how his time in Edinburgh had changed his attitudes toward guns and shooting. How recently visiting his home in Colombia and witnessing the shooting of a young boy on the doorstep of his apartment building had traumatised him for a few days, whilst his mother admonished him for being so upset. For her, it was a normal part of daily experience. 'Normal' is such an interesting word: one person's normal cannot be understood, and neither is it stable.

Final mull

The manuscript sits on the left of my laptop on my desk, back in my office in New Zealand. It has journeyed far. The chapters have been held together with a strong black clip. Yellow sticky notes peek out from between the pages. I am beginning to imagine sharing some of these stories with my students. The personal story is a powerful way to connect us with wider social, political and historical stories; these will be useful for my students to juxtapose their own stories alongside. These questions of culture.

References

Behar, R. (1996). *The vulnerable observer: Anthropology that breaks your heart*. Boston, MA: Becon Press.

Binney, J. (1997). *Redemption songs: A life of the nineteenth-century Māori leader Te Kooti Arikirangi Te Turuki*. Honolulu, Hawai'i: University of Hawai'i.

Binney, J. (2010). *Encircled lands: Te Urewera, 1820–1921*. Wellington, NZ: Bridget Williams Books.

Derrida, J. (1994). *Spectres of Marx: The state of the debt, the work of mourning, and the new international* (P. Kamuf, Trans.). New York: Routledge.

Derrida, J. (2006). *Specters of Marx*. New York: Routledge Classics.

Elsmore, B. (2000). *Like them that dream: The Māori and the Old Testament*. Auckland, NZ: Reed.

Fitzpatrick, E. (2016). It was becoming all too confusing. In J. White (Ed.), *Permission: The international interdisciplinary impact of Laurel Richardson's work*. Rotterdam, The Netherlands: Sense, pp. 23–24.

Fitzpatrick, E. (2017a). A story of becoming: Entanglement, ghosts and postcolonial counterstories. Special Issue: Decolonizing Autoethnography. *Cultural Studies «—» Critical Methodologies*. doi:10.1177/1532708617728954.

Fitzpatrick, E. (2017b). Hauntology and Pākehā: An embodied experience with my ghosts. In Z. Rocha & M. Webber (Eds.), *Mana Tangatarua: Mixed heritages, ethnic identity and biculturalism in Aotearoa/New Zealand*. London: Routledge.

Fitzpatrick, E., & Bell, A. (2016). Summoning up the ghost with needle and thread. *Departures in Critical Qualitative Research*, 5(2), 1–24.

Fitzpatrick, E., & Fitzpatrick, K. (2015). Disturbing the divide. *Qualitative Inquiry*, 21(1), 50–58. doi:10.1177/1077800414542692

Fitzpatrick, E.M., Worrel, F., Alansari, M. & Lee, A. (2017). Let us dance. Special issue, *Qualitative Inquiry*, 23(7), 495–501. doi:10.1177/1077800417718286

Maddison-MacFadyen, M. (2013). This white women has journeyed far: Serendipity, counter-stories, hauntings, and ekphrasis as a type of poetic inquiry. Special Edition: Narratives of becoming a researcher, *Morning Watch Journal of Educational and Social Analysis*, 40, 1–15.

Metge, J. (2010). *Tuamaka: The challenges of difference in Aotearoa New Zealand*. Auckland, NZ: Auckland University Press.

O'Loughlin, M. (2009). The curious subject of the child. *The subject of childhood*. New York: Peter Lang.

Taonui, R. (2013). *'Whakapapa – genealogy – What is whakapapa?' Te Ara – the Encyclopedia of New Zealand*. Retrieved from http://www.TeAra.govt.nz/en/whakapapa-genealogy/page-1

Traue, J. (1990). Ancestors of the mind: a Pakeha Whakapapa. Retrieved from http://www.recreationaccess.org.nz/files/traue_ancestors.pdf

ACKNOWLEDGEMENTS

Hyejeong Ahn would like to thank Susanna Carter for her insights and critical comments, which greatly assisted in the crafting of this manuscript. She would also like thank her husband, Martin Boyce, for encouraging her to share her private journey with English in a public forum. Hyejeong also wishes to thank the two editors of this book, Phiona Stanley and Greg Vass, for their helpful comments and support during the preparation of this manuscript.

Silvia Bénard Calva would like to thank Aline Bénard Padilla, my niece, for her help with my English writing. She is always willing to read my articles and make encouraging comments about what she names bold writing. I also want to thank my colleague, Alejandro Rodríguez Castro, for his kind suggestions to improve this piece.

Greg Vass, Michelle Bishop, Katherine Thompson, Pauline Beller, Calita Murray, Jane Tovey and Maxine Ryan would like to thank the Aboriginal community of La Perouse and surrounding area for their support, guidance and advocacy. A big thanks to all the Elders, community members, teachers, and principals involved in the Project for sharing their knowledge and stories. We would like to also acknowledge and thank the Ian Potter Foundation for helping to fund the CCCP.

David Bright would like to thank the editors, Phiona and Greg, for their patience and encouragement, as well as everyone at ICQI 2016 for their ideas and input.

Ulrike Najar and Julie Choi would like to acknowledge Chris Mertins for his assistance in drawing the image in our chapter. We also thank the community centre organizer and housing estate managers for their support and the Collier Charitable Fund for funding this study.

192 Acknowledgements

David Fa'avae would like to sincerely thank Fetaui Iosefo for continuing to glorify the Lord in all that she does and says. Her gracious ability to place others' needs before her own is a representation of her desire to maintain the va'/vā/va-tapuia/veitapui with her maker and other people in her life. 'Ofa atu Taui.

Esther Fitzpatrick thanks firstly Phiona Stanley and Greg Vass for inviting me to write this reflective chapter. What a privilege. And as always I thank my wonderful family, the ghosts and the living, in particular my inspiring partner Mike Fitzpatrick and our awesome supportive children, the marvellous Melinda Webber, the fabulous Fetaui Iosefo, and our CAE family in the South (here a big nod to Stacy Holman-Jones and Anne Harris).

Fetaui Iosefo would like to thank the 'Aiga' (family) ethics committee and Sister-hood of the 'Underpants' of whom this labour of love would not be possible. Tamasailau Suaalii-Sauni; Barbara Grant; Frances Kelly; Stacy Holman-Jones; Anne Harris; Esther Fitzpatrick and the Trister-hood: thank you all for always nourishing my soul with alofa, spiritually, value, critique and fortitude. Finally, Phiona and Greg: thank you both for always being beautiful!

Gabrielle Piggin would like to thank her family for their support, especially Maria and James and 'Grandma', and Julianne Benson for being the best initial end user. Thanks also to my colleagues Lisa Fairbrother and Susan Edwards for all the sense-making on the ninth floor. And, thank you to Greg and Phiona for all their insightful feedback and for being such brilliant editors and people in general.

Robert E. Rinehart would like to thank my son, Nick Long-Rinehart, and his Kiwi and American 'mates' for enlightening me with some of the finer subtleties of his cohort of global male cultures.

Harmony Siganporia would like to thank all the people in Dharamsala who have given so generously of themselves and their time to her. Tenzin Tsundue, Tenzin Gaphel, Tenzin Dhondup, Tenzin Nyinjey, Tenzin Jamyang, Tenzin Tsering: this one's for you.

Phiona Stanley would like to thank the chapter authors for submitting such interesting and thought-provoking chapters. Those who presented on book-related panels at the CEAD conference (2016, Cape Town) and ICQI (2017, Urbana-Champaign, Illinois) have also contributed greatly to my thinking on these ideas. Next, thank you Greg for being such a wonderful co-editor. You've been my sounding board, collaborator, and even a shoulder to cry on, and I am so, so glad you came on board with this project. Then, Hannah Shakespeare at Routledge: thank you. You have been incredibly supportive, warm, and approachable all along, and without your initial enthusiasm, this book would probably never have been more than an interesting idea. I'd also very much like to thank Anne Harris for thought-provoking and supportive feedback, conversations, and advice along the way, and also Fetaui Iosefo for her wonderful, magical connection-making behind the scenes.

C. Darius Stonebanks would like to thank his students, Ashwini and Aamir, for reading, analyzing and discussing Naipaul's *North of South* while in Malawi and his Malawian colleagues, Francis and Japhet, who contributed new perspectives on the subject of racial identity. He would also like to express gratitude for the brave Brown people who are taking ownership of voice in a Global North space where we/they are often spoken about.

Gresilda A. Tilley-Lubbs would like to acknowledge my husband, Dan Lubbs, and my Graduate Research Assistant, Jameson Jones, for their multiple careful reads and thoughtful feedback as the manuscript developed.

Greg Vass would like to thank the contributors to the book. This has been an undertaking that has provided many opportunities to think, learn, grow, and feel connected with an inspiring learning community, engaged with really interesting and important projects that are spread far and wide. Additionally, big thanks to Phiona for the offer to be involved in the project. This was not something that was on the 'to do' list, but was a privilege to contribute to in the small ways I have.

ABOUT THE AUTHORS

Dr Hyejeong Ahn works as a lecturer at Nanyang Technological University in Singapore. Her publications include *Attitudes to World Englishes: Implications for teaching English in South Korea* (Routledge). She is currently researching the practice of using English as medium of instruction in South Korean universities.

Silvia Bénard Calva has a PhD from the University of Texas at Austin. She is Professor in the Department of Sociology and Anthropology, Universidad Autónoma de Aguascalientes in Mexico. Her research interests include: identity and subjectivity (how they are constructed through biography in different socio-cultural settings), the city, and migration. Her methodological interests are within qualitative methodology, particularly autoethnography. She has published and edited many books and articles, the most recent being, as author, *Atrapada en provincia*, and as co-editor with Gresilda Tilley-Lubbs, *Re-telling our stories.*

David Bright is a lecturer in the Faculty of Education at Monash University, Australia. David's research interests include student and teacher identity, post-structural theory and post-qualitative research and writing.

Dr Julie Choi is a lecturer in Education (Additional Languages) in the Melbourne Graduate School of Education, Australia. She is co-editor of the book *Language and culture: Reflective narratives and the emergence of identity*, author of *Creating a multivocal self: autoethnography as method*, and co-editor of *Plurilingualism in teaching and learning: Complexities across contexts.*

Alice Cranney holds an honours degree in Arts (Languages), a master's degree and PhD in Education from UNSW Sydney, Australia. She is interested in identity and perception alteration that occur as a result of transnational experiences and intercultural communication, language learning. Alice's professional background is as a Spanish and History high school teacher.

David Fa'avae is a Tonga male who was born in Niue, raised in Aotearoa New Zealand, with Samoan heritage. After completing his PhD, David works as a fellow for the Institute of Education at the University of the South Pacific. He is currently serving in the region through various research projects related to teacher education and educational leadership.

Esther Fitzpatrick is a lecturer in the Faculty of Education and Social Work, University of Auckland. She originally worked as a primary school teacher and now uses various arts pedagogies in her teaching with tertiary students. She has published on issues of racial-ethnic identity in postcolonial communities, drama as a method of inquiry, and ethical issues of arts-based methodologies. Her current research uses critical autoethnography to explore emerging identities in postcolonial societies.

Fetaui Iosefo is Professional Teaching Fellow for the Faculty of Education and Social Work at the University of Auckland, New Zealand. Her current research is a critical collaborative autoethnography with ex-incarcerated. Her main areas of teaching are in philosophy, politics and education; Pasifika learners. She is passionate about; relationships Va'; Samoan indigenous reference; education; social justice; and promotes indigenous ways of knowing and being as the norm.

Dr Ulrike Najar is a lecturer in Education (Additional Languages) at the Melbourne Graduate School of Education, Australia. She is author of several journal articles on intercultural language education, such as 'The intercultural field: Interrogating context in intercultural education' and 'Weaving a method: Mobility, multilocality and the senses as foci of research on intercultural language learning'.

Gabrielle Piggin is a PhD candidate in the School of Education at UNSW Sydney, where she is untangling knots in her study of the lived experiences of women NESTs in Japanese higher education. Her research interests include Applied Linguistics, Cultural Studies and Critical Pedagogy and beyond research, her interests extend to exploring coastlines, all things pop cultural, and dog spotting with her daughter.

Robert E. Rinehart is Associate Professor at the University of Waikato, New Zealand. He coached swimming, diving and water polo for 23 years, and was himself a competitive swimmer in the United States. He is former President of the Contemporary Ethnography across the Disciplines International Association, and has written recently about poetic and experimental characteristics within ethnographic practices.

Harmony Siganporia teaches in the area of Culture and Communication at MICA, India. She has a PhD in social history, and her thesis was on the *langue* and *parole*

196 About the authors

of reformist discourse around the 'women's question' in late-19th century Western India. A practising musician, Harmony's other research interests include ethnomusicology, gender and performativity, culture and conflict, the role of music in the emplacement of exilic identities, and semiotic theory.

Phiona Stanley is Senior Lecturer in the School of Education at UNSW Sydney, Australia. Her research is about intercultural competence in international and language education, and her publications include books on *'waiguoren'* teaching English in China and *'gringos'* learning Spanish in Latin America. Her passion is spending time in nature – especially forests – and she is currently building a campervan.

A professor in Bishop's University's School of Education, in Canada, Dr. **C. Darius Stonebanks** has worked in Quebec schools from Pre-K to college. A scholar in such areas including critical practice, praxis, transformative learning, indigenous studies, qualitative methodologies, ethics, cultural studies and Islamophobia, Dr. Stonebanks infuses these analyses into his lectures. He has been awarded the divisional teaching award twice and the Chancellor's teaching award in 2016, and is currently the Primary Investigator on a SSHRC-funded ethnographic research project examining the secular nature of Canadian public schools.

Gresilda A. Tilley-Lubbs, PhD, is Associate Professor of ESL and Multicultural Education in the School of Education, Virginia Tech, USA. Her work troubles the role of researcher/teacher power and privilege in vulnerable Spanish-speaking communities. She uses alternative literary genres, including narrative, poetry, and ethnodrama to communicate the results of her qualitative research. She has published books, articles, and book chapters. She has published in both English and Spanish. Her most recent published work is a book, *Re-assembly required: Critical autoethnography and spiritual discovery.* Her research examines teacher education based on critical pedagogy, which seeks to provide opportunities for oppressed people to recognise their oppression and achieve their goals through education. She is spearheading this research with colleagues in Mexico and Spain. This project will result in books in Spanish and in English.

Greg Vass, Michelle Bishop, Katherine Thompson, Pauline Beller, Calita Murray, Jane Tovey and Maxine Ryan: see Chapter 15.

INDEX

Ache Lhamo 120
age; ageism 135
Aiga (family) ethics 72; 74
Appalachian identity 160–162; 164
assemblage 34–36
authenticity 46; 48; 62; 102
autoethnography:
    creative; evocative; interpretive 58;
        70–71; 115
    decolonising 71; 178
    collaborative; community; duo 82–84;
        171
    critical 159; 163
    methodology 39; 52; 70; 72; 102; 114;
        172
    reflexivity 44; 58; 185–186
    therapeutic 123

becoming 36–40
Bhabha, Homi 44; 46; 60; 69
body positivity 129–131; 137
Bollywood 119–120
Bourdieu, Pierre 15
Bullying 107; 114; 137

Catholic 24–28; 163
colonialism; settler-colonialism 34; 46;
        109–110; 143; 148; 159; 171; 178
Connell, Raewyn 61; 136
conscientização (Paolo Freire) 7; 81;
        147
culture/s; construction of 3–6; 10; 17; 44;
        61; 70; 94–96; 107; 115; 120; 122; 138;
        145; 164; 173; 183

cultural appropriation 7
cultural practices, set of; ossification of 10;
        118

Dalai Lama 123–124
Deleuze, Gilles 34–37; 40–41; 139
Diversify Outdoors (social movement)
        136–137

ELT (English language teaching) 2–5; 15
Embodiment 66; 101; 165
emic/etic perspectives; readings 2; 84;
        121–122
epiphanies (Norman Denzin) 7; 10; 23
ethics of care 88–89
ethnomusicology 7; 118; 196

Fat Girls Hiking 136–137
femininity; feminism 99; 101; 109;
        136–137; 152
Foucault, Michel 40; 139

gaijin/gaikokujin 94–96
    hegemonic gaijinness 99–101
gap year 2–3
gender order theory 136
Guattari, Félix; and Deleuze 34–35;
        41; 139
gun culture 107; 111; 188

Hanoi 33; 37
hauntology 74; 134; 187
hegemonic femininity 99
hegemonic masculinity 62; 136

198 Index

hiking: representations of; going alone; and gender; and safety; and 'flow' (Mihalyi Csikszentmihalyi) 134–135; 138–139
homesickness 162

I/eye 69–75
identity; identities; as constructed; cultural; 3; 37; 69; 75; 82; 106; 120; 158
    liquid; fluid 44; 60; 65–66; 70; 99
    politics 7; 61; 96; 101; 114; 118; 122; 127; 136; 143; 146; 158; 163
    researcher; writer 40; 49; 51; 96; 144; 160; 185
imaginaries 94; 96; 138
immigrant; teacher 13; 16–18; 81–82
insider; and or outsider 8; 11; 43–45; 50; 70; 94–96; 118; 121–122
institutionalised violence 6
intersectionality 96–97; 183

Language/s of power 13; 14–15; 187
    English
    French 24; 34
    German 24
    Japanese; and non-Japanese 93; 95; 98
    Mexican 24; 50
    Polish 4
    Spanish; and non-Spanish 4; 24; 45; 50; 156; 159; 162; 164; 183; 187–188
    Vietnamese 33–34
legitimacy 49; 101–102; 132
lingua franca 4

masculinity; bloke; mate 61–62; 108–110; 115; 136
meaningful participation 82
Mexicanidad 45; 48; 52
multiplicity 35–36; 143; 148

native English speaker teachers (NESTs) 5
native speakerism 20–21
Neruda, Pablo 139
Nihonjinron 95

obesity: and alarmism; and scepticism; and 129; 133; 137–139
Occidental 95
Othering 6; 45–46; 88; 103; 151
Otherness as a foil in identity construction 4; 6; 17–18; 45–46; 102; 127; 146
outsider; see also insider 29; 31; 44; 46; 51; 65; 95; 99; 111; 122; 145; 148; 151; 165; 183

Parsi; community in India 122
participatory framework 81
performative 62; 70; 75; 107; 169; 178
Peru 2–4
positionality 11; 44–45; 49; 73; 83; 94; 96–97; 100; 118
postcolonialism 46
poststructuralism; poststructuralist-initiated crisis of 9; 39
precarity in minority communities 103; 123; 126–127; 172
privilege 2; 7; 14; 53; 61; 74; 93; 99; 108; 110; 122; 127; 146; 152; 159; 163; 187
protestant 27–28; 31; 163

Rangzen 124–125
refugees 83; 120; 122
relational; concerns; ethics 7; 8; 57; 59–61; 70; 72; 84; 116; 126; 172; 175
relational self 70
researcher responsibility 54
resistance 3; 8; 22; 120; 125; 129; 173; 178

Said, Edward 34; 45; 48; 146
Samoan; people, culture, tradition, identity 60; 69; 72–73
Singapore 13; 19
small cultures (Adrian Holliday) 3; 182–183
stranger/s (George Simmel) 28–29

third space 43–44; 49; 60; 69–70
Tibet, idea of; Tibetan identities, exiles and refugees 118–120; 122
Tongan; people, culture, tradition, identity 57–66; 186
travel writing, critique of (Mary Louise Pratt) 5; 94; 145

Umey Lam 124
Unlikely Hiker 136
us versus them; disposition 6

Vietnam 33; 37

Westernness; characterizations of; 4; 7; 94; 96
Whiteness; as discursively reproduced; 8; 96; 143–144; 149–152; 161; 186
Writing; as research; about self/others; practice 1; 5–6; 31; 39–41; 50; 70–72; 80; 82–83; 88; 97; 115; 144–145; 163; 169

'yahs' 2